British Invasion Fleets

BRITISH INVASION FLEETS

The Mediterranean
and beyond
1942-1945

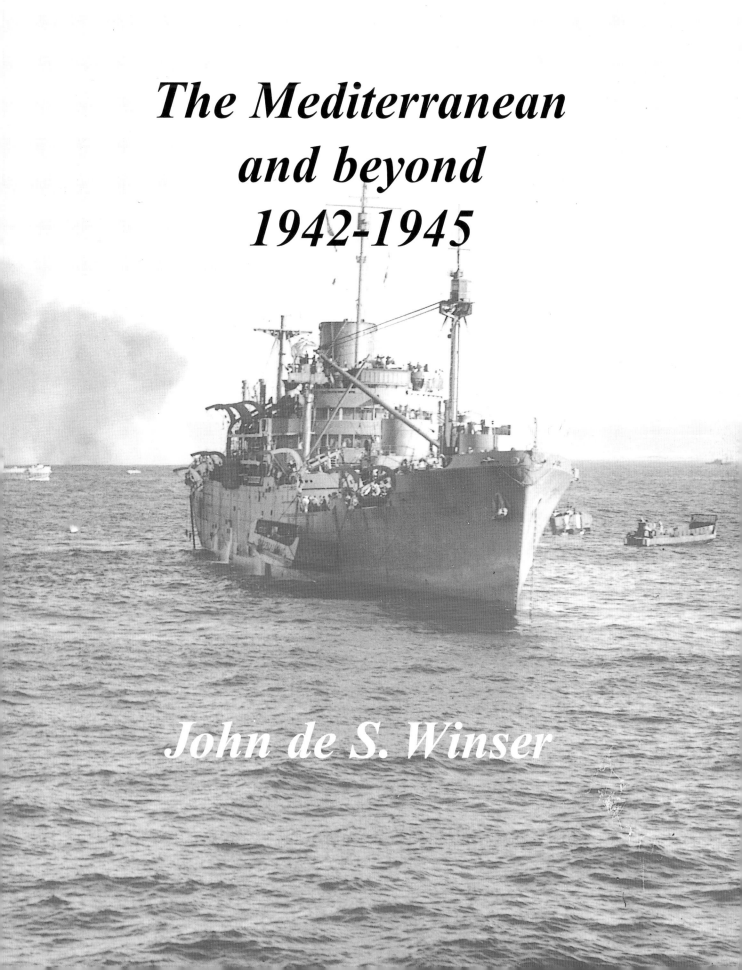

John de S. Winser

CONTENTS

© 2002 J de S Winser

ISBN 0-9543310-0-1

Published by -
The WORLD SHIP SOCIETY Limited
P O Box 706
Gravesend, KENT DA12 5UB, England

PHOTOGRAPHS
Photographs credited to the IWM (Imperial War Museum, Lambeth Road, London SE1 6HZ); MPL (Maritime Photo Library, 8 Jetty Street, Cromer, Norfolk NR27 9HF) and NMM (National Maritime Museum, Greenwich, London SE10 9NF) are on sale on application to the appropriate addresses, quoting the reference numbers shown.

Outside cover photograph: the main assault convoy of 38 troop carrying ships on its way to North Africa for the 8 November 1942 landings in Algeria: the three landing ships nearest the camera are (right to left) MONARCH OF BERMUDA, a former luxury liner; HMS LARGS, a converted French banana carrier, and HMS GLENGYLE, built as a fast cargo vessel. [IWM A12655]

Pages 2 & 3: the scene off Bark West beachhead in Sicily during the 10 July 1943 invasion: nearest the camera is GLENGYLE, with CIRCASSIA astern of her, both are Landing Ships, Infantry (LSIs); to the left of the picture is a Landing Craft, Infantry (LCI) and Motor Launch 1301, while, in the far distance, a destroyer is laying a smokescreen. [IWM A17956]

FOREWORD

by
CHRISTOPHER PAGE
Captain Royal Navy (Rtd), Head of the Naval Historical Branch, Ministry of Defence

In the short time that I have been fortunate enough to be the Head of the Naval Historical Branch of the Naval Staff, I have discovered the priceless value of accurately-researched and well-expressed reference works as an essential aid to the study of naval history. This latest work by John Winser fills a glaring gap, covering all the vessels that participated in major British invasion operations of the Second World War to supplement his well-received previous books, including "The D-Day Ships" and "BEF Ships before, at and after Dunkirk".

This work is much more than a straight listing of vessels which were there. Section A contains brief details of the purpose and outcome of each operation, while Section B is full of valuable details of routings and cargoes, as well as the particulars of the ships themselves. The reader cannot fail to be struck by the large numbers of merchant ships involved in these complicated and costly endeavours. It should serve as a fitting testament, if one were still needed, to the crucial part played by the Merchant Marine in wartime and particularly during the Second World War. In addition to these were other merchant vessels whose wartime function found them renamed 'His Majesty's' ship. Not forgotten either are the ships and craft without names, without which the troops could never have got ashore and been supplied.

These stories also hold lessons for today: in a world where the United Kingdom armed forces are adopting a progressively more expeditionary role, it helps to be reminded of the scale of effort required to transport, protect, land and supply thousands of men at long distances from home. And, notwithstanding the increased capacity of modern aircraft, it remains today, as it was 60 years ago, that if you want to deploy substantial forces, they have to go by sea and they have to be protected while en route.

Christopher Page

INTRODUCTION

This is a sequel to my World Ship Society publication "The D-Day Ships", which commemorated the 50th anniversary of the 1944 Operation "Neptune" invasion in Normandy. This book is timed to coincide with the 60th anniversary of one of the other massive Allied invasions of the Second World War - that of North Africa in November 1942. It is designed to highlight the British contribution to the assault and follow-up phases not only of that operation but also of nine other amphibious invasions, starting with three in Madagascar in the months prior to North Africa. It then moves on to cover the vast July 1943 assault on Sicily, followed two months later by the attack on mainland Italy at Salerno and, in January 1944, by an operation further up the coast at Anzio. In support of the Normandy invasion that June came Allied landings in the South of France in August, followed by the 1945 launch of British invasion fleets against Rangoon, in Burma, and, more massively, against Malaya. As "Neptune" was pronounced 'the greatest amphibious operation in the world', it might, at first sight, seem difficult to muster the same fervour for the achievements of the obviously 'less great' operations. Although none of the operations covered by this book compare in fleet size with the Normandy invasion, the variety of their composition was often infinitely more impressive. For instance, a number of the most magnificent pre-war passenger liners afloat sailed in the 38-ship convoy, with a total gross tonnage of nearly half a million, which conveyed the assault troops to the Eastern and Centre Task Force areas in the North African invasion. It followed from the UK in the wake of a 42-ship convoy, carrying the vehicles, equipment and supplies so essential to a military operation. Concentration on the achievements of Britain's Royal and Merchant Navies, does not preclude the US and continental Allied ships under British contro, whose support was equally vital to success. All were phased to reach the correct destination at the required time and all were assisted by Royal Navy vessels dedicated not only to the protection of the fleet from air, surface and underwater attack but also to the provision of bombardment and aerial support, as required. It required no fewer than 27 different warships, which joined in relays, to escort the cargo ship convoy during its 17-day voyage from the Clyde to the Sicilian invasion beachheads in 1943 and this was just one of the convoys. The overwhelming theme of many of the operations covered by this book is the sheer scale, organisational complexity and seamanship skills required to transport an army from mounting port to beachhead, over distances five or ten times those for "Neptune". I dedicate this book to those who made the invasions successful, in the earnest hope that this record does them justice.

John de S. Winser

Section A
A brief description of
the invasions

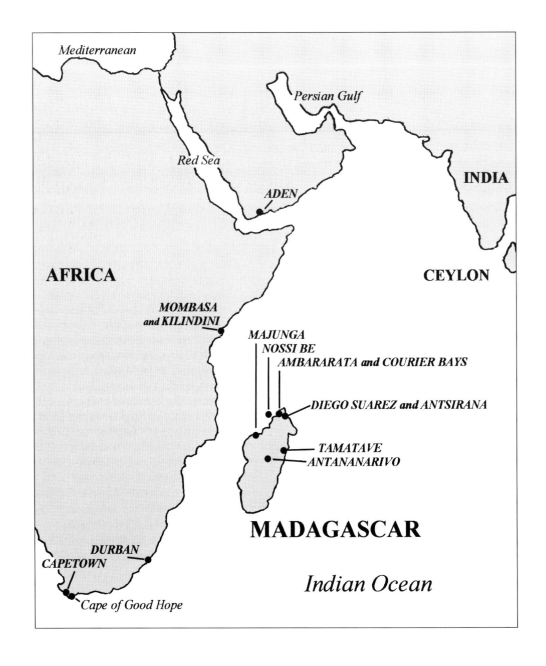

MADAGASCAR

A1. DIEGO SUAREZ, MADAGASCAR: 5 MAY 1942

Troop carrying ships en route to Madagascar, (from left to right) DUCHESS OF ATHOLL; FRANCONIA (obscuring ORONSAY); the sister ships KEREN and KARANJA; the escorting battleship RAMILLIES; the Polish SOBIESKI and, finally, WINCHESTER CASTLE. [IWM A8862]

The danger of operating ships through the Mediterranean in 1942 elevated the Cape of Good Hope route to a position of supreme importance to Britain. Located 9,000 miles from the UK, the island of Madagascar, roughly equidistant between Capetown and Aden, controlled the southern gateway to the Indian Ocean. The threat that the Vichy French regime might permit the island's use as a Japanese base for attacks on the all-important supply convoys, linking Britain with the Middle East, India and Australia, was unacceptable. To counter this and in the expectation of French resistance, a British invasion force left the UK that March to assemble at Durban, with the main participating ships being issued with charts of Burmese waters, during the voyage to South Africa, to disguise their true destination.

The probability of carrying out the planned operation, code named "Ironclad", came ever nearer with the departure from Durban on 25 April of convoy Y. This consisted of five fully-laden cargo ships (a sixth joined later) and the fleet oiler EASEDALE, to refuel the smaller warships at sea. It also included the tank landing ship BACHAQUERO, in an inaugural operational assignment which demonstrated the value of a ship with bow opening doors, and DERWENTDALE, a tanker successfully adapted to transport landing craft. The convoy escorts comprised the cruiser DEVONSHIRE, two destroyers, six corvettes and four minesweepers, which were joined later by another destroyer and two more corvettes. The troop carrying fleet of converted passenger liners left Durban on 28 April, as convoy Z. It included the commissioned sister ships KARANJA and KEREN (ex KENYA), owned by British India, with the last-named also acting as assault headquarters ship; Union-Castle's WINCHESTER CASTLE and the Polish-flag SOBIESKI, between them carrying 56 landing craft, in which to ferry the troops ashore. Other personnel were transported in three larger ships, the Canadian Pacific

The cruiser DEVONSHIRE (left) and battleship RAMILLIES off Madagascar. [IWM A8857]

The tanker BACHAQUERO demonstrates the vehicle ramp installed during her conversion into a tank landing ship: Madagascar was the first operational use of this type of vessel, developments of which became an essential ingredient of later invasion fleets. [IWM A20035]

DUCHESS OF ATHOLL; the Cunard White Star FRANCONIA and the Orient liner ORONSAY. Use was also made of the small commissioned transport ROYAL ULSTERMAN, which had, by chance, been in South Africa undergoing capstan repairs. Convoy Z's escort was made up of the battleship RAMILLIES, the aircraft carrier ILLUSTRIOUS, the cruiser HERMIONE and six destroyers. Positioned 130-220 miles to the east of Madagascar, as protection against Japanese attack from that quarter, were the Eastern Fleet battleships RESOLUTION and WARSPITE and the aircraft carrier FORMIDABLE, with their escort of five cruisers and seven destroyers.

Even though the assault fleet had already been at sea for many days, it was not until 2 May that the operation was finally approved and, on the following morning, the aircraft carrier INDOMITABLE and two destroyers augmented the assault convoy from the Eastern Fleet. The objectives were the capture of the French naval and air bases at Diego Suarez, on the north-east corner of Madagascar, and the extreme north-west of the island was chosen for the assault, even though it was known to be navigationally hazardous. Despite this, after converging, convoys Y and Z safely reached the assigned anchorages, as planned, in the early hours of 5 May, to put their troops ashore at Ambararata and Courier Bays. Assisted by information about French military dispositions, supplied by two locally resident

Englishmen who came out to meet the fleet in their sailing boat, the attacking force achieved complete surprise, despite the explosion of two sea mines. In support of the troops, as they prepared for their overland advance towards Diego Suarez, carrier-borne aircraft from ILLUSTRIOUS were flown off to attack Diego Suarez harbour, whilst the target of Albacores from INDOMITABLE was Antsirana airport. The only British maritime casualty occurred at 1140 that day, when a mine broke the back of the corvette AURICULA: an attempt to tow her to shallow water proved unsuccessful and she sank the following morning. Over 13,000 soldiers, 321 vehicles and 18 guns were landed in the first two days, including 50 Royal Marines from RAMILLIES who, on the evening of 6 May, leapt ashore from the stern of the destroyer ANTHONY at Antsirana quay, opposite Diego Suarez. On 7 May, DEVONSHIRE, HERMIONE and RAMILLIES carried out a bombardment as a prelude to the entry into Diego Suarez harbour that evening of the two last-named ships and the destroyers PALADIN and PANTHER. Within 60 hours of the initial landings, the initially strong resistance had been overcome and the objectives achieved, to bring a successful conclusion to the first British invasion of the war on any scale.

Details of the ships involved are given in Section B1.

The cargo vessel MARTAND carried motor vehicles to Madagascar in the slow assault convoy from Durban. [Capt J F van Puyvelde]

The Madagascar invasion fleet after the capture of Diego Suarez: the chart (below) names the main vessels visible in the photograph. [IWM A9404]

<table>
<tr><td></td><td></td><td>DUCHESS</td><td>Escorts</td><td>ORONSAY</td><td></td></tr>
<tr><td></td><td></td><td>of ATHOLL</td><td></td><td>FRANCONIA</td><td></td></tr>
<tr><td></td><td>EASEDALE</td><td></td><td></td><td></td><td></td></tr>
<tr><td></td><td>DEVONSHIRE</td><td></td><td></td><td></td><td></td></tr>
</table>

```
                    DUCHESS     Escorts     ORONSAY
                    of ATHOLL               FRANCONIA
            EASEDALE
            DEVONSHIRE
                                        MAHOUT
ILLUSTRIOUS (bow)   INDOMITABLE         BACHAQUERO     DERWENTDALE
        HERMIONE                    KEREN         MARTAND
            RAMILLIES               ROYAL ULSTERMAN     NAIRNBANK
                        KARANJA
        WINCHESTER CASTLE                   alongside the quay
        SOBIESKI                            CITY OF HONGKONG
            THALATTA
                                The wreck of the French sloop
GREYSTOKE CASTLE                        D'ENTRECASTEAUX
                            bombed by aircraft from ILLUSTRIOUS 5 May
```

HM Australian destroyer NESTOR was one of the warships positioned to the east of Madagascar, to provide cover against Japanese attack. [IWM A9062]

A2. MAJUNGA, MADAGASCAR:

10 SEPTEMBER 1942

In line ahead, 12 assault ships, together with an escort, approach Majunga: the vessel nearest the camera is EMPIRE PRIDE and, in her wake, the sister ships DUNERA and DILWARA. [IWM A12439]

After the successful invasion of the Diego Suarez area of northern Madagascar in May 1942, the fast minelayer MANXMAN sailed into the port with £100,000 in bullion in an endeavour to achieve full French cooperation. However, the French authorities in the remainder of the island declined voluntarily to join the Allied cause, so, in August that same year, a plan to carry out additional landings was approved. The first, code named Operation "Stream", was an assault on the west coast in the area of Majunga and, to conceal their intended destination, the ships were directed along the normal convoy routes through the Mozambique Channel, with Swahili interpreters aboard, to deal with any inquisitive dhows or neutral shipping encountered on the way. Six cargo ships setting out from Mombasa on 3 September were followed, two days later, by the personnel ships DILWARA, DUNERA, EMPIRE PRIDE and EMPIRE TROOPER. The first two were pre-war sister troopships, owned by British India; EMPIRE PRIDE was a brand new vessel, just completing her first year of service, while EMPIRE TROOPER was originally the German Hamburg-South America liner CAP NORTE, intercepted by HM cruiser BELFAST in October 1939 and taken over as a war prize. These ten ships from Mombasa were joined by eight personnel and cargo vessels which left Diego Suarez on 7 September. This convoy included Elder Dempster's ABOSSO; the Union-Castle LLANDAFF CASTLE; the formerly American EMPIRE WOODLARK and the previously Egyptian KHEDIVE ISMAIL. All made a rendezvous on the 9th, south of the Comoro Islands, with the aircraft carrier ILLUSTRIOUS and her escorts to combine into Force M, with the seaplane carrier ALBATROSS serving as headquarters ship. The first landings took place in the early hours of 10 September eight miles north-west of Majunga, with the second following a few hours later in the harbour at Majunga. Meanwhile, in Operation "Esme B", MANXMAN was allocated to land Royal Marines and South African infantrymen north of Majunga, to capture the island of Nossi Be, an objective achieved after a preliminary bombardment in which MANXMAN was joined by the cruiser CARADOC. As a diversionary operation 380 miles further south, commandos, transferred at sea from EMPIRE PRIDE to the destroyer NAPIER, were put ashore at Morondava early the same morning in Operation "Tamper". The landings were successfully completed and, after capturing Majunga, the troops moved on to occupy the capital city, Antananarivo.

Details of the ships involved are given in Section B2.

Landing craft assemble alongside the assault ship EMPIRE PRIDE (right) off Tamatave: on the left are the sister ships DUNERA and DILWARA and, in the distance, the cargo vessel OCEAN VIKING, loaded with military vehicles and supplies. [IWM A12393]

On completion of Operation "Stream" at Majunga, the assault forces rejoined their vessels for Operation "Jane", with the object of capturing Tamatave on the east coast of Madagascar. Commandos, who had reached Diego Suarez from Majunga in the personnel ship KHEDIVE ISMAIL, were transferred to the destroyers ACTIVE, ARROW and BLACKMORE for the 18 September landings, with a further platoon being transported aboard the destroyer INCONSTANT. After an initial French refusal to surrender, a display of air power and a bombardment by Royal Navy cruisers and destroyers lasted barely three minutes, before white flags appeared on the main buildings in the town. In the event, this early capitulation proved somewhat fortunate, because, from the assault ships allocated to the most northerly of the three beaches, six of the nine

landing craft broached to, largely stranding the second wave of the assault force. When called forward to her berth at Tamatave, the cargo ship OCEAN VIKING, loaded with vehicles, misjudged her approach and grounded for nearly two hours. She then proceeded to the outer harbour where she again went aground and remained firmly stuck until being refloated the following morning. In the meantime, the personnel ships DILWARA, DUNERA and EMPIRE PRIDE and the cargo vessel GASCONY entered the port and safely berthed to complete the operation, which had been carried out virtually as planned.

Details of the ships involved are given in Section B3.

Laden with troops, a landing craft passes HMS GAMBIA at Tamatave, with DAUNTLESS to the right of the picture: both cruisers are flying their battle ensigns. [IWM A12375]

A4. ALGERIA, NORTH AFRICA: 8 NOVEMBER 1942

Ships off Algiers A beachhead on the day of the assault include the Landing Ships, Infantry VICEROY OF INDIA (nearest the camera), with KARANJA astern of her, then the Dutch MARNIX VAN ST ALDEGONDE: cargo ships carrying vehicles and supplies can be seen in the far distance. [IWM A12710]

Abbreviations – LSI = Landing Ship, Infantry; LST = Landing Ship, Tank

Ever since the occupation of France by German forces in 1940, the ultimate goal had been the mounting of an Allied assault across the English Channel. Such an operation was impracticable in 1942, so an invasion of Vichy French North Africa was approved as an alternative and became the first Anglo-American operation since the December 1941 attack on Pearl Harbor had brought the USA into the war. Operation "Torch" was designed to open up the Mediterranean to Allied shipping; to create a threat to the enemy's southern flank and to permit a military advance overland towards Tunisia. Combined with a westward thrust by the British Eighth Army from Egypt, it was intended to clear the opposing armies out of Africa once and for all. The invasion, which was planned in the expectation of initial opposition from the French, involved three separate task forces. The Western Task Force consisted of an American fleet making a 14-day voyage across the Atlantic to land troops on the coast of Morocco, with its sights set on the capture of Casablanca. Three landing areas were selected – one 60 miles north-east of the city at Port Lyautey; a main and central assault at Fedala, 14 miles north-east of Casablanca, and a third at Safi, 135 miles to the south. The main convoy left the USA on 25 October 1942 and, augmented by an aircraft carrier group from Bermuda, formed itself into a fleet of over 100 transports, supply vessels and warships. The Moroccan landings were timed for 8 November, concurrently with the arrival of

two invasion fleets from the UK which, after sailing through the Strait of Gibraltar, would make final landfall in the Algiers and Oran areas of French Algeria. It is on the assault and follow-up vessels of these two British-controlled fleets, the Eastern and Centre Task Forces, that this book will concentrate.

The first assault ship to leave the UK was the Madagascar veteran LST BACHAQUERO, together with her sister ships, MISOA and TASAJERA: all three had set out from the Clyde on 21 October for Gibraltar, to await the main fleet. The following day saw the departure of 42 American, Belgian, British and Dutch "Torch" cargo ships, carrying tanks, other vehicles, guns, cased petrol, stores and, in many instances, 300 or more military personnel. Included in this convoy was the landing ship, gantry DERWENTDALE, with Madagascar service experience, and her two sister ships, DEWDALE and ENNERDALE, each carrying 14 landing craft. These were to supplement the 2-5 craft carried by most of the cargo ships themselves, for transporting ashore loads, after they had been hoisted out by derrick at the beachhead anchorages. The main personnel convoy, made up of 38 ships with a total gross tonnage approaching half a million, left the Clyde on 26 October and the following day formed into 10 columns abreast, around the cruiser SHEFFIELD and escort carrier BITER. Also acting as escorts from the UK were a destroyer; three sloops; the cutters HARTLAND and WALNEY and four frigates. This troop convoy was composed of a mixture of Royal and

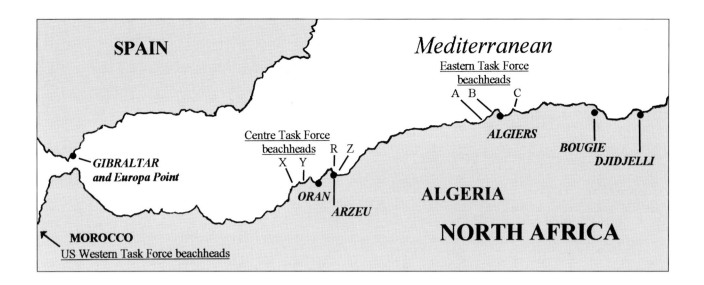

Merchant Navy LSIs, carrying between them over 375 landing craft, and personnel ships without landing craft. It included some of Britain's most impressive passenger liners, in particular DUCHESS OF BEDFORD, WARWICK CASTLE, VICEROY OF INDIA, STRATHNAVER and MONARCH OF BERMUDA, from some of the world's premier shipping companies, such as Canadian Pacific, Union-Castle, P & O and Furness, Withy. They had been converted for the task of transporting assault troops and the fleet contained not only ships sailing under the British flag but also those of the Netherlands, Poland and the USA.

For convoy identification, a prefix KM (UK/Mediterranean) was used, to which was added the letter F or S, to denote Fast or Slow. In readiness for the assault convoys to divide by destination, an additional letter was used – A for Algiers (Eastern Task Force) or O for Oran (Centre Task Force). This lettering system was followed by a numerical sequence – 1 for the assault, 2 for the follow-up and 3 onwards for the subsequent build-up convoys. Accordingly, as the assault fleet neared the entrance to the Mediterranean, slow convoy KMS1 separated into KMSA1 and KMSO1, whilst the fast convoy split into KMFA1 and KMFO1.

As part of Force H, the cruiser SIRIUS left Gibraltar on 5 November to be in her patrol area, 30 miles north of Algiers, when the landings went in. [IWM A12798]

Landing Ships, Infantry awaiting departure from the Clyde for North Africa

This page (top) Union-Castle's WARWICK CASTLE [IWM FL21322]; (centre) Glen Line's GLENGYLE, a converted cargo ship [IWM FL8888] and (bottom) P & O's VICEROY OF INDIA [IWM FL4528]: of the three, only GLENGYLE survived the operation.
Opposite page (top) the Dutch TEGELBERG [IWM FL19767]; (centre) Bibby Line's DERBYSHIRE and (bottom) P & O's STRATHNAVER [IWM FL19394].

North African invasion convoy KMF1 at sea

The convoy was made up of 38 troop carrying ships, plus escorts, and was sailing ten abreast and four deep around the cruiser SHEFFIELD and escort carrier BITER: the ships visible in full or in part are indicated on the chart below

MOOLTAN   NIEUW ZEELAND

ROYAL ULSTERMAN   ROYAL SCOTSMAN   TEGELBERG

WARWICK CASTLE   DUCHESS of BEDFORD   DURBAN CASTLE

DERBYSHIRE   LLANGIBBY CASTLE   MONARCH of BERMUDA

ULSTER MONARCH   PRINCESS BEATRIX   QUEEN EMMA

ETTRICK   Escort carrier BITER   Cruiser SHEFFIELD

ALMAACK   LEEDSTOWN   THOMAS STONE

EXCELLER   WINCHESTER CASTLE   OTRANTO   STRATHNAVER

SOBIESKI   AWATEA   KEREN

KARANJA

Top: (left to right) the Landing Ships, Infantry (LSIs) SOBIESKI and WINCHESTER CASTLE, the US Navy transport LEEDSTOWN, the cruiser SHEFFIELD and the LSI BATORY: LEEDSTOWN was lost during the invasion. [IWM A12692]

Centre: HM cruiser SHEFFIELD: in the distance, to the left, is the US Navy transport SAMUEL CHASE and, to the right, the Landing Ship, Infantry ETTRICK: the latter ship was sunk whilst returning to the UK from North Africa. [IWM A12837]

Below: the sloop ENCHANTRESS (nearest the camera) and escort carrier BITER: the last-named vessel flew off anti-submarine patrols as the convoy progressed towards the Mediterranean. [IWM12712]

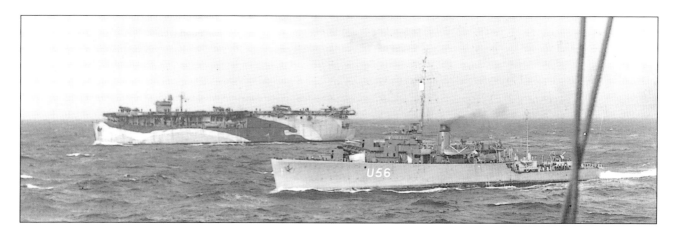

The destroyer PANTHER, viewed from the aircraft carrier FORMIDABLE: the day before the invasion, damage from a bomb explosion forced her to retire from the operation. [IWM A18312]

Still unobserved by the enemy, the armada of assault vessels and warships entering the Mediterranean from the UK, together with those joining from Gibraltar, totalled over 200. The schedule for ships passing Europa Point from 1930 on 5 November was a complex one. First to proceed were the fleet oilers BROWN RANGER and DINGLEDALE and five escorts of Force R, heading for a position well north of the beachheads, where they were to provide excellent service in refuelling the ships of Force H. In their wake came the aircraft carrier ARGUS; cruisers CHARYBDIS, SCYLLA and SHEFFIELD and their escorts, destined for a patrol area 15 miles north of the beachhead. The monitor ROBERTS was followed by the ships of Algiers-bound convoys KMSA1 and KMFA1, with the three LSTs from Gibraltar astern. The scheduled passage slot of Force H was 0430 on 6 November. This powerful force, made up of the battleships DUKE OF YORK and RODNEY; the battlecruiser RENOWN; the aircraft carriers FORMIDABLE and VICTORIOUS, with Albacores, Martlets and Seafires embarked; cruisers and destroyers, was on its way to a position some 30 miles north of Algiers, to cover the landings against any surface attack. Immediately astern came the three small LSIs ROYAL SCOTSMAN, ROYAL ULSTERMAN and ULSTER MONARCH, due to land US troops at Arzeu R beachhead and in the process of rejoining the main fleet after refuelling at Gibraltar. Coastal forces craft were followed by the ships of Oran convoys KMSO1 and KMFO1 and finally, at 0400 on 7 November, came the aircraft carrier FURIOUS, the cruiser DELHI and their escorts. It was not until all had entered the Mediterranean that the first casualty occurred. At 0543 that day, the US Navy transport THOMAS STONE, heading for Algiers in convoy KMFA1, was attacked from the air and hit in the stern by a torpedo, some 50 miles off the Spanish coast. Although the ship remained afloat, 700 of her troops were embarked in landing craft to complete the 140-mile journey to the beachhead: owing to breakdowns and adverse weather conditions, this endeavour failed and the men subsequently completed their journey aboard the escorting frigate SPEY. Later that same day, flooding caused by a bomb near miss sent the Force H destroyer PANTHER heading back to Gibraltar for repairs.

The first casualty of the operation occurred when the rudder and propellers of the US Navy transport THOMAS STONE were wrecked by an aerial torpedo: the ship survived and was towed the 140 miles to Algiers, where she is seen in this photograph.

Two Royal Fleet Auxiliary oilers were positioned in the Mediterranean to refuel the ships of covering Force H: this shot of the oiler DINGLEDALE was taken from the cruiser ARGONAUT. [IWM A12800]

Eastern Task Force: **Algiers sector**. Allocated to this sector were 35 assault ships, carrying over 31,000 Anglo-American troops, their vehicles and equipment, due to land on A (equally often referred to as Apples) and B (Beer) beachheads, to the west of Algiers, and on C (Charlie) beachhead to the east of the city. The landing craft release areas were between 5 and 7 miles from the shore and, as at every other sector, navigation

was assisted by the pre-positioning of a marker submarine. The assault ships arrived shortly before midnight, to enable the assault craft, guided by motor launches, to start proceeding ashore by the appointed time of 0100 on 8 November. Despite difficulties at B and C beaches, this operation was successful, in contrast to the situation at Algiers harbour, where the destroyers BROKE and MALCOLM were involved in

HM aircraft carrier FORMIDABLE, with Seafires being carried in outriggers on the starboard side of her flight deck, their wing span being too large for the hanger lifts: this type of aircraft was making its first appearance at sea in this operation. [IWM A12788]

The destroyer WILTON at Algiers B beachhead, with four Landing Ships, Infantry in the background: on the left is AWATEA (which was sunk three days later), with OTRANTO beyond her; to the right, KEREN, with WINCHESTER CASTLE beyond her, and, on the extreme right, the Landing Ship, Headquarters BULOLO. [IWM A12727]

Operation "Terminal". There the objective was to land troops to prevent acts of sabotage to the port installations and to the 25 French ships in the harbour. On her approach, MALCOLM was hit amidships, seriously damaged and forced to withdraw with three boilers out of action. At her fourth attempt, BROKE got alongside to land her American troops: she left after four hours but, in the process, was holed in the hull by shore gunfire to such an extent that she had to be taken in tow and subsequently foundered. With unloading continuing at the beachheads, despite deteriorating weather taking its toll of the landing craft, French resistance ceased at 1900 that day but raids by 30-50 German aircraft developed. The cruisers BERMUDA and SHEFFIELD both escaped damage from a series of torpedo attacks but the American cargo ship EXCELLER was less fortunate. She was damaged by a bomb near miss and COWDRAY was disabled, when a bomb went right through the destroyer and exploded under a boiler room. The last two air raids took place at Algiers C beachhead, where the US transport LEEDSTOWN's steering gear was wrecked when hit by

an aerial torpedo. She survived that damage but sank next day in renewed torpedo and bombing attacks, which also caused serious damage and heavy casualties aboard the anti-aircraft ship PALOMARES. When the headquarters ship BULOLO entered Algiers harbour on 9 November, she did so to an enthusiastic welcome from the assembled crowds: the city had passed into Allied control.

Centre Task Force: **Oran sector**. As Oran is situated 180 miles to the west of Algiers, the convoy sailing schedule was adjusted so that both the Algiers and Oran assault fleets would land their troops simultaneously and, in consequence, the scheduled time difference for the fast convoys to pass Europa Point was over 21 hours. At 1600 on 7 November, the fast and slow O convoys met to form into groups for the final approach to X and Y beachheads to the west of Oran and to R and Z landing areas approximately 35 miles to the east of Y. These latter two beachheads were situated in the Gulf of Arzeu and are therefore referred to in this book as Arzeu R and Z. The landings encountered unexpected difficulties in some areas but

The Dutch MARNIX VAN ST ALDEGONDE off Algiers A beachhead: she had a personnel capacity of 3,429 and carried 12 landing craft on this operation. [IWM A12705A]

KEREN arrived at Algiers B beachhead on 8 November and the following day went alongside in Algiers harbour, where this photograph was taken: she carried 1,161 troops and 26 vehicles to North Africa. [IWM NA67]

no opposition and, by 0300 on 8 November, all had been reported successful. Four LSIs came under fire from the shore: at Y beachhead, GLENGYLE was straddled and both LLANGIBBY CASTLE and MONARCH OF BERMUDA received direct hits, as did REINA DEL PACIFICO, which was one of 34 ships directed to Arzeu Z. The battleship RODNEY, already detached from Force H for this purpose, brought her main armament to bear in reply from a range of 13 miles. Over 3,000 men went ashore at X beachhead; 5,500 at Y and 29,000 at R and Z. In addition, more than 3,200 tanks and other vehicles were landed but the slow process of discharging vehicles and supplies into landing craft meant that the full clearance of some ships took more than five days. As at Algiers, it was regarded as vital that every effort be made to ensure that the port would be ready to handle Allied ships, without its facilities being damaged by sabotage. Accordingly, HARTLAND and WALNEY were assigned to land US troops in Oran harbour early in the morning of 8 November in Operation "Reservist". The profile of both Royal Navy ships clearly revealed their US origins and, for this operation, they also wore the American ensign, because of the ill will generated by the British bombardment of the French fleet in 1940. Despite this, the reception the two ships received could not have been more hostile. WALNEY entered the harbour to meet withering fire from French warships: she sustained crippling damage and massive casualties. HARTLAND also came under devastating attack both on the approach and inside the harbour: she was ablaze and had to be abandoned. Events were meanwhile proving more successful for the Royal Navy outside the harbour. On patrol five miles to the north of Oran, the cruiser AURORA engaged three French destroyers. TRAMONTANE was seen to be stopped, on fire and with her forecastle awash; TORNADE was sunk and TYPHON headed into port, damaged. BOADICEA and CALPE were also involved in this action, the first-named receiving a direct hit forward, whilst a third British destroyer, BRILLIANT, engaged and sank the French warship LA SURPRISE. On 9 November, AURORA was in action once more: with her fellow cruiser JAMAICA, she seriously damaged the French destroyer EPERVIER, which, after many

explosions and dense smoke, was beached and again caused TYPHON to put into Oran, where she was scuttled. A less satisfactory event was the loss, earlier that day, of the corvette GARDENIA, as a result of a collision with the trawler FLUELLEN. To expedite the landing of her 151 personnel, 205 vehicles, 4 guns, 240 tons cased petrol and 600 tons of stores, PACIFIC EXPORTER was able to go alongside the quay at Arzeu and, by noon on 10 November, French forces in Oran had capitulated.

Bougie. The first loaded cargo ship to be lost was GARLINGE: she was hit by a U-boat torpedo early on 10 November, whilst heading from Gibraltar to Algiers, carrying over 2,400 tons of coal for naval use. Two hours later, the destroyer MARTIN, escorting Force H, was similarly hit and then blew up. That afternoon, the sloop IBIS capsized as a result of being struck by an aerial torpedo, while escorting the aircraft carrier ARGUS, which was herself damaged in a dive-bomb attack, leaving only seven of her Seafires serviceable. That night a substantial convoy sailed eastwards from Algiers along the North African coast in Operation "Perpetual". The fleet assigned included the cruiser SHEFFIELD; monitor ROBERTS; anti-aircraft ship TYNWALD and escorts, as protection for the LSIs KARANJA and MARNIX VAN ST ALDEGONDE; the gantry ship DEWDALE; the personnel vessel CATHAY and four cargo ships. At Bougie, on 11 November, they mounted a dawn landing, which was unopposed. Because of engine defects, STRATHNAVER sailed late and her assignment was taken over by fellow LSI, AWATEA, which was ordered to proceed to Djidjelli, about 35 miles beyond Bougie, to land urgently required aircraft stores, maintenance personnel and fuel. The intention was to operate RAF fighters from Djidjelli airfield from noon that day to provide vital air defence for the area. Although the aircraft arrived, it was too rough for the seaborne landings to take place and AWATEA had to be diverted and joined the other ships at Bougie. However, the delay in providing air cover, compounded by the lack of transport to the airfield once the supplies had been put ashore, created a gap in the anti-aircraft defences, with disastrous consequences. Having completed her discharge,

After sailing eastwards along the North African coast to Bougie, the personnel ship CATHAY was hit by bombs on 11 November and, burning fore and aft, sank the following morning. [IWM A12834]

AWATEA left Bougie but, one mile out, was heavily attacked from the air, caught fire and subsequently sank, a fate which also befell CATHAY. ROBERTS was also attacked and became temporarily immobilised by three bomb hits. Elsewhere that day, U-boat activity caused the sinking not only of VICEROY OF INDIA, north of Arzeu, but also of the Dutch personnel ship NIEUW ZEELAND, east of Gibraltar: both ships were homeward-bound at the time. Whilst assisting the damaged ROBERTS at first light on 12 November,

TYNWALD was sunk by an Italian submarine and, in going to her aid, KARANJA became the target of enemy aircraft and was also lost, after smoke, steam and flames engulfed her midships section. Air attacks damaged the destroyers BICESTER and WILTON off Bougie and a U-boat torpedo seriously damaged the bow of the sloop STORK, north of the Algiers beachheads. Bomb hits on GLENFINLAS, whilst discharging her cargo of vehicles, guns, cased petrol and stores in Bougie harbour, caused her forward

This photograph, taken on 11 November, shows the dying minutes of VICEROY OF INDIA, which was torpedoed on the port side in her engine room: having landed her troops, she was proceeding unescorted because of a shortage of escort vessels. [IWM HU62985]

Bombs ignited the diesel tanks and petrol stores aboard KARANJA on 12 November: after becoming engulfed in smoke, steam and flames, her loss was inevitable. [IWM A12831]

section to settle to the bottom on 13 November. That day also saw both the cargo ship MARON, off Oran, and the Dutch destroyer ISAAC SWEERS, escorting Force H, succumb to U-boat torpedo hits.

Meanwhile, 61 merchant ships of follow-up convoys KMS2 and KMF2 had arrived off the Oran and Algiers beachheads, having left the UK on 25 October and 1 November respectively. On the approach to the Mediterranean, they had been protected against surface attacks by Force Q consisting of the cruisers CUMBERLAND and NORFOLK and three destroyers. Although the American Liberty ship LUTHER MARTIN had turned back in the early stages, neither convoy had suffered loss during the outward voyage until BROWNING, carrying cased petrol and ammunition amongst her other cargo, blew up, sending smoke and flames 300ft into the air off Oran, as a result of a U-boat attack on 12 November. The Algiers contingent reached port that day and the personnel ship NARKUNDA sailed on to arrive at Bougie on 14 November. After quickly disembarking her troops, she left but was almost immediately attacked with bombs, which burst alongside and caused so much devastation that eventually she sank. LALANDE was somewhat more fortunate, during her passage to Gibraltar after

discharging her cargo: a U-boat attack failed to sink her, despite opening up a massive hole in her hull. U-boats were now being successfully deployed against the homeward convoys after they had left the Mediterranean. They were responsible for the loss of the two large LSIs WARWICK CASTLE, on 14 November, and ETTRICK early the following day, the latter by U 155 which, in the same attack, hit the escort carrier AVENGER, causing her to blow up, and damaged the US Navy cargo ship ALMAACK. It was, however, an Italian submarine which, also on 15 November, torpedoed and sank the minesweeper ALGERINE off Bougie. These set-backs did not detract from the overhelming success of Operation "Torch" and, as early as 11 November, the main French bases in all three task force areas, from Safi in the west to Bougie and Bone in the east, were in the hands of Allied forces. The arrival of the follow-up convoys marked the conclusion of the initial phases: the regular build-up convoys which followed, brought further troops and supplies, as well as the inevitable losses, the most serious of which was P & O's latest liner STRATHALLAN.

Details of the ships involved are given in Section B4.

Personnel ships of the follow-up convoy, which reached Algiers on 12 November, with (left to right) CAMERONIA, STRATHEDEN, ORMONDE and STRATHMORE: between them they had a troop carrying capacity of almost 14,000. [IWM A12743B]

THE CENTRAL MEDITERRANEAN

THE SOUTH OF FRANCE

ST TROPEZ
TOULON
MARSEILLES

CORSICA
AJACCIO
PROPRIANO
Str of Bonifacio — MADDALENA

SARDINIA

ITALY

ROME
ANZIO

NAPLES
SALERNO

TARANTO

Tyrrhenian Sea

Mediterranean

← BONE, PHILIPPEVILLE, BOUGIE, ALGIERS and ORAN

REGGIO DI CALABRIA
TERMINI
PALERMO
SICILY

Str of Messina
CATANIA
AUGUSTA
SYRACUSE
Acid North   Eastern
Acid South   Task
Bark East   Force
Bark South   beachheads

Western Task
Force beachheads

Bark West

BIZERTA
TUNIS

SOUSSE

TUNISIA

MALTA

SFAX

**CENTRAL
MEDITERRANEAN
AREA**

TRIPOLI   BENGHAZI →

24

A5. SICILY: 10 JULY 1943

The Landing Ships, Infantry KEREN (right) and STRATHNAVER on their way to Sicily with assault troops from Egypt: in the far distance are numerous cargo ships of the slow convoy. [IWM A17975]

Abbreviations – LCT = Landing Craft, Tank; LSI = Landing Ship, Infantry; LST = Landing Ship, Tank

Following the success of the North African landings, Casablanca was selected as the venue for a January 1943 conference between President Roosevelt and Prime Minister Churchill. At this, it was agreed that the central Mediterranean island of Sicily would be the next major objective for Allied assault forces. The capture of this Italian island would not only secure through shipping communications in the Mediterranean but also serve as a base from which to conduct future operations against mainland Italy. In pursuit of this Sicilian objective, an Allied fleet of some 2,500 ships and landing craft was assigned for Operation "Husky". From their loading ports in the USA, in the UK, in North Africa, in Malta and in the Middle East, the assault convoys converged on an area to the south-east of Malta, before reaching eight adjoining beachheads, three American and five British, in the southern part of Sicily, in the early hours of 10 July, 1943. Cent, Dime and Joss beachheads in the Licata and Gela areas of the island were exclusively the responsibility of the US Western Task Force. Included in this American fleet of over 450 assault vessels and 130 supporting warships were four small Royal Navy LSIs; the monitor HMS ABERCROMBIE and a number of British landing craft. This book concentrates on the assault and follow-up vessels of the British-controlled Eastern Task Force, allocated to landing areas code named Acid North (nearest to Syracuse), Acid South, Bark East, Bark South and (nearest to the US Sectors) Bark West.

To allow for the long voyage time around the Cape, the ships assigned to carry assault personnel from the Middle East to Sicily left the UK as early as March 1943. The fleet, which included many of the Madagascar or North Africa veterans, such as DILWARA, DUCHESS OF BEDFORD, MONARCH OF BERMUDA, STRATHNAVER, SOBIESKI and WINCHESTER CASTLE, finally reaching Egypt in May. It conducted preparatory exercises in the Gulf of Aqaba area before final embarkation took place at Suez. After the Canal transit, the fleet of 18 British, Dutch, Norwegian and Polish LSIs and personnel ships left Port Said on 5 July in convoy MWF36 (Malta Westbound Fast No 36), accompanied by the headquarters ship BULOLO and escorted by the anti-aircraft cruiser CARLISLE and ten British and Greek destroyers. During its passage westwards, this convoy caught up the slow convoy, MWS36, formed of cargo ships, some of which had started loading their vehicles, landing craft and stores at Alexandria, Beirut, Haifa or Port Said as early as 2 June, before assembling at Alexandria, ready for a 3 July departure. All but one of the 32 participants were of wartime construction, 14 of them being US-flag Liberty ships, which were regarded as generally superior in gear and equipment to the eight British 'Ocean' vessels in the convoy. MWS36 was escorted by a total of ten destroyers, corvettes and sloops, as well as by the monitor EREBUS, the Dutch gunboat SOEMBA and the auxiliary anti-aircraft ship ALYNBANK. During its seven-day passage, the convoy suffered just one casualty. SHAHJEHAN was torpedoed by U-boat on 6 July, 70 miles north-east of Benghazi: she went down early the following day after fire engulfed her from her funnel forward, while she was under tow to Tobruk. Her sinking deprived the military not only of her cargo of vehicles, cased petrol and stores but also of four dock operating companies, whose personnel were badly needed to unload the ships on arrival. Strenuous efforts had been made to conceal and mislead the enemy about the destination of the invading fleet. It was remarkable that the convoys

A fully laden US Liberty ship heads for Sicily: across No 2 hatch, she carries two landing craft for transporting ashore her vehicles and stores, after they have been hoisted out by ship's derricks at the beachhead anchorage.
[IWM A17902]

should have been so free from attack, especially as the assembly of such a large fleet would undoubtedly have been reported by enemy agents in Egypt and a German aircraft was observed shadowing the early stages of one of the convoys. The fast ships got through without interference: between them, these two assault convoys, and the follow-up ships setting out from Egypt behind them, carried 66,000 troops, 10,000 vehicles and 60,000 tons of stores. These totals include 2,600 personnel and 846 vehicles and tanks aboard LCTs, which joined on 7 July, and the tanks and personnel embarked in 13 LSTs which met the slow convoy the following evening, all from Libya. The destination of the ships of Force A was the Acid beachheads south of the port of Syracuse, the capture of which was one of the early objectives of the landing forces.

The slow assault convoy carrying the military vehicles, stores and equipment of Force V from the UK was split into two groups. The advance section, KMS18A (UK/ Mediterranean Slow No 18 Section A), was composed of seven LSTs, which broke their voyage in Algiers. From there, on 5 July, they joined an eighth LST (406) and the cargo ships, making up section KMS18B, as they passed along the North African coast in an easterly direction. Before the two parts combined to form KMS18, this fleet lost two of its number to torpedo attack. CITY OF VENICE was hit on the evening of 4 July, with ST ESSYLT becoming a second victim of U 375 less than one hour later. The following afternoon, 50 miles east of Algiers, a further U-boat attack caused DEVIS to go down stern-first after a fierce fire. The first two ships lost, together with five of the other vessels, had been required for immediate unloading on arrival at the beachhead and were therefore due to transfer to fast convoy KMF18 from the Clyde, when it caught up on 9 July. This fast convoy, made up of 12 ships with a troop capacity in excess of 16,000, included Cunard White Star's ASCANIA; seven of the large landing ships which had participated in the North African invasion; the three named LSTs, BOXER, BRUISER and

THRUSTER, and the Force V headquarters ship HILARY, plus escorts. All were heading for Bark West beachhead, where, as at all the sectors, a submarine had been positioned to act as navigational marker.

Many of the military units of Force B, travelling from Tunisia and Malta, were aboard landing ships and craft, being given the benefit of the shortest sea crossing to Sicily. Vehicle loading took place at Sousse and personnel embarkation at Sfax and it was whilst sailing between these two ports with her vehicles on board that LST 429 caught fire, exploded and was lost on 3 July. The landing ships and craft set out from Sfax on 7 and 8 July in the company of the four small LSIs, PRINCESS BEATRIX, QUEEN EMMA, ROYAL SCOTSMAN and ROYAL ULSTERMAN and of their headquarters ship LARGS. The fleet was augmented by further craft, which joined from Malta on 9 July. En route to Bark South beachhead, a further casualty occurred: the strain of the passage out to the Mediterranean from the UK was too much for the hull of LCT 547 and she capsized, taking her six Sherman tanks down with her.

To afford the maximum possible protection from underwater and air attack, the convoy escorts were allocated into 13 different groups, lettered A-D and P-X. As an example of the organisational complexity, the escorting of assault convoy KMS18B, between its departure from the Clyde on 24 June and arrival off the Sicilian coast on 10 July, involved no fewer than 27 different warships. When the convoy set out from the UK, it was escorted by group B, consisting of the sloop ERNE; the cutter BANFF; the frigate TEVIOT and the corvettes BERGAMOT, BRYONY, HONEYSUCKLE, OXLIP, RHODODENDRON and the Indian HYDERABAD. On 5 July, this group was relieved by nine destroyers of group S, formed of CALPE, CLEVELAND, FARNDALE, HAYDON, TYNEDALE, VICEROY and the Polish KRAKOWIAK, from Algiers; PUCKERIDGE, from Bone, and later LEDBURY. To

The Landing Ship, Headquarters HILARY, prior to her 28 June departure from the Clyde with the fast Force V assault convoy for Sicily. [IWM A17348]

release group S to refuel on 7-8 July, the convoy was covered by the group T destroyers ATHERSTONE, HOLCOMBE, LIDDESDALE and the Polish SLAZAK and by the minesweepers CADMUS, CIRCE, ESPIEGLE and FLY, all from Bizerta. Group S, less LEDBURY and VICEROY, returned to take over from group T on the evening of 8 July, with ANTHONY as late replacement for VICEROY, which put into Malta for repairs. Dependent upon its size and importance, a similar programme was required to protect every other convoy throughout its passage to the beachheads.

In addition to the coastal bombardment monitors, cruisers, gunboats, destroyers and craft allocated to the landing beachheads, a powerful fleet had been assembled to cover the operation against any Italian surface vessel activity. The aircraft carriers FORMIDABLE and INDOMITABLE and the battleships

NELSON, RODNEY, VALIANT and WARSPITE of Force H, together with their escorting destroyers, were positioned to the south-east of Sicily, it being considered that four British battleships could adequately deal with six Italian counterparts. Force Z, including the battleships HOWE and KING GEORGE V and cruisers DIDO and SIRIUS, was held in reserve to the west of Sicily but was not required on the day of the landings; they did, however, undertake diversionary bombardments on 11-12 July in Operation "Fracture".

Sailing out of Malta on the eve of the invasion was Admiral Sir Bertram Ramsay aboard his Eastern Task Force flagship ANTWERP. Accompanied by Admiral Lord Louis Mountbatten, Chief of Combined Operations, he witnessed the convergence of the massive armada before it reached the enemy coast, the outline of which came into the view of the leading ships

The Hunt class destroyer LEDBURY served as escort to three different assault convoys, during part of their transit through the Mediterranean to the Sicilian coast. [MPL 1996]

Vessels at Bark West on the first day of the operation, with (left to right) a BOXER class Landing Ship, Tank (LST); the Landing Ships, Infantry DURBAN CASTLE and (nearest the camera) GLENGYLE and (in the distance to the right) other LSTs. This photograph was taken shortly after that appearing on pages 2 and 3. [IWM A17957]

Landing Craft, Tank discharging onto one of the Sicilian beaches, with soldiers of the Highland Division up to their waists in water: the prominent numbers displayed are operational not craft numbers. [IWM A17916]

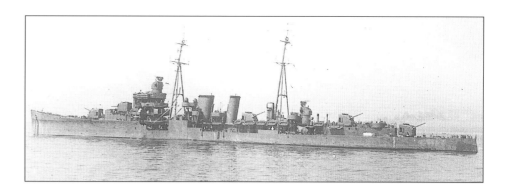

At the beachhead on 10 July, the cruiser DELHI fired three salvoes against shore targets, then provided anti-aircraft protection. [MPL 1205]

just after sunset that evening. As midnight approached, Allied glider aircraft passed overhead and, early on 10 July, the first ships of the assault fleet reached their assigned positions. Within five hours, the landings in the Eastern Task Force area had been successfully accomplished, partly due to the detailed planning and tactical surprise and partly as a result of the weakness of the Italian opposition. However, it was not long before the assembled fleet was subjected to heavy air attacks. As soon as they had disembarked their personnel, the large ships left the beachheads but the Norwegian personnel ship BERGENSFJORD, carrying the Syracuse naval port party, remained and became a target when 40 German aircraft bombed the beachhead that afternoon. She suffered some damage and casualties, as did LST 407 and the US Liberty ship GEORGE ROGERS CLARK, which was straddled by

bombs. Despite being clearly marked and fully floodlit to reveal her hospital ship status, TALAMBA was dive-bombed that night and sank five miles off the Acid beachheads. The British Army Commander, General Montgomery, and his staff landed in Sicily from ANTWERP on 11 July, a day on which further air attacks were aimed at the shipping anchorages. Cargo discharge had already been completed when a bomb exploded in JOSEPH G CANNON's after hold but the Liberty ship survived and was able to reach Malta under her own steam. In contrast, ammunition was still aboard the Dutch vessel BAARN when her forward hold was set on fire: after the failure of a towage attempt by the cruiser CARLISLE, BAARN was sent to the bottom by gunfire from the destroyer TARTAR. The latter's sister ship, NUBIAN, opened the port of Syracuse to allied shipping that day and, during the evening of 12 July, the

The destroyer ESKIMO in the Acid area on 11 July: closer inshore cargo ships lie at anchor, with the Dutch BAARN blazing furiously as a result of an air attack and the cruiser CARLISLE standing by: the following day, ESKIMO was herself damaged by a bomb. [IWM A18092]

Above: off the port of Augusta, the minesweeper SEAHAM took the surrender of the Italian submarine BRONZO and is seen here on 12 July with her prize in tow, en route to Syracuse. [IWM A18094]

Left: the Belgian personnel ship LEOPOLDVILLE. [NMM P23213]

LSI ULSTER MONARCH put ashore commandos in Augusta, enabling that port to be occupied. Air raids had persisted that day and, during one of these, cased petrol on board OCEAN PEACE caught fire as a result of several bomb near misses and, after a massive explosion, the ship settled to the bottom. Three destroyers suffered damage on the 12th, ESKIMO from a bomb hit and BRISSENDEN and BLANKNEY from a collision whilst on anti-submarine patrol: the latter ship remained operational but the other two were forced to retire to Malta for repairs. In the vicinity of Augusta the Italian submarine BRONZO surrendered to the minesweeper SEAHAM, which proudly brought her into Syracuse. On 13 July, the monitor EREBUS, which had been providing bombardment support in the Augusta area during the two previous days, turned her attention to Catania airfield and that night commandos went ashore from the LSI PRINS ALBERT at the southern end of Catania Bay.

The opening of Syracuse enabled the 12 large personnel ships of the follow-up convoy from Egypt, MWF37, to berth in the port and ALMANZORA, EMPIRE TROOPER, ORBITA and the Belgian LEOPOLDVILLE were the largest to do so on 13 July. This was the day that three other follow-up convoys also reached Sicily. From the east came 31 cargo ships of convoy MWS37 which, within a few hours of arriving from Alexandria, lost the Liberty ship TIMOTHY PICKERING to air attack off Acid South beachhead. Convoys KMF19 and KMS19 from the UK had a combined total of 44 ships carrying "Husky" personnel, equipment and supplies: its Force X contingent sailed direct to Sicily, whereas the ships of Force Y were held back at Algiers and Malta, until military requirements dictated their being called forward. The first Force Y personnel ship to arrive in Sicily was CAMERONIA on 16 July, with BANFORA, FRANCONIA, LETITIA and ORMONDE following three days later. It was not until the end of the month that the last Force Y cargo ship reached the beachheads and, by the time they had all been discharged, the conquest of Sicily was nearly complete and the Allies could actively prepare for the assault on mainland Italy.

Details of the ships involved are given in Section B5.

The Landing Ship, Headquarters BULOLO (centre) and (in the distance) Liberty ships discharging their military equipment and supplies, aided by tank landing ships and craft. [IWM A18095]

A6. SALERNO, ITALY: 9 SEPTEMBER 1943

The scene off the Salerno beachhead, with the cruiser MAURITIUS in the centre of the picture. [IWM A19157]

Abbreviations – LCI = Landing Craft, Infantry; LCT = Landing Craft, Tank; LSI = Landing Ship, Infantry; LST = Landing Ship, Tank

The unexpectedly rapid progress of the Allied forces in Sicily and indications of an imminent Italian surrender, spurred on the early completion of plans for the invasion of mainland Italy. On 3 September 1943 came the unopposed Operation "Baytown" crossing, by the British Eighth Army, of the narrow Straits of Messina to Reggio di Calabria, using LSTs and LCTs. These troops were then to head northwards to link up with a major Allied invasion force to be put ashore in Salerno Bay. This location was selected because of its proximity to the major port of Naples. Its beaches were suitable for landings; there were no strong fixed defences and the area was within fighter aircraft range from Sicily. For this assault, code named "Avalanche", United States troops formed the Southern Attack Force, while the British Army's X Corps comprised the Northern Attack Force, the territorial division being the River Sele. In

One of 53 British Landing Ships, Tank to take part in this operation, LST 63 is seen here making her way to Salerno, laden with military vehicles on deck and below. [IWM A19148]

The cruiser MAURITIUS off the Italian coast to provide bombardment support. [IWM A19154]

operation, there was a considerable degree of interchange of British and US vessels between the two task forces. This study concerns itself with the British-controlled assault and follow-up vessels, which made up more than 50% of the fleet, and relates to the British Northern Attack Force, except where indicated otherwise.

The main invasion embarkation area for the troops and their equipment was North Africa and the port of origin was shown up in the first letter of the convoy identifications – F for Bizerta, N for Oran and T for Tripoli or Sousse. After S, for Salerno, as the second designator came the convoy speed, Fast, Medium or Slow, followed by the numerical sequence. In the case of vessels scheduled to join at intermediate points, a suffix X or Y was applied. The first convoy to set out direct to Salerno left on 5 September: it was NSF1 (Oran/Salerno Fast No 1) formed of the main American fleet of 19 assault vessels; 16 escorts and 8 minesweepers, heading for the southern beachhead area. It included the LSIs DUCHESS OF BEDFORD, MARNIX VAN ST ALDEGONDE and ORONTES and the three British LSTs BOXER, BRUISER and

As a Landing Ship, Infantry, DEVONSHIRE was part of the Northern Attack Force. [NMM P22158]

Although designed as an aircraft maintenance carrier, UNICORN carried 30 Seafire and three Swordfish aircraft for the operation. [IWM A18349]

THRUSTER. Sailing with them, as part of the escort, was ULSTER QUEEN, which was fitted for fighter direction duty, as was PALOMARES, one of the intermediate joiners from Algiers the following day. The equivalent convoy for the northern area was TSF1 originating in Tripoli on 6 September and including the headquarters vessel HILARY, the large LSIs DEVONSHIRE, GLENGYLE and SOBIESKI and nine smaller LSIs, three of which joined from Palermo. Other convoys brought a small number of cargo ships; 53 British LSTs, for both beachheads, and 114 LCIs and LCTs.

The invasion was timed for the morning of 9 September, on the eve of which came the announcement of Italy's surrender but the immediate relief within the assault fleet was short-lived, because Salerno was strongly defended by the German army, which was rapidly reinforcing its strength in southern Italy. To cover against surface attack from the Italian fleet, the battleships VALIANT and WARSPITE and aircraft carriers FORMIDABLE and ILLUSTRIOUS of Force H had been directed to the area on an assignment, which was now rendered unnecessary. However, the fleet carriers were still required to provide air cover for the smaller carriers of Force V, whilst their own fighters were protecting the beachhead. The main vessels of Force V were UNICORN and the escort carriers ATTACKER, BATTLER, HUNTER and STALKER. Designed as an aircraft maintenance carrier and only completed that year, UNICORN was making a rare appearance as a conventional aircraft carrier. She left Malta on 8 September, in company with the cruisers CHARYBDIS, EURYALUS and SCYLLA and the four escort carriers, to be in position next day some 45 miles south-west of the beachhead area.

German air attacks were launched against the invasion fleet, even before its arrival at Salerno. During the evening of 6 September an estimated 180 aircraft attacked the vessels assembled in Bizerta Bay but, thwarted by a smokescreen, they inflicted no damage. Termini, on the north coast of Sicily, was a refuelling stop for the smaller vessels. Whilst waiting there fully loaded late on 8 September, LST 417 was struck aft by an aerial torpedo and sustained such severe damage that she had to be beached. Earlier that day, the first sinking had occurred when LCT 624 received a bomb hit, whilst in convoy off the Isle of Capri: her high-octane fuel immediately burst into flames and the craft went down in seconds. Other LSTs and landing craft suffered damage from the fierce resistance mounted by the Germans against the initial assault. Supported by tanks and armoured cars, the enemy slowly fell back, leaving few mines and demolitions but the operation did not progress as rapidly as had been expected. Five days after the main landings, a powerful German counter-attack was repulsed and, within three weeks, the main objective had been achieved: the port of Naples passed into Allied hands and, in spite of systematic and extensive demolitions, was capable of limited immediate use. The only major ship loss at Salerno occurred as a result of an air attack on 13 September, when a bomb exploded between the bridge and funnel of the hospital ship NEWFOUNDLAND. She survived the ensuing fire and remained afloat but the unavailability of a salvage tug made her a navigational hazard to the ships of the build-up fleet and she was deliberately sunk the following day, with 70 shells being fired at her by the US destroyer PLUNKETT.

Details of the ships involved are given in Section B6.

A7. ANZIO, ITALY: 22 JANUARY 1944

Only recently completed, HMS SPARTAN is seen here bombarding enemy shore positions at Anzio: seven days after the initial assault, the cruiser was hit by a glider bomb and capsized with heavy loss of life. [IWM A21460]

Abbreviations —- LCI = Landing Craft, Infantry; LCT = Landing Craft, Tank; LSI = Landing Ship, Infantry; LST = Landing Ship, Tank

The fierce resistance put up by German forces in Italy prevented the Allies from making the sought-after progress northwards after the September 1943 landings at Salerno. In a bold attempt to relieve the pressure further south by cutting the enemy's supply lines, it was decided that another invasion force would storm ashore further north at Anzio, only a mere 40 miles from the capital city of Rome. Operation "Shingle" was mounted from Naples and Salerno, from where most of the fleet set out the previous day, in preparation for the early morning landings on 22 January 1944. The

assault operation was divided into two sections, with (American) Force X to the south and (British) Force P to the north of Anzio. This study highlights the activities of the British-controlled assault and follow-up vessels of both forces and the US Liberty ships carrying British stores.

The American convoys formed parts 2-8 of Task Group 81. The US Rangers, directed to capture the port of Anzio, before demolitions could render it unusable, were embarked in part 2 aboard the LSIs PRINCESS BEATRIX, ROYAL ULSTERMAN and WINCHESTER CASTLE, while the landing ships ASCANIA and CIRCASSIA were included in part 4. The Force P

CIRCASSIA served as a Landing Ship, Infantry for these landings. [IWM FL8122]

The Cunard White Star liner ASCANIA carried American troops from Naples to Anzio's X beachhead. [IWM FL1101]

assault contingent was formed of five groups, designated A-E, with the Landing Ship, Headquarters BULOLO and the LSIs DERBYSHIRE, GLENGYLE and SOBIESKI leaving Naples (Pozzuoli) on 21 January in group D. The LSTs and craft, carrying the Force P personnel and equipment, moved to the beachhead as follows – 10 LCT in group A; 12 LSTs in B; 18 LSTs and 24 LCI in C; 7 LCI in D and 9 LCI in E.

Timed to coincide with a large-scale Allied offensive from the south, the landings achieved complete surprise. However, this early advantage was not exploited and was consequently lost. No link up took place with those advancing from the south and German opposition hemmed the assault forces in around the beachhead, with the British on the left flank and the US Army on the right. Although no British ships were lost on D-Day, LST 11 was damaged by a bomb near miss; LST 320 was holed by shore gunfire and LST 363, carrying 315 personnel, 73 vehicles and a balloon, was attacked from the air. Also that day, PALOMARES, serving as stand-by fighter direction ship, was immobilised by a mine explosion and required tug towage back to Naples. Air attacks intensified and, on 23 January, the forward magazines of JANUS blew up, after the destroyer was struck by an aerial torpedo:

survivors were rescued by her sister ship, JERVIS, even though she had just lost a few feet of her bow as a result of a glider bomb hit. The following day, three hospital carriers were attacked with bombs: LEINSTER was damaged; ST ANDREW escaped unharmed, despite three near misses, but her sister, ST DAVID, took a direct hit and went down by the stern. A shuttle service of LSTs and LCTs was established between Naples and Anzio, where unloading was concentrated on the port and the US beachhead. On 26 January, LST 422 sank with heavy loss of life, after being mined and gutted by fire, whereas HILARY A HERBERT survived not only an aircraft crashing on her but also a later bomb explosion. Three days later, another US Liberty ship, SAMUEL HUNTINGTON, was extensively damaged, and subsequently blew up, the same evening that a glider bomb caused massive casualties aboard the newly completed cruiser SPARTAN, which then capsized. The stubbornness of the German resistance can be gauged from the fact that it was not until early June that the Allies finally reached Rome, four months later than originally planned.

Details of the ships involved are given in Section B7.

The hospital carrier ST DAVID was bombed by a German aircraft on 24 January and sank by the stern in five minutes.

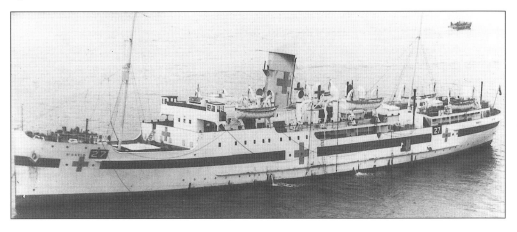

Some of the ship's 20 Wildcat aircraft on the deck of the escort carrier PURSUER: immediately astern are ATTACKER, KHEDIVE and the force flagship, the cruiser ROYALIST. [IWM A25184]

A8. THE SOUTH OF FRANCE: 15 AUGUST 1944

Abbreviations – LCT = Landing Craft, Tank; LSI = Landing Ship, Infantry; LST = Landing Ship, Tank

Operation "Neptune", the long-awaited invasion across the English Channel to France, commenced on 6 June 1944, with five beachheads being established on the Normandy coast. In an attempt to divert some German forces away from the country's north coast; to create a firm bridgehead in southern France and to capture Marseilles, one of the world's major ports, another invasion was mounted in the Mediterranean. Originally under the name "Anvil", for security reasons it had been renamed Operation "Dragoon" by the time the assault forces landed on 15 August. Under American control, it was predominantly composed of US troops, backed up by Free French forces, the only British soldiers involved being participants in the airborne assault, carried out simultaneously with the amphibious landings. Nevertheless, the initial British Royal and Merchant Navy contribution was considerable and involved over 350 vessels, representing more than one third of the total: it is to these British-controlled assault and follow-up vessels that this study is confining itself.

The assault area, centred on St Tropez, extended some 30 miles along the Cote d'Azur. It was divided into four sectors, code named (from east to west) Camel, Delta, Alpha and Sitka. The Sitka force PRINCEs BAUDOUIN, DAVID and HENRY, with escort including the cruiser DIDO and destroyer LOOKOUT, were directed to land commandos on the islands of Port Cros and Levant: the heavy guns on the latter posed a threat to the invading fleet, until discovered to be dummies. These ships sailed in convoy SY1, in company with PRINS ALBERT and PRINCESS BEATRIX. The first four of the LSIs just named had taken part in the Normandy invasion, after which they had been swiftly despatched to Naples, the main mounting port for this new assault. Convoys from there were allocated the prefix S, which, except for SY1, was followed by the Fast, Medium or Slow designators and convoy number. The second section of convoys running to different destination beachheads was suffixed A and the third section B. Accordingly, KEREN, carrying 1,114 troops, formed part of SF1 assault fleet to Camel beachhead; ASCANIA and DILWARA between them transported 3,800 personnel to Delta in SF1A and DERBYSHIRE and DUNERA landed a similar number in Alpha area after arriving in SF1B. The Corsican ports of Ajaccio and Propriano were used as staging points by SY1 and a number of the other convoys. Although they were observed several times by enemy reconnaissance aircraft, no attacks were launched against any of the ships whilst en route to the beachheads and the complex shipping movements proceeded as planned, with the first vessels arriving during the night of 14-15 August, ready for the early morning assault.

The gunboats APHIS and SCARAB were allocated to the Special Operations Group, to perform diversionary functions, as were ANTWERP and STUART PRINCE, although these two were detached, initially to serve as

The Canadian Landing Ship, Infantry PRINCE HENRY landed her 279 commandos on the Isle of Levant, off the south coast of France. [IWM A21733]

aircraft navigational beacons. HM battleship RAMILLIES and ten British cruisers, including DIDO, formed part of the bombardment and anti-aircraft fleet, four of them to protect a combined British and US Navy force of nine escort carriers, positioned about 30 miles south of the French coast on spotting, strafing and bombing assignments. The Royal Navy contribution to this consisted of ATTACKER, EMPEROR, HUNTER, KHEDIVE, PURSUER, SEARCHER and STALKER. At the beachhead on 15 August, three shells struck LCT 307 on her port side aft and LCTs 339, 552 and 625 were also damaged, 552 taking a direct hit in her engine room. In Alpha sector the minesweepers ARIES, BRIXHAM, POLRUAN, ROTHESAY and STORNOWAY came under attack from small patrol vessels but managed to destroy all five, without damage to themselves. Later that day, the landing ship, gantry, DEWDALE, was narrowly missed by a rocket bomb: she and her sister ship ENNERDALE, in addition to transporting landing craft, were filled with fuel oil, diesel and water to replenish other vessels during their stay at the beachhead.

By the end of the first day, 60,150 troops and 6,737 vehicles had been put ashore, including the first French armoured contingent, which had embarked at Oran in convoys prefixed A and in Special Convoy No 2, to which the LSI WINCHESTER CASTLE and the LSTs BRUISER and THRUSTER were assigned. Two French infantry divisions arrived from Taranto, in the heel of Italy, on 16 August, in convoy TF1. It was formed of eleven large LSIs and personnel ships, including CAMERONIA, CIRCASSIA and DURBAN CASTLE; the Dutch VOLENDAM and the Polish BATORY and SOBIESKI, the last-named taking part in her sixth invasion operation. Their equipment and supplies reached Alpha and Delta beachheads the same day aboard 40 British cargo vessels, which also sailed from Taranto, 16 of them having loaded at the Adriatic port of Brindisi. They had formed convoy TM1 and their number included OCEAN RIDER carrying a part replacement cargo, following a hold fire during loading at Taranto. Within 30 minutes of arrival, FORT MAISONNEUVE and ESSEX TRADER were hit by anti-personnel bombs, which inflicted many casualties aboard the latter ship. Overall, the losses had proved minimal and the success of the operation was confirmed by the late August capture of Marseilles and the naval base of Toulon. By then, Allied forces were moving rapidly northwards to link up with those from Normandy, as intended.

Details of the ships involved are given in Section B8.

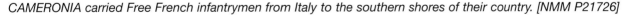

CAMERONIA carried Free French infantrymen from Italy to the southern shores of their country. [NMM P21726]

THE FAR EAST

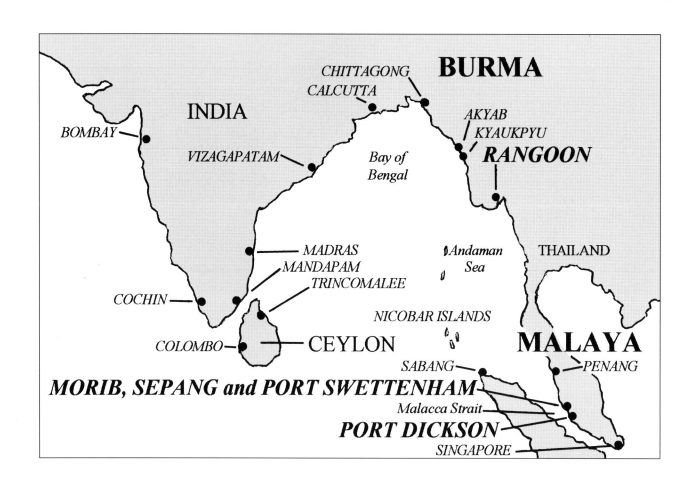

MORIB, SEPANG and PORT SWETTENHAM

As a Royal Navy Landing Ship, Infantry, GLENROY took part in the assaults on both Rangoon and Malaya in 1945. [Wright & Logan]

DUNERA heading for the entrance to the Rangoon River, as seen from one of her escorts: other ships of the main assault convoy are just visible to the right of the picture. [IWM SE3926]

Abbreviations – LCT = Landing Craft, Tank; LSI = Landing Ship, Infantry

After taking part in the July 1943 invasion of Sicily, seven large assault ships had transitted the Suez Canal to proceed eastwards to India. They were to train with troops in preparation for large-scale amphibious operations against the Japanese but all hope of major assaults being mounted was eliminated when they were ordered back for overriding invasion commitments in the Mediterranean. It was not until 1945 that suitable large ships were again available in India, by which time the converted passenger liner for use as a large LSI was a thing of the past: this type of assault vessel became exclusively based on those of cargo ship design.

Landings had been carried out along the Burmese coast since the beginning of that year but, in order to feed reinforcement troops, equipment and supplies to the British Army, fighting its way through Burma, it was now necessary to seize the port of Rangoon from the Japanese. This was the objective of Operation

"Dracula", timed to beat the start of the monsoon with an assault date of 2 May. In preparation for this, between 27 and 30 April, four invasion convoys left the port of Kyaukpyu, in western Burma, and two others left nearby Akyab, some 250 miles from Rangoon. Forming convoy Able were 16 fleet minesweepers and accompanying danlayers, assigned the task of clearing and marking the approaches to the Rangoon River, up to the lowering position 30 miles from the assault area. Convoys Dog, Easy and Fox were made up of the smaller and slower vessels, while convoy Charlie included the LSI BARPETA and three cargo ships carrying vehicles and stores from Chittagong, Calcutta and Kyaukpyu. The headquarters ship LARGS; the cruiser PHOEBE; the personnel ship and hospital carrier RAJULA and the LSIs GLENROY, PERSIMMON, PRINS ALBERT and SILVIO were amongst the last to leave in Baker, the main convoy. They had all sailed out east after forming part of the Normandy invasion fleet in June 1944, although delays in PERSIMMON's readiness, as the newly-built PAMPAS, had prevented her from taking part in the

The cruiser PHOEBE and (right) the personnel ship RAJULA at Kyaukpyu. [IWM SE3919]

With some difficulty, a 25pdr gun is put ashore from Landing Craft, Tank 1242 on the banks of the Rangoon River. Passing in the background is LCT 1054 [IWM SE3915]

early stages of the operation. SILVIO was by then a commissioned ship, having the previous year sailed as the Red Ensign EMPIRE HALBERD.

Air support for the invading forces was provided by the escort carriers EMPEROR, HUNTER, KHEDIVE and STALKER, all of which left Kyaukpyu on 30 April, in company with their flagship, the cruiser ROYALIST. To intercept any escaping Japanese forces, the destroyers RACEHORSE, REDOUBT and ROEBUCK were positioned south of the Rangoon River in Operation "Gable" and, in an action on 30 April, they engaged and sank nine small vessels. A bombarding force, including the battleships HMS QUEEN ELIZABETH and the French RICHELIEU, was also ordered to the area on an associated operation code named "Bishop", with a view to preventing interference from any Japanese naval units. It was known that Elephant Island at the entrance to the Rangoon River had been equipped with a significant number of coastal and anti-aircraft guns but, when the assault went in early on the morning of 2 May, absolutely no opposition was encountered. The planning had been based on faulty intelligence and it soon became apparent that Japanese forces had evacuated the whole area some days before. In view of the changed circumstances, the assault troops re-embarked the following day and ventured in craft 30 miles up river to the city of Rangoon, which was found also to be devoid of Japanese defenders. Mines in the river did, however, pose a problem and LCT 1238 became a victim, suffered casualties and was lost. By 6 May, HMS PHOEBE and 25 other ships of varying sizes were able to make the passage upstream to Rangoon and, two days later, the first merchant vessels berthed

With a carrying capacity of 1,822, the personnel ship NEVASA formed part of the first convoy carrying follow-up troops to Rangoon. [IWM SE7171]

Landing Craft, Infantry 120 lands Indian troops. [IWM SE3322]

alongside at the capital. The follow-up convoys operated under the KR (Kyaukpyu/Rangoon) prefix: KRF1 included the personnel ship NEVASA and four of the LSIs, on their second round trip after carrying the initial assault troops. Despite the work of the sweepers, whilst returning downstream from Rangoon on 8 May, SILVIO was mined, having possibly strayed outside the swept channel. She remained seaworthy but permanent hull repairs were too extensive to be carried out in India or South Africa and the ship was therefore ordered back to the UK. No further such incidents occurred and this allowed the unhindered passage of the initial build-up convoys and of the Commander-in-Chief, East Indies Fleet who reached the Burmese capital on 11 May aboard HMS ULSTER QUEEN.

Details of the ships involved (not only in the assault and follow-up but also in the initial build-up convoys) are given in Section B9.

Two Landing Craft, Gun (Large) move up the Rangoon River towards the Burmese capital city: nearest the camera is LCG(L) 5. [IWM SE3927]

Part of ROCKSAND's complement of 19 landing craft can be seen stowed and water borne. [IWM SE5440]

Abbreviations – LCT = Landing Craft, Tank; LSI = Landing Ship, Infantry; LST = Landing Ship, Tank

After hostilities in Europe ended in May 1945, all available resources could be concentrated in the Far East for the continuing war against Japan. The recapture of Singapore was expected no later than March 1946 and would be achieved after an overland advance through Malaya. No US resources could be allocated to assist this, because 1,384 of their assault vessels and transports were required for a November 1945 landing on the southern Japanese island of Kyushu, where up to a quarter of a million American casualties were predicted. Independent British preparations were therefore approved for a September operation, code named "Zipper", against the west coast of Malaya.

The shortage of landing ships and craft dictated that this operation, to be carried out by Indian army divisions, should be conducted in two parts, with a separation of three days and 40 miles between them. The first part was to be launched simultaneously in the Sepang area and over the Morib beaches, 28 miles south-east of Port Swettenham. The second part was to take place on the beaches near Port Dickson, from a fleet due to assemble off Morib the previous day. A

complex series of convoys, prefixed JM, was set up from all major ports in India (except Karachi) and from Colombo and Trincomalee in Ceylon, with the bulk of the landing ships for the initial force setting out from the Indian south-east coast port of Madras. The third letter of the JM convoy designations denoted the originating port – A for Bombay, B Cochin, C Trincomalee, D Mandapam, E Madras, F Vizagapatam and G for Colombo. Next came the numerical convoy sequence, suffixed, if necessary, by A or B, when a large movement was split into two parts, and finally the Fast or Slow speed indicator. Thus, convoy JMA2BS was India/Malaya, from Bombay, No 2 convoy, B section, at slow speed. A further series of (GM) convoys was organised to set out from Rangoon, with the convoys merging as they headed southwards to form a massive armada of more than 550 assault, follow-up and support vessels. Because of the distances involved, Bombay to Morib being 2,315 miles, the assault troops would be on board the larger vessels for 7-12 days and in the landing craft for as much as three weeks, which called for a feat of considerable endurance on the part of both men and craft.

The setting of D-Day for 9 September required a Bombay departure date for the first cargo ships of 27

August. When news was received of the Japanese surrender, the operational arrangements were too far advanced to accommodate major changes and, in any case, there was no guarantee that the cease-fire would be observed by all Japanese forces, certainly until the instrument of surrender had finally been signed in Tokyo Bay on 2 September. Consequently "Zipper" continued to be regarded as an assault operation but the massively changed circumstances resulted in a quarter of the fleet being detached and diverted. To be appropriately placed as soon as the surrender was signed, the cruisers CLEOPATRA and LONDON were despatched to Sabang in Operation "Beecham"; the battleship NELSON, supporting vessels and two medium LSIs sailed to liberate Penang in Operations "Jurist" and "Flashlight" and the large LSIs GLENGYLE and LLANSTEPHAN CASTLE, joined by the escort carrier SMITER, proceeded to Hong Kong as part of Operation "Armour". Another fleet, heading for Singapore in Operations "Tiderace" and "Shackle", included the entire GM troop and supply movement, which had been due to sail from Rangoon as part of Operation "Zipper".

The remainder of the "Zipper" fleet proceeded as planned, except that the ships now could sail undarkened, and the slow assault convoy from Bombay, JMA1S, duly left on 27 August. It consisted of ten cargo ships, carrying between them around 900 vehicles and 3,000 tons of cased petrol and other stores. In accordance with the usual practice, most of them were fitted to carry 200-300 personnel, for whom accommodation would normally be provided in the 'tween decks of the after holds. On the second day out, one ship of the convoy was forced to turn back, after becoming the only vessel of the entire invasion fleet to be damaged by gunfire. MALIKA's cargo of Bofors guns had been delivered to the quayside with instructions that they be loaded. They were duly loaded, not only into the ship's hold, as intended, but also with

ammunition, which certainly had not been the intention. The movement of the ship at sea caused a shell to be fired, puncturing MALIKA's hull below the water-line and an inspection of the holds of the other ships revealed that the guns aboard SAMGARA and SAMGAUDIE also needed to be made safe. Heading out from Madras on 1 September was convoy JME1S of 30 vessels, including 25 LSTs with a total lifting capacity of 4,800 personnel, 880 vehicles and 850 tons of stores. A further 1,100 personnel, 168 vehicles and 1,050 tons of stores could be catered for by the 48 LCTs, from Madras, via Mandapam, in JMD1 convoys.

GLENROY, PERSIMMON, ROCKSAND and SEFTON embarked their assault troops at Madras, while Vizagapatam was the loading port of SANSOVINO, a sister ship of the last two just named. The fact that, two days out, PERSIMMON had one of her landing craft carried away, gives an indication of the sea state prevailing during the voyage. All these large LSIs joined up with the personnel ships carrying the immediate follow-up troops. These included ALMANZORA, CITY OF CANTERBURY and the Dutch TEGELBERG from Madras and RANCHI and the formerly French FELIX ROUSSEL from Cochin. Despite their reduced numbers, the merging convoys of the invasion fleet stretched for approximately 40 miles as the vessels proceeded through the Malacca Strait between Malaya and Sumatra. Even with the long distances involved and the prevalent monsoon, the assault vessels and their naval escorts arrived at the scheduled time. Air cover was provided by fighters from the escort carriers AMEER, EMPEROR, EMPRESS, HUNTER, KHEDIVE and STALKER: spare aircraft were to have been available aboard BEGUM but she went aground on departure from Trincomalee and returned to port. The day prior to the first landings, EMPRESS, having sustained damage to her catapult, was also withdrawn. The battleships HMS NELSON and the French RICHELIEU were amongst the vessels allocated for

On passage to Malaya, the personnel ship CITY OF CANTERBURY experienced difficulty in maintaining the required speed; she fell behind the rest of the assault convoy and the cutter LULWORTH was assigned as her escort. [NMM P22095]

Released from the fleet assigned for the invasion of the Japanese main island in 1946, the Landing Ship, Infantry SEFTON returns to the UK having discarded her assault craft. [Wright & Logan]

bombardment purposes but, after leaving Penang on 7 September, NELSON's manoeuvrability was seriously impaired by electrical failures and both ships were consequently held in reserve and did not take up their assigned bombardment positions.

The initial assault proceeded as planned, with the invading forces being under orders to take no offensive action, unless they encountered enemy opposition. The first vessels arrived in the assault area at 0325 on 9 September: craft from PERSIMMON and SEFTON were lowered at 0445 and, after a six-mile run-in, touched down on their respective beaches in assault formation two hours later. Much to the vast relief of all concerned, they were unopposed and consequently no preliminary bombardment was carried out. The invasion force was spared the crippling losses feared from suicide attacks by motor boats and aircraft but the condition of the landing beaches still presented considerable hazards, as did sea mines. Indeed, on the approaches the previous day, the destroyers BLEASDALE and CALPE each exploded one mine and PENN two. Nevertheless, at the Morib and Sepang beachheads, 25,000 troops and 1,043 vehicles were put ashore on the first day, in contrast to the originally planned totals of 44,000 and 1,200 respectively. For the 12 September assault, ships anchored at the lowering position off the Port Dickson beaches at 0430. There, a total of 15,000 troops and 729 vehicles were landed and, the following day, a surrender ceremony of the Japanese forces in Malaya took place at Kuala Lumpur. A sizeable follow-up movement brought further equipment and supplies to the "Zipper" area on 19 September. By that date, many of the personnel ships, which had brought troops in the early convoys, had been directed on to Singapore, to assist with the repatriation of released prisoners of war and civilian internees.

Details of the ships originally assigned (and the ports to which those detached were diverted) are given in Section B10.

The invasion of the main Japanese island of Honshu, code named Operation "Coronet", was due to take place in April 1946, with the object of forcing the unconditional surrender of the Japanese. The plan outlined in July 1945 called for a British Commonwealth force of at least two divisions in the early stages of the invasion, followed by a further two or three divisions soon afterwards. Besides the units of the British Pacific Fleet already in the area and the additional warships earmarked, ships of the East Indies Fleet would be used in support. The requirement was also identified for 100 British cargo ships, for operations and essential maintenance: the assault ships were allocated between Forces A and B.

Force A was to be formed at Brunei, mostly from the ships used in "Zipper", to transport the Australian division. It would consist of the headquarters ships BULOLO, NITH and WAVENEY; the LSIs GLENROY, PERSIMMON, ROCKSAND, SAINFOIN, SANSOVINO and SEFTON; the landing ships, dock HIGHWAY and NORTHWAY and 48 LSTs. Force B was to be formed on the west coast of the USA, to transport a British division across the Pacific, after its troops had been supplied and trained with American equipment. This force was allocated, as headquarters ships, KEREN (after conversion from an LSI), LOTHIAN and the frigates ETTRICK and MEON; the LSIs CICERO, GALTEE MORE, GLENEARN, GLENGYLE, SILVIO and SIR HUGO; the landing ships, dock EASTWAY and OCEANWAY and another 48 LSTs. Other LSIs were being prepared in Europe but, mercifully, the surrender of Japan meant that no such invasion was required.

Section B
Details of the ships
involved

Between 1942 and 1944, the Union-Castle liner WINCHESTER CASTLE (above) served as an assault ship for the invasions of Madagascar, North Africa, Sicily, Anzio and the South of France. [IWM FL12489] This service achievement was exceeded by the Polish SOBIESKI (below), which was not only part of the fleet for all the invasions listed above but was also a participant in the Salerno and Malaya landings. [IWM FL12635]

FRANCONIA.

B1. DIEGO SUAREZ, MADAGASCAR: 5 MAY 1942

Ships carrying personnel, equipment and supplies

NAME OF SHIP Gross tonnage/Year of build Owner or *Managers, if British, or Nationality (and owner) - *WARTIME FUNCTION [HM = His Majesty's commissioned ship: MT Ship = Cargo ship assigned primarily for carrying military vehicles]*

BACHAQUERO 4,890/37 Lago - *HM TANK LANDING SHIP, CLASS I*: left Durban 25 Apr in assault convoy Y: experienced difficulty in maintaining convoy speed: arrived Courier Bay 5 May: discharged guns and vehicles after delay in locating a suitable beaching area

CITY OF HONGKONG 9,606/24 *City - *MT/STORE SHIP*: left Durban 26 Apr for the beachhead: arrived Diego Suarez 9 May

DUCHESS OF ATHOLL 20,119/28 Canadian Pacific - *PERSONNEL SHIP (capacity 3,056)*: left Durban 28 Apr in assault convoy Z carrying personnel of the floating reserve: arrived at the beachhead 5 May

EMPIRE KINGSLEY 6,996/41 *Salvesen - *MT SHIP*: left Durban 25 Apr in assault convoy Y: arrived at the beachhead 5 May and Diego Suarez 9 May

FRANCONIA 20,175/23 Cunard White Star - *PERSONNEL SHIP (capacity 2,102)*: left Durban 28 Apr in assault convoy Z: arrived at the beachhead 5 May

GREYSTOKE CASTLE 5,853/28 Lancashire - *STORE SHIP*: from Durban, carrying reserves of ammunition, arrived at the beachhead 7 May and Diego Suarez 9 May

KARANJA 9,891/31 British India - *HM INFANTRY ASSAULT SHIP, CLASS I (personnel capacity 1,100)*: left Durban 28 Apr in assault convoy Z: arrived Ambararata Bay 5 May: carried personnel, 32 vehicles, 11 motor cycles and 55 tons stores

KEREN 9,890/30 British India KENYA - *HM INFANTRY ASSAULT SHIP, CLASS I (personnel capacity 1,100)*: also serving as headquarters ship, left Durban 28 Apr in assault convoy Z: arrived Ambararata Bay 5 May: carried personnel, 30 vehicles, 54 motor cycles and 40 tons stores

MAHOUT 7,921/25 Brocklebank - *MT SHIP*: left Durban 25 Apr in assault convoy Y: arrived at the beachhead 5 May: carried 86 vehicles

MARTAND 7,967/39 Brocklebank - *MT SHIP*: left Durban 25 Apr in assault convoy Y: arrived at the beachhead 5 May and Diego Suarez 9 May

NAIRNBANK 5,156/25 *Weir - *MT SHIP*: left Durban 25 Apr in assault convoy Y: arrived at the beachhead 5 May and Diego Suarez 9 May

ORONSAY 20,043/25 Orient - *PERSONNEL SHIP (capacity 4,381)*: left Durban 28 Apr in assault convoy Z carrying personnel of the floating reserve: arrived at the beachhead 5 May

ROYAL ULSTERMAN 3,244/36 Burns & Laird - *HM*

Above: DUCHESS OF ATHOLL and (right) ORONSAY: five months later, both became submarine victims on consecutive days.

PERSONNEL SHIP: left Durban 28 Apr in assault convoy Z: arrived Courier Bay 5 May

SOBIESKI 11,030/39 Polish (Gdynia-America) - *PERSONNEL SHIP (capacity 1,500)*: left Durban 28 Apr in assault convoy Z: arrived at the beachhead 5 May: carried personnel, 24 vehicles, 40 motor cycles and 282 tons stores

THALATTA 5,671/22 Norwegian (Wilhelmsen) - *MT SHIP*: left Durban 25 Apr in assault convoy Y: arrived at the beachhead 5 May: carried 59 vehicles

WINCHESTER CASTLE 20,012/30 Union-Castle - *PERSONNEL SHIP (capacity 1,100)*: left Durban 28 Apr in assault convoy Z: arrived Courier Bay 5 May: carried personnel, 32 vehicles, 28 motor cycles and 162 tons stores

Other merchant ships including Royal Fleet Auxiliaries

ATLANTIS 15,135/13 *Royal Mail - HOSPITAL SHIP*: left Durban 30 Apr: arrived Courier Bay 5 May: with 320 patients aboard, left for Diego Suarez 8 May and Durban 12 May

DERWENTDALE 8,398/41 Admiralty - *LANDING CRAFT SHIP, subsequently became known as LANDING SHIP, GANTRY*: carrying 14 landing craft, left Durban 25 Apr in assault convoy Y: experienced difficulty in maintaining convoy speed: arrived at the beachhead 5 May

EASEDALE 8,032/42 Admiralty - *OILER*: left Durban 25 Apr in assault convoy Y: refuelled destroyers and smaller ships en route to the beachhead

MAHOUT. [Capt J F van Puyvelde]

Naval vessels in support

BATTLESHIPS

RAMILLIES - left Durban 28 Apr with assault convoy Z: detached for the covering position 4 May: provided bombardment support 7 May: entered Diego Suarez harbour same evening (Force F)

RESOLUTION - left Seychelles 2 May: provided cover 130-220 miles east of Madagascar (Eastern Fleet)

WARSPITE - left Seychelles 30 Apr: provided cover 130-220 miles east of Madagascar (Eastern Fleet)

AIRCRAFT CARRIERS

FORMIDABLE - left Seychelles 1 May: provided cover 130-220 miles east of Madagascar (Eastern Fleet)

ILLUSTRIOUS - left Durban 28 Apr: joined assault convoy Z 29 Apr: detached for the covering position 4 May: flew off aircraft to attack the French naval base at Diego Suarez 5 May (Force F)

INDOMITABLE - left Seychelles 29 Apr: joined assault convoy Z 3 May: detached for the covering position 4 May: flew off aircraft to attack the French air base at Antsirana 5 May (Eastern Fleet)

CRUISERS

CALEDON - left Seychelles 2 May: provided cover 130-220 miles east of Madagascar (Eastern Fleet)

DEVONSHIRE - left Durban 25 Apr with assault convoy Y: was stand-by bombardment ship at convoy anchorage 5 May: positioned east of Diego Suarez 6 May: provided bombardment support 7 May (Force F)

DRAGON - left Seychelles 2 May: provided cover 130-220 miles east of Madagascar (Eastern Fleet)

EMERALD, **ENTERPRISE** - both left Seychelles 30 Apr: provided cover 130-220 miles east of Madagascar (Eastern Fleet)

HERMIONE - left Durban 28 Apr: joined assault convoy Z 29 Apr: detached for the covering position 4 May: provided diversionary bombardment 5 May: carried out a patrol east of Diego Suarez 6 May: provided bombardment support 7 May: entered Diego Suarez harbour same evening (Force F)

NEWCASTLE - left Seychelles 1 May: provided cover 130-220 miles east of Madagascar (Eastern Fleet)

MINELAYER

MANXMAN - left Durban 10 May carrying £100,000 in

HM battleship RAMILLIES at sea off Madagascar during the operation. [IWM A8858]

The cruiser NEWCASTLE. [IWM A9063]

bullion for use in effecting French cooperation: arrived Diego Suarez 13 May

DESTROYERS

ACTIVE - left Durban 25 Apr with assault convoy Y: detached for the covering position 4 May (Force F)

ANTHONY - assigned to assault convoy Y 25 Apr but joined late after boiler cleaning at Durban: provided bombardment support: landed 50 Royal Marines at Antsirana 6 May (Force F)

DECOY - left Seychelles 1 May: provided cover 130-220 miles east of Madagascar (Eastern Fleet)

DUNCAN - left Durban 25 Apr with assault convoy Y: detached for the covering position 4 May (Force F)

FORTUNE - left Seychelles 2 May: provided cover 130-220 miles east of Madagascar (Eastern Fleet)

FOXHOUND - left Seychelles 1 May: provided cover 130-220 miles east of Madagascar (Eastern Fleet)

GRIFFIN, HOTSPUR - both left Seychelles 2 May: provided cover 130-220 miles east of Madagascar (Eastern Fleet)

INCONSTANT, JAVELIN - both left Durban 28 Apr with assault convoy Z: detached for the covering position 4 May (Force F)

LAFOREY, LIGHTNING - both left Durban 28 Apr: joined assault convoy Z: provided bombardment support at Antsirana (Force F)

LOOKOUT - left Durban 28 Apr: joined assault convoy Z 29 Apr: detached for the covering position 4 May (Force F)

NESTOR, NORMAN - both Australian: left Seychelles 1 May: provided cover 130-220 miles east of Madagascar (Eastern Fleet)

PAKENHAM - left Durban 28 Apr with assault convoy Z: provided bombardment support (Force F)

PALADIN, PANTHER - both left Seychelles 29 Apr:

joined assault convoy Z 3 May: detached for the covering position 4 May: entered Diego Suarez harbour 7 May (Eastern Fleet)

CORVETTES

AURICULA - left Durban 25 Apr with assault convoy Y: arrived at the beachhead 5 May: back broken by mine explosion 1140 same day: sank 0820 6 May during an attempt by the corvette FREESIA to tow her to shallow water (Force F)

CYCLAMEN - left Durban 26 Apr with the MT ship CITY OF HONGKONG to arrive at the beachhead 5 May (Force F)

FREESIA - left Durban 25 Apr with assault convoy Y: arrived at the beachhead 5 May: made a failed attempt to tow the corvette AURICULA to shallow water 6 May (Force F)

FRITILLARY - left Durban 25 Apr with assault convoy Y to arrive at the beachhead 5 May (Force F)

GENISTA - left Durban 26 Apr with the MT ship CITY OF HONGKONG to arrive at the beachhead 5 May (Force F)

JASMINE, NIGELLA, THYME - all left Durban 25 Apr with assault convoy Y to arrive at the beachhead 5 May (Force F)

MINESWEEPERS

CROMARTY - left Durban 25 Apr with assault convoy Y to arrive at the beachhead 5 May: positioned east of Diego Suarez 6 May: provided bombardment support (Force F)

CROMER - left Durban 25 Apr with assault convoy Y to arrive at the beachhead 5 May: positioned east of Diego Suarez 6 May (Force F)

POOLE - left Durban 25 Apr with assault convoy Y to arrive at the beachhead 5 May (Force F)

ROMNEY - left Durban 25 Apr with assault convoy Y to arrive at the beachhead 5 May: positioned east of Diego Suarez 6 May (Force F)

DILWARA. [MPL 3732]

B2 & 3. MAJUNGA and TAMATAVE, MADAGASCAR: 10 and 18 SEPTEMBER 1942

Ships carrying personnel, equipment and supplies

NAME OF SHIP Gross tonnage/Year of build Owner or *Managers - *WARTIME FUNCTION [MT Ship = Cargo ship assigned primarily for carrying military vehicles]*

ABOSSO 11,330/35 Elder Dempster - *PERSONNEL SHIP (capacity 2,053)*: left Diego Suarez 7 Sep in "Stream" convoy D: arrived Majunga 10 Sep (Force M)

ADVISER 6,348/39 *T & J Harrison - *MT SHIP*: left Mombasa 3 Sep in "Stream" convoy F to arrive Majunga 10 Sep (Force M)

CHARLTON HALL 5,200/40 C G Dunn - *MT SHIP*: left Mombasa 3 Sep in "Stream" convoy E to arrive Majunga 10 Sep (Force M)

DELIUS 6,065/37 Lamport & Holt - *MT SHIP*: left Diego Suarez 7 Sep in "Stream" convoy D to arrive Majunga 10 Sep (Force M)

DILWARA 11,080/36 British India - *PERSONNEL SHIP (capacity 1,030)*: embarked personnel at Diego Suarez: left Mombasa 5 Sep in "Stream" convoy G: arrived Majunga 10 Sep (Force M): left there 13 Sep in "Jane" convoy H: arrived Tamatave 18 Sep

DUNERA 11,162/37 British India - *PERSONNEL SHIP (capacity 1,165)*: embarked personnel at Diego Suarez: left Mombasa 5 Sep in "Stream" convoy G: arrived Majunga 10 Sep (Force M): left there 13 Sep in "Jane" convoy H: arrived Tamatave 18 Sep

EMPIRE PRIDE 9,248/41 *Bibby - *PERSONNEL SHIP (capacity 1,291)*: stand-by headquarters ship: embarked personnel at Diego Suarez: left Mombasa 5 Sep in "Stream" convoy G: at sea, transferred commandos to the destroyer NAPIER 8 Sep: arrived Majunga 10 Sep (Force M): left there 13 Sep in "Jane" convoy H: arrived Tamatave 18 Sep

EMPIRE SQUIRE 7,044/42 *Robinson - *MT SHIP*: left Diego Suarez 7 Sep in "Stream" convoy D to arrive Majunga 10 Sep (Force M)

EMPIRE TROOPER 13,994/22 *British India ex German CAP NORTE - *PERSONNEL SHIP (capacity 1,264)*: left Mombasa 5 Sep in "Stream" convoy G to arrive Majunga 10 Sep (Force M)

EMPIRE WOODLARK 7,793/13 *Canadian Pacific ex US EMMA ALEXANDER - *PERSONNEL SHIP*: left Diego Suarez 7 Sep in "Stream" convoy D to arrive Majunga 10 Sep (Force M)

GASCONY 4,716/25 Royal Mail - *MT SHIP*: loaded at Diego Suarez: left Mombasa 3 Sep in "Stream" convoy F to arrive Majunga 10 Sep (Force M): left there 13 Sep in "Jane" convoy H: arrived Tamatave 18 Sep

KHEDIVE ISMAIL 7,513/22 *British India ex Egyptian - *PERSONNEL SHIP (capacity 1,223)*: left Diego Suarez 7 Sep in "Stream" convoy D to arrive Majunga 10 Sep

(Force M): left there 12 Sep: arrived Diego Suarez 15 Sep: transferred commandos to the destroyers ACTIVE, ARROW and BLACKMORE 16 Sep

KOLA 1,538/24 British India - *CASED PETROL SHIP*: left Mombasa 3 Sep in "Stream" convoy E to arrive Majunga 10 Sep (Force M)

LLANDAFF CASTLE 10,799/26 Union-Castle - *PERSONNEL SHIP*: left Diego Suarez 7 Sep in "Stream" convoy D to arrive Majunga 10 Sep (Force M)

OCEAN VESPER 7,174/42 *Connell & Grace - *MT SHIP*: left Diego Suarez 7 Sep in "Stream" convoy D to arrive Majunga 10 Sep (Force M)

OCEAN VIKING 7,174/41 *Bolton - *MT SHIP*: loaded at Diego Suarez: left Mombasa 3 Sep in "Stream" convoy F to arrive Majunga 10 Sep (Force M): left there 13 Sep in "Jane" convoy H: arrived Tamatave 18 Sep and, in attempting to berth, was aground in the inner harbour for nearly two hours same day: refloated but grounded again in the outer harbour until the following morning, refloating assisted by the destroyer ACTIVE and minesweeper CROMER

ROSS 4,978/36 Sutherland - *MT SHIP*: left Mombasa 3 Sep in "Stream" convoy F to arrive Majunga 10 Sep (Force M)

WANDERER 5,079/25 *T & J Harrison - *MT SHIP*: left Diego Suarez 7 Sep in "Stream" convoy D to arrive Majunga 10 Sep (Force M)

Other merchant ships including Royal Fleet Auxiliaries

BRITISH ENERGY 7,209/31 British Tanker - *TANKER*: left Mayotte 8 Sep: joined "Stream" convoy E to arrive Majunga 10 Sep

DORSETSHIRE 9,717/20 Bibby - *HOSPITAL SHIP*: left Diego Suarez 10 Sep: arrived Majunga 11 Sep

EASEDALE 8,032/42 Admiralty - *OILER*: left Mombasa 3 Sep in "Stream" convoy F: arrived Majunga 10 Sep

VASNA 4,820/17 British India - *HOSPITAL SHIP*: left Mombasa 6 Sep: arrived Majunga 10 Sep and Tamatave 18 Sep

Naval vessels in support

BATTLESHIP
WARSPITE - left Kilindini 13 Sep: joined the aircraft carrier ILLUSTRIOUS and escort 16 Sep: joined "Jane" convoy H 17 Sep: arrived Tamatave 18 Sep

AIRCRAFT CARRIER
ILLUSTRIOUS - left Kilindini 6 Sep: joined "Stream" convoy G 9 Sep to arrive Majunga 10 Sep: left Diego Suarez 16 Sep: joined "Jane" convoy H 17 Sep and provided air support at Tamatave 18 Sep

SEAPLANE CARRIER
ALBATROSS - as headquarters ship, left Kilindini 5 Sep: joined "Stream" convoy G: arrived Majunga 10 Sep: left there 13 Sep in "Jane" convoy H: arrived Tamatave 18 Sep

CRUISERS
BIRMINGHAM - left Kilindini 6 Sep: joined "Stream" convoy G 9 Sep: arrived Majunga 10 Sep: left there 13 Sep and Diego Suarez 16 Sep: joined "Jane" convoy H: arrived Tamatave 18 Sep: provided bombardment support same day

CARADOC - left Diego Suarez: arrived Hellville on the island of Nossi Be 10 Sep: provided bombardment support same day (Operation "Esme B")

DAUNTLESS - left Kilindini 3 Sep with "Stream" convoy F to arrive Majunga 10 Sep: left there 13 Sep and Diego Suarez 15 Sep: joined "Jane" convoy H: arrived Tamatave 18 Sep

ENTERPRISE - left Kilindini 5 Sep with "Stream" convoy G: detached to Diego Suarez, arrived 10 Sep

WANDERER. [Capt J F van Puyvelde]

GAMBIA - left Diego Suarez 7 Sep: joined "Stream" convoy D to arrive Majunga 10 Sep: left Diego Suarez 15 Sep: joined "Jane" convoy H 17 Sep: arrived Tamatave 18 Sep: provided bombardment support same day

JACOB VAN HEEMSKERCK - Dutch: to provide anti-aircraft protection, left Kilindini 6 Sep: joined "Stream" convoy G 9 Sep to arrive Majunga 10 Sep: joined "Jane" convoy H 17 Sep to arrive Tamatave 18 Sep

MONITOR
EREBUS - left Kilindini 3 Sep with "Stream" convoy E: arrived Majunga 10 Sep

MINELAYER
MANXMAN - left Diego Suarez 9 Sep: carried Royal Marines and South African infantrymen to Hellville on the island of Nossi Be 10 Sep: provided bombardment support same day (Operation "Esme B")

DESTROYERS
ACTIVE - left Diego Suarez 16 Sep, carried commandos to "Jane" beachhead 18 Sep then berthed at Tamatave same day: assisted the cargo ship OCEAN VIKING same day and 19 Sep

ARROW, BLACKMORE - both left Kilindini 5 Sep: joined "Stream" convoy G to arrive Majunga 10 Sep: left Diego Suarez 16 Sep: carried commandos to "Jane" beachhead 18 Sep then berthed at Tamatave same day

FORTUNE - left Kilindini 5 Sep: joined "Stream" convoy G to arrive Majunga 10 Sep: left there 11 Sep: left Kilindini with the battleship WARSPITE 13 Sep: called Diego Suarez 16 Sep: joined "Jane" convoy H: arrived Tamatave 18 Sep

FOXHOUND, HOTSPUR - both left Diego Suarez 7 Sep to provide anti-submarine cover: joined "Jane" convoy H: arrived Tamatave 18 Sep

INCONSTANT - left Diego Suarez 16 Sep: carried commandos to "Jane" beachhead 18 Sep

NAPIER - Australian: left Kilindini 6 Sep: at sea, embarked commandos from the personnel ship EMPIRE PRIDE 8 Sep and landed them near Morondava, 380 miles south of Majunga, on a diversionary raid 10 Sep (Operation "Tamper"): left Majunga for Diego Suarez 13 Sep: joined "Jane" convoy H: arrived Tamatave 18 Sep

NEPAL - Australian: left Kilindini 5 Sep: joined "Stream" assault convoy G to arrive Majunga 10 Sep: left Kilindini with the battleship WARSPITE 13 Sep: called Diego Suarez 16 Sep: joined "Jane" convoy H: arrived Tamatave 18 Sep

NIZAM, NORMAN - both Australian: left Diego Suarez 7 Sep to provide anti-submarine cover: arrived Diego Suarez 14 Sep: left there 15 Sep: joined "Jane" convoy H: arrived Tamatave 18 Sep

TJERK HIDDES, VAN GALEN - both Dutch: left Kilindini 6 Sep: joined "Stream" convoy G 9 Sep: arrived Majunga 10 Sep

CORVETTE
FREESIA - left Diego Suarez 15 Sep with "Jane" convoy H to arrive Tamatave 18 Sep

MINESWEEPERS
CROMER - left Kilindini 3 Sep with "Stream" convoy F: arrived Majunga 10 Sep: left there for Diego Suarez 12 Sep: joined "Jane" convoy H: arrived Tamatave 18 Sep: assisted the cargo ship OCEAN VIKING 19 Sep

CROMARTY, ROMNEY - both left Kilindini 3 Sep with "Stream" convoy F: arrived Majunga 10 Sep: left there for Diego Suarez 12 Sep: joined "Jane" convoy H: arrived Tamatave 18 Sep

AUXILIARY NETLAYER
BRITTANY - left Mombasa 3 Sep with "Stream" convoy F: arrived Majunga 10 Sep: commenced laying nets same day

WHALERS
LURCHER - left Kilindini 3 Sep with "Stream" convoy F to arrive Majunga 10 Sep: left there 12 Sep with "Jane" convoy H to arrive Tamatave 18 Sep

MASTIFF - left Kilindini 3 Sep with "Stream" convoy F to arrive Majunga 10 Sep

FOXHOUND formed part of an eight-destroyer anti-submarine screen. [IWM A18777]

B4. ALGERIA, NORTH AFRICA: 8 NOVEMBER 1942

BATORY. [A Duncan]

Named ships carrying personnel, equipment and supplies

NAME OF SHIP Gross tonnage/Year of Build Owner or *Managers, if British, or Nationality (and owner or *managers) - *WARTIME FUNCTION* [HM = His Majesty's commissioned ship: MT Ship = Cargo ship assigned primarily for carrying military vehicles: WSA = War Shipping Administration]

AKABAHRA 1,524/29 Norwegian (Hannevig) - *STORE SHIP*: left Port Talbot 25 Oct and the Clyde 30 Oct in convoy KX5 for Gibraltar: left there 11 Nov: arrived Algiers 14 Nov for onward routing to Philippeville: carried 81 tons cased petrol and 1,078 tons stores

ALCINOUS 6,189/25 Dutch (Oceaan) - *MT SHIP*: loaded at Birkenhead: left there 20 Oct and the Clyde 22 Oct in assault convoy KMS1: arrived Arzeu Z beachhead 8 Nov: entered Arzeu harbour 10 Nov: carried 352 personnel, 2 tanks, 124 other vehicles, 30 guns, 207 tons cased petrol and 382 tons stores

ALMAACK 6,736/40 US - *US NAVY CARGO SHIP*: loaded at New York but cargo re-stowed in the UK: left the Clyde 26 Oct in assault convoy KMF1: arrived Algiers C beachhead 8 Nov: entered Algiers harbour 9 Nov: left for the homeward passage 13 Nov: damaged by a torpedo from U 155 when 130 miles west of Gibraltar 0330 15 Nov: arrived Gibraltar in tow 17 Nov

ALPERA 1,777/20 Mossgiel - *STORE SHIP*: left Barry 27 Oct and the Clyde 30 Oct in convoy KX5 for Gibraltar: left there 11 Nov: arrived Oran 12 Nov: carried 1,795 tons stores

ALPHARD 5,483/37 Dutch (Goudriaan) - *MT SHIP*: loaded at Birkenhead: left there 18 Oct and the Clyde 22 Oct in assault convoy KMS1: arrived Arzeu Z beachhead 8 Nov: entered Arzeu harbour 11 Nov: carried 307 personnel, 138 vehicles, 15 guns, 239 tons cased petrol and 558 tons stores

ALRESFORD 2,472/22 *Hunter - *MILITARY COLLIER*: left Cardiff 17 Oct and the Clyde 21 Oct in advance convoy KX4A but, unable to maintain convoy speed, turned back: left the Clyde 30 Oct in convoy KX5 for Gibraltar: left there 11 Nov: arrived Algiers 14 Nov: carried 3,232 tons coal

ANDREW HAMILTON 7,191/42 US (WSA) - *MT/STORE SHIP*: joined follow-up convoy KMS2 (which originated Loch Ewe 25 Oct): arrived Oran 11 Nov: carried 9 personnel, 101 vehicles, 12 guns, 6 tons cased petrol and 2,099 tons stores

ARGENTINA 20,614/29 US (Maritime Commission) - *PERSONNEL SHIP*: left the Clyde 1 Nov in follow-up convoy KMF2: arrived Oran 11 Nov

ARTEMAS WARD 7,177/42 US (WSA) - *MT/STORE SHIP*: left the Clyde: joined follow-up convoy KMS2 (which originated Loch Ewe 25 Oct): arrived Algiers 12 Nov: arrived Bougie 15 Nov: carried 9 personnel, 173

vehicles, 10 guns, 257 tons cased petrol and 2,355 tons stores

ARUNDEL CASTLE 19,118/21 Union-Castle - *PERSONNEL SHIP (capacity 2,219)*: left Glasgow 31 Oct and the Clyde 1 Nov in follow-up convoy KMF2: arrived Algiers 12 Nov

AURORA 1,695/20 Dutch (Koniklijke Nederlandsche) - *STORE SHIP*: left Port Talbot 27 Oct and the Clyde 30 Oct in convoy KX5 for Gibraltar: left there 11 Nov: arrived Algiers 14 Nov for onward routing to Philippeville: carried 80 tons cased petrol and 985 tons stores

AWATEA 13,482/36 Union SS of New Zealand - *LANDING SHIP, INFANTRY (LARGE) (personnel capacity 2,506)*: left the Clyde 26 Oct in assault convoy KMF1: arrived Algiers B beachhead 8 Nov: left Algiers 10 Nov for Djidjelli, in place of STRATHNAVER, to land urgently required RAF stores, maintenance personnel and fuel: diverted and arrived Bougie 11 Nov: completed discharge same day and left for Gibraltar: one mile out, attacked from the air at 1640: the ship caught fire after bombs struck her two forward hatches: her engine room became flooded as a result of two further hits on her port side below the water-line: the explosion of a delayed-action bomb set the ship alight from her bridge to her bow: with flames spreading in No 2 hold, ammunition starting to explode, the ship's side red hot and the vessel settling perceptibly, AWATEA was abandoned off Cape Carbon: survivors were rescued by the destroyer BICESTER, frigate ROTHER, corvette PENTSTEMON and trawler MULL, with the destroyer WILTON and trawler HOY also assisting: when last reported, AWATEA was blazing from her bow to her foremost funnel and drifting towards the shore: by 2300 she had disappeared in deep water (Operation "Perpetual")

BACHAQUERO 4,890/37 Lago - *HM LANDING SHIP, TANK*: loaded at Glasgow 17-18 Oct: left the Clyde 21 Oct in advance convoy KX4A for Gibraltar: arrived Oran X beachhead 8 Nov: involved in collision with the MT ship WALT WHITMAN same day

BATORY 14,287/36 Polish (Gdynia-America) - *LANDING SHIP, INFANTRY (LARGE) (personnel capacity 1,700)*: left the Clyde 26 Oct in assault convoy KMF1: arrived Oran X beachhead 8 Nov: one of the ship's landing craft caught fire and was abandoned 0505 same day

BAYOU CHICO 5,401/20 US (WSA) - *MT SHIP*: joined follow-up convoy KMS2 (which originated Loch Ewe 25 Oct): arrived Oran 11 Nov: carried 8 personnel, 149 vehicles and 600 tons cased petrol

BENALBANACH 7,153/40 *Thomson - *MT SHIP*: loaded at Birkenhead: left the Clyde 22 Oct in assault convoy KMS1: arrived Oran X beachhead 8 Nov:

carried 278 personnel, 22 tanks, 106 other vehicles, 6 guns, 77 tons cased petrol and 141 tons stores: seven vehicles lost when the raft carrying the first load ashore sank

BERNARD CARTER 7,191/42 US (WSA) - *MT/STORE SHIP*: joined follow-up convoy KMS2 (which originated Loch Ewe 25 Oct): arrived Oran 11 Nov: carried 9 personnel, 157 vehicles, 5 guns and 1,347 tons stores

BERTO 1,493/18 Norwegian (Berge) - *STORE SHIP*: left Silloth 24 Oct and the Clyde 30 Oct in convoy KX5 for Gibraltar: left there 11 Nov: arrived Algiers 14 Nov for onward routing to Bone: carried 206 tons cased petrol and 1,077 tons stores

BJORKHAUG 2,094/19 Norwegian (Aarseth) - *STORE SHIP*: left Silloth 28-29 Oct and the Clyde 30 Oct in convoy KX5 for Gibraltar: left there 11 Nov: arrived Algiers 14 Nov for onward routing to Bone: carried 1,860 tons stores

BRAZIL 20,614/29 US (Maritime Commission) - *PERSONNEL SHIP*: left the Clyde 1 Nov in follow-up convoy KMF2: arrived Oran 11 Nov

BROWNING 5,332/19 Lamport & Holt - *MT/STORE SHIP*: left Barrow 21 Oct and Loch Ewe 25 Oct in follow-up convoy KMS2: carried 9 personnel, 141 vehicles, 292 tons cased petrol and 1,395 tons stores, including ammunition: arrived Arzeu 11 Nov and was moving to Oran when, at 1420 12 Nov, she was torpedoed on her starboard side in No 1 hold as she entered Oran Bay: the hold caught fire and at 1525 a tremendous explosion sent smoke and flames 300ft into the air and, by the time the smoke had cleared, the ship had sunk: her lifeboats were towed into Oran by the trawler FLUELLEN: the U-boat responsible was U 593 not 595 as originally thought

CALUMET 7,268/23 Elder Dempster - *MT SHIP*: left Newport 10 Oct and Loch Ewe 25 Oct in follow-up convoy KMS2: arrived Algiers 12 Nov: carried 8 personnel, 165 vehicles, 8 guns and 277 tons stores

CAMERONIA 16,297/20 Anchor - *PERSONNEL SHIP (capacity 3,681)*: left Glasgow 30 Oct and the Clyde 1 Nov in follow-up convoy KMF2: arrived Algiers 12 Nov

CATHAY 15,225/25 P & O - *PERSONNEL SHIP (capacity 3,611)*: left Glasgow 22 Oct and the Clyde 26 Oct in assault convoy KMF1 carrying part of the floating reserve: arrived Algiers B beachhead 8 Nov: left Algiers 10 Nov: arrived Bougie 11 Nov: at 1330 same day, with 1,200 personnel still aboard, she was hit by a bomb and suffered further damage in air attacks three hours later: at 2200 the vessel caught fire and was burning fore and aft by 0100 12 Nov: at 0700 same day, after an explosion (possibly a torpedo from the Italian submarine ARGO), the ship settled down in the water and, three hours later, was lying on the bottom on her

CATHAY was one of six P & O Group passenger liners lost in the operation. [World Ship Photo Library]

starboard side, completely gutted (Operation "Perpetual")

CHARLES H CRAMP 6,220/20 US (American South African) - *MT SHIP*: loaded at Birkenhead: left the Clyde 22 Oct in assault convoy KMS1: arrived Arzeu Z beachhead 8 Nov and entered Arzeu harbour 10 Nov: carried 293 personnel, 161 vehicles, 26 guns, 201 tons cased petrol and 309 tons stores

CHATTANOOGA CITY 5,687/21 US (Isthmian) - *MT SHIP*: loaded at Liverpool: left the Clyde 22 Oct in assault convoy KMS1: arrived Arzeu Z beachhead 8 Nov: carried 295 personnel, 151 vehicles, 30 guns, 188 tons cased petrol and 663 tons stores

CIRCASSIA 11,136/37 Anchor - *PERSONNEL SHIP (capacity 2,406)*: left Glasgow 30 Oct and the Clyde 1 Nov in follow-up convoy KMF2: arrived Algiers 12 Nov

CITY OF CHRISTCHURCH 6,009/15 Ellerman & Bucknall - *MT SHIP*: left Newport 18 Oct and Loch Ewe 25 Oct in follow-up convoy KMS2: arrived Oran 11 Nov: carried 9 personnel, 169 vehicles, 1 gun, 295 tons cased petrol and 576 tons stores

CITY OF NORWICH 6,726/13 *Hall - *MT/STORE SHIP*: left Glasgow 5 Oct and Loch Ewe 25 Oct in follow-up convoy KMS2: arrived Oran 11 Nov: arrived Bougie 14 Nov: carried 10 personnel, 141 vehicles, 20 guns, 744 tons cased petrol and 635 tons stores

CITY OF WORCESTER 5,469/27 *Hall - *MT/STORE SHIP*: left Birkenhead 9 Oct and the Clyde 22 Oct in assault convoy KMS1: arrived Algiers B beachhead 8 Nov: carried 21 personnel, 78 vehicles, 22 guns, 242 tons cased petrol and 839 tons stores

CLAN LAMONT 7,250/39 Clan - *STORE SHIP*: originally destined for Malta: left the Clyde 1 Nov in

follow-up convoy KMF2 for Gibraltar and Bougie: carried 21 vehicles, 1,765 tons cased petrol, 5,271 tons stores and 216 tons coal

CLAN MACTAGGART 7,622/20 *Turnbull, Martin - *MT SHIP*: left Faslane 20 Oct and the Clyde 22 Oct in assault convoy KMS1: arrived Oran Y beachhead 8 Nov: carried 310 personnel, 164 vehicles, 23 guns, 45 tons cased petrol and 445 tons stores: left for the homeward passage 14 Nov: when 100 miles west of Gibraltar at 0453 16 Nov, vessel was struck on the starboard bow abreast No 1 hatch by a torpedo from U 92, followed at 0523 by another hit abaft the bridge beside No 3 hatch: ship was abandoned and survivors taken aboard the corvette COREOPSIS

COXWOLD 1,124/38 Yorkshire Dale - *CASED PETROL SHIP*: left the Clyde 21 Oct in advance convoy KX4A for Gibraltar: arrived Bougie 13 Nov and Bone 16 Nov: carried 1,347 tons cased petrol

DELILIAN 6,423/23 Donaldson - *MT SHIP*: left Faslane 21 Oct and the Clyde 22 Oct in assault convoy KMS1: arrived Arzeu Z beachhead 8 Nov: carried 330 personnel, 93 vehicles, 17 guns, 174 tons cased petrol and 341 tons stores

DEMPO 17,024/31 Dutch (Rotterdamsche Lloyd) - *PERSONNEL SHIP (capacity 2,550)*: left the Mersey 25 Oct and the Clyde 26 Oct in assault convoy KMF1: arrived Algiers C beachhead 8 Nov: a bomb near miss at 1620 9 Nov caused minor leaks: another attack, at 1640 same day, caused damage to the ship's auxiliary motors

DERBYSHIRE 11,660/35 Bibby - *LANDING SHIP, INFANTRY (LARGE) (personnel capacity 3,085)*: left the Clyde 26 Oct in assault convoy KMF1: arrived Arzeu Z beachhead 8 Nov

DERWENTHALL 4,934/40 West Hartlepool - *MT/STORE SHIP*: left the Mersey 7 Oct: joined follow-up convoy KMS2 (which originated Loch Ewe 25 Oct): arrived Algiers 12 Nov: arrived Bougie 15 Nov: carried 9 personnel, 162 vehicles, 10 guns, 34 tons cased petrol and 3,002 tons stores

DORELIAN 6,431/23 Donaldson - *MT/STORE SHIP*: left Glasgow 6 Oct and Loch Ewe 25 Oct in follow-up convoy KMS2: arrived Algiers 12 Nov: carried 10 personnel, 178 vehicles, 479 tons cased petrol and 530 tons stores

DUCHESS OF BEDFORD 20,123/28 Canadian Pacific - *LANDING SHIP, INFANTRY (LARGE)*: left the Clyde 26 Oct in assault convoy KMF1: arrived Arzeu Z beachhead 8 Nov: carried 3,044 personnel

DUCHESS OF RICHMOND 20,022/28 Canadian Pacific - *PERSONNEL SHIP (capacity 3,837)*: left the Clyde 1 Nov in follow-up convoy KMF2: arrived Algiers 12 Nov

DUNNOTTAR CASTLE 15,007/36 Union-Castle - *PERSONNEL SHIP (capacity 2,568)*: left Liverpool 25 Oct and the Clyde 1 Nov in follow-up convoy KMF2: arrived Oran 11 Nov

DURBAN CASTLE 17,388/38 Union-Castle - *LANDING SHIP, INFANTRY (LARGE) (personnel capacity 2,419)*: left the Clyde 26 Oct in assault convoy KMF1: arrived Arzeu Z beachhead 8 Nov

EDWARD RUTLEDGE 7,177/42 US (WSA) - *MT SHIP*: loaded at Birkenhead: left the Clyde 22 Oct in assault convoy KMS1: arrived Arzeu Z beachhead 8 Nov: entered Arzeu harbour 10 Nov: carried 49 personnel, 17 tanks, 61 other vehicles, 21 guns, 224 tons cased petrol and 500 tons stores

EGRET 1,391/37 British & Continental - *CASED PETROL SHIP*: left the Clyde 30 Oct in convoy KX5 for Gibraltar: left there 18 Nov: arrived Philippeville 29 Nov: carried 1,157 tons cased petrol

EMPIRE BAXTER 7,024/41 *Reardon Smith - *MT SHIP*: left Cardiff 7 Oct and Loch Ewe 25 Oct in follow-

up convoy KMS2: arrived Algiers 12 Nov: carried 10 personnel, 153 vehicles and 8 tons stores

EMPIRE BUCKLER 7,046/42 *Houlder - *MT/STORE SHIP*: left the Mersey 20 Oct and Loch Ewe 25 Oct in follow-up convoy KMS2: arrived Oran 11 Nov: carried 9 personnel, 136 vehicles, 600 tons cased petrol and 843 tons stores

EMPIRE CONFIDENCE 5,023/35 *Royal Mail ex German DUSSELDORF - *MT SHIP*: left Swansea 19 Oct and the Clyde 22 Oct in assault convoy KMS1: arrived Arzeu Z beachhead 8 Nov: entered Arzeu harbour 10 Nov: carried 28 personnel, 98 vehicles, 10 guns, 223 tons cased petrol and 377 tons stores

EMPIRE KAMAL 7,862/38 *P & O ex German HOHENFELS - *STORE SHIP*: originally destined for Malta: left Newport 30 Oct and the Clyde 1 Nov in follow-up convoy KMF2 for Gibraltar and Casablanca (US Western Task Force area)

EMPIRE MORDRED 7,024/42 *Nisbet - *MT SHIP*: left Glasgow 21 Oct and the Clyde 22 Oct in assault convoy KMS1: arrived Arzeu Z beachhead 8 Nov: entered Arzeu harbour 10 Nov: carried 55 personnel, 119 vehicles, 277 tons cased petrol and 483 tons stores

EMPIRE RUSKIN 7,037/42 *Thompson - *MT/STORE SHIP*: left Glasgow 21 Oct: joined follow-up convoy KMS2 (which originated Loch Ewe 25 Oct): arrived Oran 11 Nov: carried 9 personnel, 125 vehicles and 1,113 tons stores

EMPIRE SPLENDOUR 7,335/42 *Heyn - *MT/STORE SHIP*: left Glasgow 7 Oct and Loch Ewe 25 Oct in follow-up convoy KMS2: arrived Algiers 12 Nov: carried 10 personnel, 176 vehicles, 3 guns, 266 tons cased petrol and 1,343 tons stores

EMPRESS OF CANADA 21,517/22 Canadian Pacific - *PERSONNEL SHIP*: left the Clyde 1 Nov in follow-up convoy KMF2: arrived Oran 11 Nov

ENSIS 6,207/37 Anglo-Saxon - *MILITARY TANKER*: left Stanlow 20 Oct and Loch Ewe 25 Oct in follow-

DURBAN CASTLE.
[A Duncan]

convoy KMS2: arrived Oran 11 Nov: carried 7,619 tons bulk oil

ETTRICK 11,279/38 P & O - *LANDING SHIP, INFANTRY (LARGE) (personnel capacity 1,700)*: left the Clyde 26 Oct in assault convoy KMF1: arrived Arzeu Z beachhead 8 Nov: left for the homeward passage: at 0320 15 Nov, was torpedoed by U 155 130 miles west of Gibraltar: vessel was abandoned at 0345 and sank stern first at 0836 same day: survivors were rescued by the destroyer GLAISDALE

EVVIVA 1,597/21 Norwegian (Hansen) - *CASED PETROL SHIP*: left Preston 28 Oct and the Clyde 30 Oct in convoy KX5 for Gibraltar: left there 11 Nov: arrived Bougie 16 Nov: carried 1,027 tons cased petrol

EXCELLER 6,535/41 US (American Export) - *MT SHIP*: loaded in the USA but cargo re-stowed in the UK: left the Clyde 26 Oct in assault convoy KMF1: arrived Algiers C beachhead 8 Nov: slightly damaged by a bomb near miss same day: entered Algiers harbour 9 Nov

FINTRA 2,089/18 South Georgia - *STORE SHIP*: left Barrow 28 Oct and the Clyde 30 Oct in convoy KX5 for Gibraltar: carried 826 tons cased petrol and 786 tons stores: intended for Oran but diverted to Port Lyautey (US Western Task Force area)

FORT AUGUSTUS 7,134/42 *Watts, Watts - *MT SHIP*: left Glasgow 25 Oct and the Clyde same day to join follow-up convoy KMS2: arrived Algiers 12 Nov: carried 9 personnel, 159 vehicles and 176 tons stores

GLENFINLAS 7,479/17 Glen Line - *MT SHIP*: left Glasgow 6 Oct and the Clyde 22 Oct in assault convoy KMS1 carrying part of the floating reserve: arrived Algiers B beachhead 8 Nov: left Algiers 10 Nov: arrived Bougie 11 Nov: carried 127 personnel, 135 vehicles, 12 guns, 82 tons cased petrol and 541 tons stores: at 1210 13 Nov, hit by at least three bombs on the starboard side forward, whilst discharging in Bougie harbour: ship listed heavily to port, righted herself then settled rapidly on the bottom forward: unloading continued from the undamaged holds (Operation "Perpetual")

ETTRICK. [IWM H374]

GLENGYLE 9,919/39 Glen Line - *HM LANDING SHIP, INFANTRY (LARGE)*: left the Clyde 26 Oct in assault convoy KMF1: arrived Oran Y beachhead 8 Nov: carried 642 personnel, 18 vehicles and 34 tons stores: straddled by shore gunfire same day

GUDRUN MAERSK 2,294/37 *Brocklebank ex Danish - *CASED PETROL SHIP*: left Swansea 14 Oct and Loch Ewe 25 Oct in follow-up convoy KMS2: arrived Algiers 12 Nov: carried 3,226 tons cased petrol

HARDINGHAM 7,269/42 *J & C Harrison - *MT SHIP*: left Glasgow 23 Oct: joined follow-up convoy KMS2 (which originated Loch Ewe 25 Oct): arrived Oran 11 Nov: carried 8 personnel, 148 vehicles, 500 tons cased petrol and 30 tons stores

HARPALYCUS 5,629/35 J & C Harrison - *MT/STORE SHIP*: left Swansea 17 Oct and Loch Ewe 25 Oct in follow-up convoy KMS2: arrived Oran 11 Nov: carried 9 personnel, 158 vehicles, 979 tons cased petrol and 188 tons stores

HARPALYCUS was one of more than 80 cargo ships, which carried vehicles and supplies in the assault and follow-up convoys. [Capt J F van Puyvelde]

KARANJA. [A Duncan]

HAVILDAR 5,407/40 Asiatic - *MT SHIP*: left Birkenhead 19 Oct and the Clyde 22 Oct in assault convoy KMS1: arrived Arzeu Z beachhead 8 Nov: entered Arzeu harbour 10 Nov: carried 83 personnel, 37 tanks, 61 other vehicles, 6 guns, 3 tons cased petrol and 221 tons stores

HILDUR I 1,497/19 Norwegian (*Pehrson & Wessel) - *STORE SHIP*: left Barrow 29 Oct and the Clyde 30 Oct in convoy KX5 for Gibraltar: carried 747 tons cased petrol and 786 tons stores: intended for Oran but diverted to Port Lyautey (US Western Task Force area)

HORACE BINNEY 7,191/42 US (WSA) - *MT SHIP*: partly loaded in the USA: joined follow-up convoy KMS2 (which originated Loch Ewe 25 Oct): arrived Oran 11 Nov: carried 6 tanks, 43 other vehicles, 515 tons cased petrol and 40 tons stores

JADE 930/38 Robertson - *CASED PETROL SHIP*: left Preston 25 Oct and the Clyde 30 Oct in convoy KX5 for Gibraltar: left there 11 Nov: arrived Algiers 14 Nov for onward routing to Philippeville: carried 955 tons cased petrol

JEAN JADOT 5,859/29 Belgian (Lloyd Royal) - *MT SHIP*: left Birkenhead 8 Oct and the Clyde 22 Oct in assault convoy KMS1: arrived Algiers B beachhead 8 Nov: carried 10 personnel, 176 vehicles, 26 guns, 143 tons cased petrol and 705 tons stores

JOHN DAVENPORT 7,176/42 US (WSA) - *MT SHIP*: left the Clyde: joined follow-up convoy KMS2 (which originated Loch Ewe 25 Oct): arrived Algiers 12 Nov: carried 9 personnel, 162 vehicles, 8 guns and 4 tons stores

JOHN P POE 7,191/42 US (WSA) - *MT SHIP*: joined follow-up convoy KMS2 (which originated Loch Ewe 25 Oct): arrived Oran 11 Nov: carried 9 personnel, 143 vehicles, 2 tons cased petrol and 807 tons stores

JOHN SERGEANT 7,191/42 US (WSA) - *MT SHIP*: partly loaded in the USA: left the Mersey: joined follow-up convoy KMS2 (which originated Loch Ewe 25 Oct): arrived Oran 11 Nov: carried 3 tanks, 33 other vehicles, 550 tons cased petrol and 76 tons stores

JUNECREST 6,945/42 Crest - *MT SHIP*: left Glasgow 5 Oct and Loch Ewe 25 Oct in follow-up convoy KMS2: arrived Algiers 12 Nov: carried 10 personnel, 173 vehicles and 232 tons stores

KARANJA 9,891/31 British India - *HM LANDING SHIP, INFANTRY (LARGE)*: left the Clyde 26 Oct in assault convoy KMF1: arrived Algiers A beachhead 8 Nov: carried 860 personnel, also vehicles, motor cycles and cased petrol: left Algiers 10 Nov: arrived Bougie 11 Nov: at 0515 12 Nov, ship hit by two bombs whilst proceeding to the assistance of the anti-aircraft ship TYNWALD: fire in KARANJA's diesel tanks and petrol stores engulfed her midships section in smoke, steam and flames: at 0830 same day, after the unauthorised lowering of lifeboats by some troops, the order to abandon ship was given (Operation "Perpetual")

KEREN 9,890/30 British India KENYA - *HM LANDING SHIP, INFANTRY (LARGE)*: left the Clyde 26 Oct in assault convoy KMF1: arrived Algiers B beachhead 8 Nov: carried 1,161 personnel and 26 vehicles

KROMAN 1,897/12 Polish (Baltic Shipping) - *MILITARY COLLIER*: left Cardiff 17 Oct and the Clyde 21 Oct in advance convoy KX4A for Gibraltar: arrived Oran 20 Nov: carried 2,037 tons coal

LALANDE 7,453/20 Lamport & Holt - *MT SHIP*: from Birkenhead, left the Clyde 22 Oct in assault convoy KMS1: arrived Algiers A beachhead 8 Nov: carried 78 personnel, 162 vehicles, 8 guns and 4 tons stores: left for the homeward passage 12 Nov: when 77 miles east of Gibraltar, hit forward on the starboard side by a torpedo, possibly from U 73, at 0414 14 Nov: ship abandoned with a 50ft x 20ft hole in No 1 hold: crew taken aboard the corvette MARIGOLD but ship remained afloat and was towed to Gibraltar

LAMBROOK 7,038/42 Austin Friars - *MT SHIP*: from the Mersey, left Loch Ewe 25 Oct in follow-up convoy KMS2: arrived Algiers 12 Nov: carried 10 personnel, 149 vehicles, 6 tons cased petrol and 183 tons stores

LANARKSHIRE 9,816/40 *Turnbull, Martin - *STORE SHIP*: originally destined for Malta: left the Mersey 29 Oct and the Clyde 1 Nov in follow-up convoy KMF2 for Gibraltar and Bougie: carried 11 vehicles, 1,601 tons cased petrol, 4,865 tons stores and 150 tons coal

LEEDSTOWN 9,135/33 US (Grace) ex SANTA LUCIA - *US NAVY TRANSPORT*: loaded at New York: left the Clyde 26 Oct in assault convoy KMF1: arrived Algiers C beachhead 8 Nov: steering gear wrecked by an aerial torpedo: sank at 1615 9 Nov as a result of receiving further damage in torpedo and bomb attacks: survivors taken to Algiers by the corvette SAMPHIRE

LETITIA 13,595/25 Donaldson Atlantic - *PERSONNEL SHIP*: left the Clyde 26 Oct in assault convoy KMF1: arrived Arzeu Z beachhead 8 Nov

LEWANT 1,942/30 Polish (SS Agency) - *CASED PETROL SHIP*: left Preston 12 Oct and Loch Ewe 25 Oct in follow-up convoy KMS2: arrived Algiers 12 Nov: carried 2,486 tons cased petrol

LEWIS MORRIS 7,181/42 US (WSA) - *MT SHIP*: partly loaded in the USA: joined follow-up convoy KMS2 (which originated Loch Ewe 25 Oct): arrived Oran 11 Nov: carried 42 vehicles, 1 gun, 281 tons cased petrol and 100 tons stores

LLANGIBBY CASTLE 11,951/29 Union-Castle - *LANDING SHIP, INFANTRY (LARGE)*: left the Clyde 26 Oct in assault convoy KMF1: arrived Oran Y beachhead 8 Nov: carried 1,646 personnel, 20 vehicles and 62 tons stores: damaged amidships by shore gunfire at 0917 same day

LOCHEE 964/37 Dundee, Perth & London - *CASED PETROL SHIP*: left Swansea 18 Oct and the Clyde 21 Oct in advance convoy KX4A for Gibraltar: left there 11 Nov: arrived Oran 12 Nov: carried 1,204 tons cased petrol

LOCHMONAR 9,412/24 Royal Mail - *MT SHIP*: left Birkenhead 8 Oct and the Clyde 22 Oct in assault convoy KMS1: arrived Algiers B beachhead 8 Nov: carried 79 personnel, 171 vehicles, 18 guns, 289 tons cased petrol and 451 tons stores

LORIGA 6,665/19 Pacific Steam - *MT/STORE SHIP*: left the Mersey 9 Oct and Loch Ewe 25 Oct in follow-up convoy KMS2: arrived Algiers 12 Nov: carried 9 personnel, 9 tanks, 179 other vehicles, 5 guns, 625 tons cased petrol and 1,550 tons stores

LUTHER MARTIN 7,191/42 US (WSA) - *MT SHIP*: joined follow-up convoy KMS2 (which originated Loch Ewe 25 Oct): dropped out of convoy 27 Oct and turned back

LYCAON 7,350/13 *Alfred Holt - *MT SHIP*: left Glasgow 20 Oct and the Clyde 22 Oct in assault convoy KMS1: arrived Arzeu Z beachhead 8 Nov: entered

LYCAON. [A Duncan]

Arzeu harbour 13 Nov: carried 56 personnel, 103 vehicles, 18 guns, 232 tons cased petrol and 131 tons stores

MACHARDA 7,998/38 Brocklebank - *MT SHIP*: from Greenock, left the Clyde 22 Oct in assault convoy KMS1: arrived Algiers C beachhead 8 Nov: entered Algiers harbour 9 Nov: carried 280 personnel, 98 vehicles, 10 guns, 83 tons cased petrol and 231 tons stores

MAHSUD 7,540/17 Brocklebank - *MT/STORE SHIP*: from Faslane, left the Clyde 13 Oct and Loch Ewe 25 Oct in follow-up convoy KMS2: arrived Algiers 12 Nov: carried 9 personnel, 143 vehicles, 8 guns, 868 tons cased petrol and 1,641 tons stores

MANCHESTER PORT 7,071/35 Manchester Liners - *MT SHIP*: from Birkenhead, left the Clyde 22 Oct in assault convoy KMS1: arrived Algiers A beachhead 8 Nov: carried 305 personnel, 116 vehicles, 19 guns and 10 tons stores

MARGA 1,583/23 Norwegian (Bruusgaard) - *CASED PETROL SHIP*: left Swansea 24 Oct and the Clyde 30 Oct in convoy KX5 for Gibraltar: left there 18 Nov for Algiers: carried 1,335 tons cased petrol

MARK TWAIN 7,194/42 US (WSA) - *MT SHIP*: from Birkenhead, left the Clyde 22 Oct in assault convoy KMS1: arrived Oran X beachhead 8 Nov: landed 55 personnel, 17 tanks, 68 other vehicles, 12 guns and 61 tons stores

MARNIX VAN ST ALDEGONDE 19,355/30 Dutch (Nederland) - *LANDING SHIP, INFANTRY (LARGE) (personnel capacity 3,429)*: left the Clyde 26 Oct in assault convoy KMF1 carrying part of the floating reserve: arrived Algiers A beachhead 8 Nov: left Algiers 10 Nov: arrived Bougie 11 Nov: left there before unloading completed, owing to the danger from air attacks (Operation "Perpetual")

MARON 6,487/30 Alfred Holt - *MT SHIP*: left Glasgow 6 Oct and the Clyde 22 Oct in assault convoy KMS1: arrived Algiers C beachhead 8 Nov: entered Algiers harbour 9 Nov: carried 284 personnel, 94 vehicles, 6 guns, 275 tons cased petrol and 273 tons stores: left for the homeward passage 12 Nov: off Oran at 1505 13 Nov, vessel was torpedoed and sank by the bow in nine minutes: survivors were picked up by the corvette MARIGOLD: the sinking was originally credited to U 81 but is now thought to have been U 73

MARY SLESSOR 5,027/30 Elder Dempster - *MT SHIP*: left Manchester 19 Oct and the Clyde 22 Oct in assault convoy KMS1: arrived Oran X beachhead 8 Nov: carried 394 personnel, 58 vehicles, 8 guns, 51 tons cased petrol and 47 tons stores

MATTHEW P DEADY 7,176/42 US (WSA) - *MT SHIP*: partly loaded in the USA: joined follow-up convoy

KMS2 (which originated Loch Ewe 25 Oct): arrived Oran 11 Nov: carried 10 tanks, 26 other vehicles and 54 tons cased petrol

MELMORE HEAD 5,273/18 *Heyn - *MT/STORE SHIP*: left Port Talbot 7 Oct and Loch Ewe 25 Oct in follow-up convoy KMS2: arrived Algiers 12 Nov: carried 5 personnel, 136 vehicles, 34 tons cased petrol and 2,107 tons stores

MEROPE 1,162/18 Dutch (Koninklijke Nederlandsche) - *STORE SHIP*: left Port Talbot 24 Oct and the Clyde 30 Oct in convoy KX5 for Gibraltar: left there 11 Nov: arrived Oran 12 Nov for onward routing to Philippeville: carried 80 tons cased petrol and 1,061 tons stores

META 1,575/30 Clydesdale - *CASED PETROL SHIP*: left Barrow 27 Oct and the Clyde 30 Oct in convoy KX5 for Gibraltar: left there 11 Nov: arrived Oran 12 Nov: carried 1,553 tons cased petrol

MISOA 4,800/37 Lago - *HM LANDING SHIP, TANK*: loaded at Glasgow 17-18 Oct: left the Clyde 21 Oct in advance convoy KX4A for Gibraltar: arrived Arzeu Z beachhead 8 Nov

MONARCH OF BERMUDA 22,424/31 Furness, Withy - *LANDING SHIP, INFANTRY (LARGE)*: left the Clyde 26 Oct in assault convoy KMF1: arrived Oran Y beachhead 8 Nov: carried 2,683 personnel and 127 tons stores: hit by shore gunfire at 1110 same day

MOOLTAN 20,952/23 P & O - *PERSONNEL SHIP*: left Avonmouth 24 Oct and the Clyde 26 Oct in assault convoy KMF1: arrived Arzeu Z beachhead 8 Nov: carried 3,600 personnel

NAIRUNG 5,414/42 Asiatic - *MT/STORE SHIP*: left Penarth 18 Oct and Loch Ewe 25 Oct in follow-up convoy KMS2: arrived Oran 11 Nov: carried 9 personnel, 121 vehicles, 81 tons cased petrol and 1,430 tons stores

NARKUNDA 16,632/20 P & O - *PERSONNEL SHIP (capacity 2,678)*: left the Clyde 1 Nov in follow-up convoy KMF2: arrived Algiers 12 Nov: arrived Bougie 14 Nov: left at 1600 same day for the homeward passage but bomb bursts near her port side, at 1658 that day, wrecked her bridge, tore plates from her side and caused flooding in her No 4 hold and forward stokehold: survivors were taken aboard the minesweeper CADMUS and the ship sank by the bow, with a heavy list to port, at 2042 that evening

NIEUW ZEELAND 11,069/28 Dutch (KPM) - *PERSONNEL SHIP (capacity 1,933)*: left Avonmouth 23 Oct and the Clyde 26 Oct in assault convoy KMF1: arrived Arzeu Z beachhead 8 Nov: left for the homeward passage 10 Nov: hit on the port side in the engine room by a torpedo from U 380 at 1142 11 Nov,

MONARCH OF BERMUDA was the largest of the passenger liners assigned to the assault fleet.

whilst about 70 miles east of Gibraltar: sank stern first at 1210 same day: the tug SALVONIA and destroyers ALBRIGHTON, ISAAC SWEERS and PORCUPINE were sent to assist and rescue survivors

OCEAN ATHLETE 7,178/42 Ministry of War Transport - *MT/STORE SHIP*: left Penarth 19 Oct and Loch Ewe 25 Oct in follow-up convoy KMS2: arrived Oran 11 Nov: carried 9 personnel, 155 vehicles, 2 guns, 808 tons stores and 1,250 tons coal

OCEAN COAST 1,173/35 Coast - *CASED PETROL SHIP*: from the Mersey, left the Clyde 21 Oct in advance convoy KX4A for Gibraltar: left there 11 Nov: arrived Algiers 14 Nov: carried 1,386 tons cased petrol

OCEAN FAME 7,173/42 *Seager - *MT/STORE SHIP*: left Cardiff 17 Oct: joined follow-up convoy KMS2 (which originated Loch Ewe 25 Oct): arrived Oran 11 Nov: carried 9 personnel, 162 vehicles, 871 tons stores and 1,257 tons coal

OCEAN LIBERTY 7,174/42 *Mitchell Cotts - *MT/STORE SHIP*: left Glasgow 21 Oct: joined follow-up convoy KMS2 (which originated Loch Ewe 25 Oct): temporarily detached from convoy 27 Oct to re-stow deck cargo which shifted in heavy weather: arrived Oran 11 Nov: carried 8 personnel, 136 vehicles, 41 guns and 1,354 tons stores

OCEAN MERCHANT 7,178/42 *Morel - *MT/STORE SHIP*: left Barry 19 Oct: joined follow-up convoy KMS2 (which originated Loch Ewe 25 Oct): arrived Oran 11 Nov: carried 9 personnel, 136 vehicles, 1 gun and 1,531 tons stores

OCEAN RIDER 7,178/42 *Larrinaga - *MT SHIP*: left Glasgow 11 Oct and the Clyde 22 Oct in assault convoy KMS1: arrived Algiers B beachhead 8 Nov: carried 10 personnel, 123 vehicles, 4 guns, 240 tons cased petrol and 28 tons stores

OCEAN STRENGTH 7,173/42 *Denholm - *MT/STORE SHIP*: left Barry 7 Oct and Loch Ewe 25 Oct in follow-up convoy KMS2: arrived Algiers 12 Nov: carried 9 personnel, 8 tanks, 145 other vehicles, 31 tons cased petrol and 2,215 tons stores

OCEAN TRADER 7,178/42 *Glen Line - *MT SHIP*: left Barry 5 Oct and Loch Ewe 25 Oct in follow-up convoy KMS2: arrived Algiers 12 Nov: two vehicles wrecked and others damaged in a fire in No 2 hold which discovered 2 Nov and smouldered for two days: carried 11 personnel, 136 vehicles, 50 tons cased petrol and 244 tons stores

OCEAN VENGEANCE 7,174/42 *Raeburn & Verel - *MT/STORE SHIP*: left Manchester 7 Oct and Loch Ewe 25 Oct in follow-up convoy KMS2: arrived Algiers 12 Nov: carried 10 personnel, 11 tanks, 96 other vehicles, 4 guns and 2,074 tons stores

OCEAN VETERAN 7,174/42 *Gould - *MT/STORE SHIP*: left Glasgow 25 Oct and the Clyde same day in follow-up convoy KMS2: arrived Algiers 12 Nov: carried 8 personnel, 14 tanks, 124 other vehicles, 2 guns and 2,318 tons stores

OCEAN VICEROY 7,174/42 *Henderson - *MT SHIP*: left Glasgow 12 Oct and the Clyde 22 Oct in assault convoy KMS1: arrived Algiers A beachhead 8 Nov: carried 10 personnel, 130 vehicles and 26 tons stores

OCEAN VIRTUE 7,174/42 *Prince - *MT/STORE SHIP*: from the Mersey, joined follow-up convoy KMS2 (which originated Loch Ewe 25 Oct): arrived Algiers 12 Nov: carried 7 personnel, 129 vehicles, 110 tons cased petrol and 2,083 tons stores

OCEAN VISCOUNT 7,174/42 *Bibby - *MT SHIP*: left Glasgow 21 Oct: joined follow-up convoy KMS2 (which originated Loch Ewe 25 Oct): arrived Oran 11 Nov: carried 9 personnel, 139 vehicles, 1 gun and 739 tons stores

OCEAN VISTA 7,174/42 *Saint - *MT/STORE SHIP*: left Manchester 6 Oct and Loch Ewe 25 Oct in follow-up convoy KMS2: arrived Oran 11 Nov: arrived Bougie 14 Nov: carried 9 personnel, 121 vehicles, 20 guns, 579 tons cased petrol and 1,489 tons stores

OCEAN VOLGA 7,174/42 *Thomson - *MT SHIP*: left Swansea 9 Oct and the Clyde 22 Oct in assault convoy KMS1 carrying part of the floating reserve: arrived Algiers B beachhead 8 Nov: left there 10 Nov: arrived Bougie 11 Nov: carried 9 personnel and 132 vehicles (Operation "Perpetual")

OCEAN WANDERER 7,178/42 *Donaldson & Black - *MT SHIP*: from Birkenhead, left the Clyde 22 Oct in assault convoy KMS1: arrived Algiers A beachhead 8 Nov: carried 30 personnel, 129 vehicles, 16 guns, 5 tons cased petrol and 4 tons stores

ORBITA 15,495/15 Pacific Steam - *PERSONNEL SHIP (capacity 1,265)*: left the Clyde 26 Oct in assault convoy KMF1: arrived Arzeu Z beachhead 8 Nov: carried 2,000 personnel

ORMONDE 14,982/17 Orient - *PERSONNEL SHIP (capacity 2,631)*: left the Clyde 1 Nov in follow-up convoy KMF2 to arrive Algiers 12 Nov

ORPHEUS 1,030/20 Dutch (Koninklijke Nederlandsche) - *STORE SHIP*: left Silloth 26 Oct and the Clyde 30 Oct in convoy KX5 for Gibraltar: left there 11 Nov: arrived Algiers 14 Nov for onward routing to Bone: carried 101 tons cased petrol and 604 tons stores

OTRANTO 20,026/25 Orient - *LANDING SHIP, INFANTRY (LARGE) (personnel capacity 3,964)*: left the Clyde 26 Oct in assault convoy KMF1: arrived Algiers B beachhead 8 Nov: evaded two torpedoes whilst homeward bound on 11 Nov

PACIFIC EXPORTER 6,734/28 *Furness, Withy - *MT SHIP*: left Swansea 19 Oct and the Clyde 22 Oct in

assault convoy KMS1: arrived Arzeu Z beachhead 8 Nov: entered Arzeu harbour 9 Nov: carried 151 personnel, 205 vehicles, 4 guns, 240 tons cased petrol and 600 tons stores

PENDEEN 4,174/23 Chellew - *MILITARY COLLIER*: left Glasgow 30 Oct and the Clyde same day in convoy KX5 for Gibraltar and Algiers: carried 5,759 tons coal

POLO 1,950/19 Ellerman's Wilson - *CASED PETROL SHIP*: left Ardrossan 30 Oct and the Clyde same day in convoy KX5 for Gibraltar and Algiers: carried 1,746 tons cased petrol

PRINCE DE LIEGE 2,588/38 Belgian (Dens) - *CASED PETROL SHIP*: left Silloth 12 Oct: joined follow-up convoy KMS2 (which originated Loch Ewe 25 Oct): arrived Algiers 12 Nov: carried 2,603 tons cased petrol

PRINCESS BEATRIX 4,135/39 Dutch (Zeeland) PRINSES BEATRIX - *HM LANDING SHIP, INFANTRY (MEDIUM) (personnel capacity 400)*: left the Clyde 26 Oct in assault convoy KMF1: arrived Oran X beachhead 8 Nov

QUEEN EMMA 4,135/39 Dutch (Zeeland) KONINGIN EMMA - *HM LANDING SHIP, INFANTRY (MEDIUM) (personnel capacity 400)*: left the Clyde 26 Oct in assault convoy KMF1: arrived Oran X beachhead 8 Nov

RECORDER 5,982/30 *T & J Harrison - *MT SHIP*: left Manchester 18 Oct and the Clyde 22 Oct in assault convoy KMS1: arrived Arzeu Z beachhead 8 Nov: carried 62 personnel, 81 vehicles and 44 tons stores

REINA DEL PACIFICO 17,702/31 Pacific Steam - *LANDING SHIP, INFANTRY (LARGE) (personnel capacity 2,500)*: left the Clyde 26 Oct in assault convoy KMF1: arrived Arzeu Z beachhead 8 Nov: hit by shore gunfire same day

REVERDY JOHNSON 7,191/42 US (WSA) - *MT/STORE SHIP*: left the Clyde 30 Oct in convoy KX5 for Gibraltar: arrived Oran 12 Nov: carried 142 vehicles, 112 tons cased petrol and 1,470 tons stores

RICHARD HENRY LEE 7,191/41 US (WSA) - *MT/STORE SHIP*: joined follow-up convoy KMS2 (which originated Loch Ewe 25 Oct): arrived Oran 11 Nov:

PACIFIC EXPORTER.
[A Duncan]

STRATHMORE.

carried 9 personnel, 121 vehicles, 713 tons cased petrol and 453 tons stores

RONAN 1,489/38 Gibson - *CASED PETROL SHIP*: left Silloth 19 Oct and the Clyde 21 Oct in advance convoy KX4A for Gibraltar: left there 11 Nov: arrived Algiers 14 Nov for onward routing to Bone: carried 1,642 tons cased petrol

ROYAL SCOTSMAN 3,244/36 Burns & Laird - *HM LANDING SHIP, INFANTRY (HAND HOISTING) (personnel capacity 500)*: left the Clyde 26 Oct in assault convoy KMF1: one landing craft carried away on passage 28 Oct: called Gibraltar for fuel 6 Nov: rejoined convoy 7 Nov: arrived Arzeu R beachhead 8 Nov

ROYAL ULSTERMAN 3,244/36 Burns & Laird - *HM LANDING SHIP, INFANTRY (HAND HOISTING) (personnel capacity 500)*: left the Clyde 26 Oct in assault convoy KMF1: called Gibraltar for fuel 6 Nov: rejoined convoy 7 Nov: arrived Arzeu R beachhead 8 Nov

ST ESSYLT 5,634/41 South American Saint - *MT SHIP*: left Birkenhead 19 Oct and the Clyde 22 Oct in assault convoy KMS1: arrived Arzeu Z beachhead 8 Nov: carried 293 personnel, 5 tanks, 85 other vehicles, 18 guns, 9 tons cased petrol and 109 tons stores

SALACIA 5,495/37 Donaldson - *MT SHIP*: left Faslane 21 Oct and the Clyde 22 Oct in assault convoy KMS1: arrived Oran Y beachhead 8 Nov: carried 302 personnel, 140 vehicles, 29 guns, 48 tons cased petrol and 445 tons stores

SAMUEL CHASE 10,000/41 US ex AFRICAN METEOR - *US NAVY TRANSPORT (personnel capacity 1,446)*: left the Clyde 26 Oct in assault convoy KMF1: arrived Algiers C beachhead 8 Nov

SELBO 1,778/21 Murrell - *CASED PETROL SHIP*: left Silloth 28-29 Oct and the Clyde 30 Oct in convoy KX5 for Gibraltar: left there 18 Nov for Algiers and onward routing to Bone: carried 1,524 tons cased petrol

SILVERLAUREL 6,142/39 Silver - *STORE SHIP*: originally destined for Malta: left the Mersey 29 Oct and the Clyde 1 Nov in follow-up convoy KMF2 for Gibraltar and Oran: carried 12 vehicles, 1,666 tons cased petrol, 4,476 tons stores and 151 tons coal

SOBIESKI 11,030/39 Polish (Gdynia-America) - *LANDING SHIP, INFANTRY (LARGE) (personnel capacity 1,500)*: left the Clyde 26 Oct in assault convoy KMF1: arrived Algiers B beachhead 8 Nov

SOBO 5,353/37 Elder Dempster - *MT SHIP*: left Birkenhead 6 Oct and the Clyde 22 Oct in assault convoy KMS1: near missed in an aerial torpedo attack at 0600 7 Nov: arrived Algiers B beachhead 8 Nov: carried 421 personnel, 141 vehicles, 4 guns, 118 tons cased petrol and 527 tons stores

STANHILL 5,969/42 Stanhope - *MT SHIP*: from Faslane, left the Clyde 22 Oct in assault convoy KMS1 carrying part of the floating reserve: arrived Algiers B beachhead 8 Nov: left there 10 Nov: arrived Bougie 11 Nov: carried 32 personnel, 91 vehicles, 16 guns, 82 tons cased petrol and 486 tons stores (Operation "Perpetual")

STRATHEDEN 23,722/37 P & O - *PERSONNEL SHIP (capacity 4,090)*: left the Clyde 1 Nov in follow-up convoy KMF2: arrived Algiers 12 Nov

STRATHMORE 23,428/35 P & O - *PERSONNEL SHIP (capacity 3,590)*: left the Clyde 1 Nov in follow-up convoy KMF2: arrived Algiers 12 Nov

VICEROY OF INDIA.

STRATHNAVER 22,283/31 P & O - *LANDING SHIP, INFANTRY (LARGE) (personnel capacity 3,739)*: left the Clyde 26 Oct in assault convoy KMF1 carrying part of the floating reserve: arrived Algiers B beachhead 8 Nov: after being delayed by engine defects, left 11 Nov: arrived Bougie 12 Nov (Operation "Perpetual")

TASAJERA 4,308/38 Lago - *HM LANDING SHIP, TANK*: left the Clyde 21 Oct in advance convoy KX4A for Gibraltar: arrived Arzeu Z beachhead 8 Nov

TEGELBERG 14,150/37 Dutch (KPM) - *LANDING SHIP, INFANTRY (LARGE) (personnel capacity 3,264)*: left the Clyde 26 Oct in assault convoy KMF1: arrived Arzeu Z beachhead 8 Nov

THESEUS 6,527/08 *Alfred Holt - *MT SHIP*: left Birkenhead 19 Oct and the Clyde 22 Oct in assault convoy KMS1: arrived Arzeu Z beachhead 8 Nov: entered Arzeu harbour 10 Nov: carried 51 personnel, 114 vehicles, 18 guns, 240 tons cased petrol and 328 tons stores

THOMAS HOOKER 7,176/42 US (WSA) - *MT/STORE SHIP*: from the Clyde, joined follow-up convoy KMS2 (which originated Loch Ewe 25 Oct): arrived Oran 11 Nov: landed 4 personnel, 111 vehicles, 116 tons stores and 914 tons coal

THOMAS STONE 9,260/41 US ex PRESIDENT VAN BUREN - *US NAVY TRANSPORT*: loaded at New York: left the Clyde 26 Oct in assault convoy KMF1 for Algiers C beachhead: carried 1,449 personnel and 133 vehicles: 50 miles off the Spanish coast, at 0543 7 Nov, the ship's port counter was struck by an aerial torpedo, wrecking her rudder and propellers: 700 personnel embarked in 24 landing craft for the 140-mile journey to the beachhead, escorted by the frigate SPEY, but adverse weather and breakdowns resulted in their being taken aboard SPEY: with the destroyer VELOX standing by, THOMAS STONE was taken in tow by the

destroyer WISHART and tug ST DAY at 2115 same day: the personnel arrived at the beachhead aboard SPEY 8 Nov and their ship was towed into Algiers harbour 11 Nov

TIBA 5,239/38 Dutch (Vrachtvaart) - *MT SHIP*: left Birkenhead 7 Oct and the Clyde 22 Oct in assault convoy KMS1: arrived Algiers B beachhead 8 Nov: carried 38 personnel, 113 vehicles, 24 guns, 117 tons cased petrol and 553 tons stores

TORR HEAD 5,021/37 *Heyn - *MT/STORE SHIP*: left Manchester 7 Oct and Loch Ewe 25 Oct in follow-up convoy KMS2: arrived Algiers 12 Nov: carried 12 personnel, 183 vehicles, 16 guns, 313 tons cased petrol and 1,990 tons stores

ULSTER MONARCH 3,791/29 Belfast - *HM LANDING SHIP, INFANTRY (HAND HOISTING)*: left the Clyde 26 Oct in assault convoy KMF1: called Gibraltar for fuel 6 Nov: rejoined convoy 7 Nov: arrived Arzeu R beachhead 8 Nov: carried 492 personnel

URLANA 6,852/41 British India - *MT SHIP*: left Glasgow 20 Oct and the Clyde 22 Oct in assault convoy KMS1 carrying part of the floating reserve: arrived Algiers B beachhead 8 Nov: left there 10 Nov: arrived Bougie 11 Nov: carried 7 personnel, 146 vehicles, 19 guns, 109 tons cased petrol and 582 tons stores (Operation "Perpetual")

URUGUAY 20,183/28 US (Maritime Commission) - *PERSONNEL SHIP*: left the Clyde 1 Nov in follow-up convoy KMF2: arrived Oran 11 Nov

VICEROY OF INDIA 19,627/29 P & O - *LANDING SHIP, INFANTRY (LARGE) (personnel capacity 3,519)*: left the Clyde 26 Oct in assault convoy KMF1: arrived Algiers A beachhead 8 Nov: left for the homeward passage 10 Nov: at 0428 11 Nov, torpedoed on the port side in the engine room by U 407 north of Arzeu: the destroyer BOADICEA was sent to take the ship in tow but she went down by the stern at 0807 same day

WALT WHITMAN 7,176/42 US (WSA) - *MT SHIP*: from Birkenhead, left the Clyde 22 Oct in assault convoy KMS1: arrived Oran X beachhead 8 Nov: involved in collision with the landing ship BACHAQUERO same day: carried 54 personnel, 84 vehicles, 15 guns, 6 tons cased petrol and 51 tons stores

WARWICK CASTLE 20,107/30 Union-Castle - *LANDING SHIP, INFANTRY (LARGE) (personnel capacity 2,600)*: left Glasgow 25 Oct and the Clyde 26 Oct in assault convoy KMF1: arrived Arzeu Z beachhead 8 Nov: left for the homeward passage: was torpedoed on the port side in holds Nos 2 and 3 by U 413, whilst west of Lisbon at 0850 14 Nov: at 0900 the ship was struck by a second torpedo, thought to have exploded inside the ship after entering through the hole made by the first: after settling by the head, she sank at 1015 same day, the destroyer VANSITTART was amongst the rescuing vessels

WEST POINT 4,999/20 Cereal Trade & Shipping - *MT/STORE SHIP*: left Manchester 8 Oct and Loch Ewe 25 Oct in follow-up convoy KMS2: arrived Algiers 12 Nov: carried 9 personnel, 12 tanks, 166 other vehicles, 40 tons cased petrol and 1,484 tons stores

WILLIAM FLOYD 7,176/42 US (WSA) - *MT SHIP*: from Birkenhead, left the Clyde 22 Oct in assault convoy KMS1: arrived Arzeu Z beachhead 8 Nov: entered Arzeu harbour 12 Nov: carried 71 personnel, 17 tanks, 103 other vehicles, 15 guns, 202 tons cased petrol and 420 tons stores

WILLIAM WIRT 7,191/42 US (WSA) - *MT/STORE SHIP*: from Newport, left the Clyde 22 Oct in assault convoy KMS1: entered Arzeu harbour 8 Nov: carried 54 personnel, 91 vehicles, 765 tons cased petrol and 514 tons stores

WINCHESTER CASTLE 20,012/30 Union-Castle - *LANDING SHIP, INFANTRY (LARGE) (personnel*

capacity 1,100)*: left the Clyde 26 Oct in assault convoy KMF1: arrived Algiers B beachhead 8 Nov

ZEBULON B VANCE 7,177/42 US (WSA) - *MT SHIP*: from Manchester, left the Clyde 22 Oct in assault convoy KMS1: arrived Arzeu Z beachhead 8 Nov: lifting gear collapsed same day: entered Arzeu harbour 13 Nov: arrived Oran 14 Nov to complete discharge: carried 46 personnel, 97 vehicles, 6 guns, 216 tons cased petrol and 421 tons stores

Other merchant ships including Royal Fleet Auxiliaries

ABBEYDALE 8,299/37 Admiralty - *OILER*: joined follow-up convoy KMS2 10 Nov: arrived Arzeu 11 Nov

BRISK 1,594/23 Norwegian (*Olsen) - *NAVAL COLLIER*: left Ellesmere Port 1 Oct and the Clyde 21 Oct in advance convoy KX4A for Gibraltar and onward routing to Oran: carried 1,967 tons coal

BRITISH LADY 6,098/23 British Tanker - *OILER*: joined follow-up convoy KMS2 to refuel ships at sea

BROWN RANGER 3,417/41 Admiralty - *OILER*: left Gibraltar 5 Nov: fuelling for Force H (Force R)

DERWENTDALE 8,398/41 Admiralty - *LANDING SHIP, GANTRY*: carrying 14 landing craft, left the Clyde 22 Oct in assault convoy KMS1: arrived Arzeu Z beachhead 8 Nov

DEWDALE 8,265/41 Admiralty - *LANDING SHIP, GANTRY*: carrying 14 landing craft, oil fuel and petrol, left the Clyde 22 Oct in assault convoy KMS1: arrived Algiers A beachhead 8 Nov: arrived Algiers 9 Nov and refuelled several destroyers and corvettes: left there 10 Nov: arrived Bougie 11 Nov and refuelled the fleet there: deck, bridge, funnel and a lifeboat damaged by aircraft machine-gun and cannon fire 12 Nov (Operation "Perpetual"): a 60ft x 26ft hole was torn in

The Royal Fleet Auxiliary oiler BROWN RANGER. [Wright & Logan]

the ship's side by a bomb direct hit at Algiers 1925 20 Nov

DINGLEDALE 8,145/41 Admiralty - *OILER*: left Gibraltar 5 Nov: fuelling for Force H (Force R)

ENNERDALE 8,219/41 Admiralty - *LANDING SHIP, GANTRY*: carrying 14 landing craft from the Mersey, left the Clyde 22 Oct in assault convoy KMS1: suffered defect with her hoisting equipment on arrival Algiers B beachhead 8 Nov

GARLINGE 2,012/18 Constants - *NAVAL COLLIER*: left Grimsby 10 Oct and the Clyde 21 Oct in advance convoy KX4A for Gibraltar: carried 2,427 tons coal: left Gibraltar 7 Nov for Algiers: at 0051 10 Nov, hit between her engine room and stokehold by a torpedo from U 81: the ship immediately rolled under the water: survivors were rescued by the examination vessel MINNA

ORKLA 2,177/22 South Georgia - *NAVAL COLLIER*: left Cardiff 14 Oct and the Clyde 30 Oct in convoy KX5 for Gibraltar: left there 18 Nov for Algiers: carried 2,709 tons coal

WILLODALE 1,777/09 Bromage - *NAVAL COLLIER*: left the Mersey 23 Oct and the Clyde 30 Oct in convoy KX5 for Gibraltar and arrived Algiers: carried 2,025 tons coal

Unnamed naval vessels carrying personnel and equipment

LANDING CRAFT, TANK
LCT 164, **169**, **170** - all left Gibraltar 7 Nov: arrived Arzeu Z beachhead 9 Nov, together with one other, drawn from LCT 135, 152, 160: all six arrived Algiers 15 Nov

Naval vessels in support

BATTLESHIPS
DUKE OF YORK - left Gibraltar 6 Nov: on patrol 30 miles north of Algiers 8 Nov (Force H)

NELSON - arrived Gibraltar 6 Nov: served as flagship Naval Commander, Expeditionary Force from 8 Nov: was available as replacement battleship, if required (Force H)

RODNEY - left Gibraltar 6 Nov: detached from Force H 7 Nov: patrolled off the coast north of Oran and provided bombardment support 8-10 Nov

BATTLECRUISER
RENOWN - left Gibraltar 6 Nov: on patrol 30 miles north of Algiers 8 Nov (Force H)

AIRCRAFT CARRIERS
ARGUS - left Gibraltar 5 Nov: joined assault convoy

KMS1: maintained continuous daylight fighter patrol over the convoy 7 Nov: on patrol 15 miles north of the Algerian coast 8 Nov: maintained a continuous daylight patrol of four Seafires 8-10 Nov when RAF took over the air cover of Algiers: provided fighter protection for the Bougie convoys: attacked by dive-bombers which inflicted a hit on the port after end of the flight deck at 1705 10 Nov: undamaged by aerial torpedo attacks same day: experienced further air attacks in which torpedo tracks passed beneath the ship at 1710 11 Nov

FORMIDABLE - left the Clyde 30 Oct: positioned 30 miles north of Algiers and provided air support 8 Nov (Force H)

FURIOUS - left Gibraltar 7 Nov: provided air support off Oran 8 Nov

VICTORIOUS - left the Clyde 30 Oct: positioned 30 miles north of Algiers and provided air support 8 Nov (Force H)

ESCORT CARRIERS
AVENGER - left the UK 22 Oct with assault convoy KMS1: maintained continuous daylight fighter patrol over the convoy 7 Nov: on patrol 15 miles north of the Algierian coast 8 Nov: subjected to an unsuccessful aerial torpedo attack 9 Nov: left for Gibraltar 12 Nov: at 0320 15 Nov, when 130 miles west of Gibraltar escorting a homeward convoy, was torpedoed by U 155 and blew up: survivors were rescued by the destroyer GLAISDALE

BITER - left the UK 26 Oct with assault convoy KMF1: flew anti-submarine patrols 30 Oct-3 Nov: provided air support off Oran 8 Nov

DASHER - left Gibraltar 6 Nov: joined assault convoy KMF1: detached 7 Nov: provided air support off Oran 8 Nov

CRUISERS
ARGONAUT - left Gibraltar 6 Nov: on patrol 30 miles north of Algiers 8 Nov (Force H)

AURORA - left Gibraltar 4 Nov: joined assault convoy KMF1 5 Nov: led assault ships to Oran then patrolled five miles off the coast 8 Nov: provided bombardment support same day: at 0542 same day, opened fire on the French destroyer TRAMONTANE, which was seen to be crippled and on fire at 0555: at 0659 same day, opened fire on two other French destroyers: TORNADE was seen to be stopped, on fire and with her forecastle awash, and TYPHON headed for Oran, damaged: patrolled ten miles off the coast with the battleship RODNEY: at 0959 9 Nov, sighted and opened fire on French destroyer EPERVIER, which was beached after many explosions and dense smoke, and TYPHON, which again returned to Oran, where she was scuttled: provided bombardment support 10 Nov

BERMUDA - left Gibraltar 6 Nov: provided

BULOLO was converted to serve as a Landing Ship, Headquarters: this type of vessel was found to be an essential requirement for all major amphibious operations. [IWM FL4326]

bombardment support with 12-gun salvoes off Algiers C beachhead 8 Nov: subjected to repeated aerial torpedo attacks same day (Force H)

CHARYBDIS - left Gibraltar 5 Nov: joined assault convoy KMS1 6 Nov: on patrol 15 miles north of the Algierian coast 8 Nov (Force O): positioned off Bougie 11 Nov

CUMBERLAND - left Azores 4 Nov to provide cover for the follow-up convoys (Force Q)

DELHI - left Gibraltar 7 Nov: provided anti-aircraft support for the carriers BITER, DASHER and FURIOUS off Oran 8 Nov: intercepted French naval vessels off Oran 9 Nov

JAMAICA - left Gibraltar 3 Nov: joined assault convoy KMF1 4 Nov: led the assault ships to Arzeu Z beachhead 8 Nov: sent a boarding party to the French merchant ship CEVENNES same day: in Oran Bay, opened fire on the French destroyers EPERVIER and TYPHON at 1025 9 Nov (see the cruiser AURORA above): provided bombardment support 10 Nov then patrolled off Oran with the battleship RODNEY

NORFOLK - left Azores 4 Nov to provide cover for the follow-up convoys (Force Q)

SCYLLA - left Gibraltar 5 Nov: joined assault convoy KMS1 6 Nov: on patrol 15 miles north of the Algerian coast 8 Nov (Force O): rescued survivors from the sloop IBIS 10 Nov: positioned off Bougie 11 Nov

SHEFFIELD - left the UK 26 Oct with assault convoy KMF1: refuelled the convoy escorts CLARE, ENCHANTRESS, IBIS, ROTHER and SPEY 1-3 Nov then detached from convoy: called Gibraltar for fuel 5 Nov: joined assault convoy KMS1 6 Nov: transferred 785 US personnel to the destroyers MALCOLM then BROKE 1700 7 Nov: on patrol 15 miles north of the Algierian coast, where she was subjected to repeated aerial torpedo attacks 8 Nov: left Algiers 10 Nov: sustained slight damage in collision with the minesweeper CADMUS 0411 11 Nov: arrived Bougie same day (Operation "Perpetual")

SIRIUS - left Gibraltar 5 Nov: on patrol 30 miles north of Algiers 8 Nov (Force H)

MONITOR

ROBERTS - left Gibraltar 5 Nov: joined assault convoy KMS1 6 Nov for the Algiers area: arrived Algiers 9 Nov: left there 10 Nov: arrived Bougie 11 Nov: during an air attack at 1715, suffered three bomb hits, the first exploding under the ship, the second penetrating the port side abaft the funnel and the third striking the superstructure on the starboard side, causing extensive damage and fire: with her fans out of action, the engine and boiler rooms had to be evacuated and the vessel stopped: rescued survivors from the anti-aircraft ship TYNWALD 12 Nov then berthed alongside at Bougie same day (Operation "Perpetual")

LANDING SHIPS, HEADQUARTERS

BULOLO - left the Clyde 26 Oct in assault convoy KMF1: arrived Algiers B beachhead 8 Nov: carried 160

LARGS - ex French CHARLES PLUMIER: left the Clyde 26 Oct in assault convoy KMF1: arrived Arzeu Z beachhead 8 Nov

AUXILIARY ANTI-AIRCRAFT SHIPS
ALYNBANK - left the UK 22 Oct with assault convoy KMS1: arrived Oran beachhead 8 Nov

PALOMARES - left Gibraltar 3 Nov: joined assault convoy KMF1 5 Nov: arrived Algiers B beachhead 8 Nov: suffered a bomb hit on the after gun deck off Algiers 1620 9 Nov: ship engulfed in flames abaft the mainmast, with steering gear out of action and heavy casualties: fires were extinguished at 1725 same day: a whaler sent to LAMERTON to collect medical supplies sank: steering repaired 10 Nov and ship went alongside in Algiers: transferred to the corvette SAMPHIRE, for burial at sea, the crew members killed in the 9 Nov air attack

POZARICA - left Gibraltar 3 Nov: joined assault convoy KMF1 5 Nov: arrived Algiers A beachhead 8 Nov: rescued survivors from the minesweeper ALGERINE 15 Nov: arrived Bougie same day

TYNWALD - left Gibraltar 5 Nov: joined the assault convoy 6 Nov: arrived Algiers C beachhead 8 Nov to provide not only anti-aircraft support but also to act as radar guard ship and to direct aircraft from the carrier AVENGER: left Algiers 10 Nov: arrived Bougie 11 Nov to provide anti-aircraft support and direct aircraft from the carrier ARGUS: at 0505 12 Nov, whilst standing by the monitor ROBERTS, TYNWALD was torpedoed on the starboard side by the Italian submarine ARGO: she settled by the head onto the sea bed, survivors being picked up by ROBERTS and the corvette SAMPHIRE (Operation "Perpetual")

DESTROYERS
ACHATES - left Gibraltar 3 Nov: joined assault convoy KMF1 4 Nov: detached 6 Nov to escort the aircraft carriers to the Oran area: in action against submarines off Oran 8 Nov

ALBRIGHTON - joined follow-up convoy KMS2 2 Nov: rescued survivors from the personnel ship NIEUW ZEELAND 11 Nov

AMAZON - left Gibraltar 3 Nov: joined assault convoy KMF1: detached 6 Nov to escort the aircraft carriers to the Oran area

ANTELOPE - left Gibraltar 3 Nov: joined assault convoy KMF1 4 Nov: arrived Oran X beachhead 8 Nov: intercepted the French passenger ship ERIDAN off Oran same day and placed an armed guard on board: also intercepted three other French vessels, including the cargo ships AGEN and MONTAIGNE, all three of which beached themselves and were sabotaged

ASHANTI - (Force H)

AVON VALE - left Gibraltar 7 Nov: joined the aircraft carriers in the Oran area then joined follow-up convoys KMF2 and KMS2: arrived Oran 11 Nov

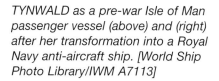

TYNWALD as a pre-war Isle of Man passenger vessel (above) and (right) after her transformation into a Royal Navy anti-aircraft ship. [World Ship Photo Library/IWM A7113]

BEAGLE - left Gibraltar 2 Nov to join Force H: detached with the battleship RODNEY 7 Nov to arrive Oran beachhead 8 Nov

BICESTER - from Gibraltar, joined assault convoy KMF1 6 Nov: arrived Algiers A beachhead 8 Nov: escorted the landing ship AWATEA towards Djidjelli 10-11 Nov but diverted to Bougie: went alongside AWATEA 11 Nov then rescued her survivors same day: suffered casualties in a near miss off Bougie 12 Nov (Operation "Perpetual")

BLYSKAWICA - Polish: left Gibraltar 5 Nov: joined assault convoy KMF1 6 Nov: arrived Algiers B beachhead 8 Nov: stood by the sloop IBIS 10 Nov: escorted the landing ship STRATHNAVER into Bougie 12 Nov: slightly damaged in two air attacks same day

BOADICEA - left Gibraltar 2 Nov to join Force H: joined assault convoy KMF1 6 Nov: arrived Oran beachhead 8 Nov: suffered flooding in her shell room as a result of a direct hit forward, whilst in action against the French destroyers TORNADE and TYPHON off Oran the same day: sent to assist the landing ship VICEROY OF INDIA 11 Nov

BOREAS - left Gibraltar to join Force H: detached with the battleship RODNEY 7 Nov to arrive Oran beachhead 8 Nov: on patrol off Arzeu 11 Nov

BRAMHAM - from Gibraltar, joined assault convoy KMF1 6 Nov: arrived Algiers A beachhead 8 Nov: left Algiers 10 Nov: escorted the landing ship STRATHNAVER into Bougie 12 Nov

BRILLIANT - left Gibraltar 2 Nov to join Force H: joined assault convoy KMF1 6 Nov to Oran Y beachhead: sank the French warship LA SURPRISE off Oran 0630 8 Nov and rescued her survivors: intercepted and turned back a merchant ship bound for Oran 10 Nov

BROKE - left the UK 21 Oct with advance convoy KX4A to Gibraltar: left there 5 Nov: joined assault convoy KMS1 6 Nov: embarked from the cruiser SHEFFIELD over 350 US troops 1700 7 Nov: on the fourth attempt, she charged the boom and entered Algiers harbour at 0530 8 Nov: she went alongside and landed her troops but, holed in the hull by gunfire and badly damaged, withdrew at 0930 and was taken in tow by the destroyer ZETLAND: with the wind and sea rising, her crew transferred to ZETLAND and BROKE foundered north of Arzeu on 9 Nov (Operation "Terminal")

BULLDOG - left Gibraltar 2 Nov to join Force H: detached with the battleship RODNEY 7 Nov to arrive Oran beachhead 8 Nov

CALPE - left Gibraltar 7 Nov: in action against the French destroyers TORNADE and TYPHON off Oran 8 Nov: escorted the French merchant ships CEVENNES and JAMAIQUE from Oran to Arzeu same day

CLARE - left the UK 26 Oct with assault convoy KMF1 27 Oct: refuelled from the cruiser SHEFFIELD 1 Nov: joined assault convoy KMS1 6 Nov for the Algiers beachhead: stood by the sloop IBIS 10 Nov

CLEVELAND - joined follow-up convoy KMS2 2 Nov

COWDRAY - from Gibraltar, joined assault convoy KMF1 6 Nov: arrived Algiers C beachhead 8 Nov: stokehold disabled by a direct hit in a dive-bombing attack at 1715 same day: the bomb entered the forecastle, went through ship's bottom and exploded under No 1 boiler room: vessel was taken in tow by the minesweeper ALGERINE and beached at 1600 9 Nov: subsequently salved and towed into Algiers harbour by the tug HENGIST 16 Nov

ESCAPADE - temporarily joined assault convoy KMF1 2 Nov: joined follow-up convoy KMF2 7 Nov

ESKDALE - joined follow-up convoy KMS2 2 Nov

ESKIMO - (Force H)

FARNDALE - left Gibraltar 7 Nov: assigned to Arzeu R and Z beachheads: provided bombardment support 8 Nov

ISAAC SWEERS - Dutch: joined assault convoy KMF1 2 Nov: detached to Force H 5 Nov: rescued survivors from the personnel ship NIEUW ZEELAND 11 Nov: hit by two torpedoes from U 431 north of Algiers at 0536 13 Nov: the ship caught fire and sank: survivors were rescued by the trawler LOCH OSKAIG

ITHURIEL - (Force H)

LAMERTON - left Gibraltar 5 Nov: joined assault convoy KMF1 6 Nov: arrived Algiers B beachhead 8 Nov: assisted the anti-aircraft ship PALOMARES 9 Nov: landed troops at Bone 12 Nov

LOOKOUT - (Force H)

MALCOLM - left the UK 21 Oct with advance convoy KX4A to Gibraltar: embarked seven Royal Marines (to capture important material) and left there 5 Nov: joined assault convoy KMS1 6 Nov: took aboard from the cruiser SHEFFIELD over 350 US troops 1700 7 Nov: whilst endeavouring to land troops in Algiers harbour, was hit amidships on the approach and forced to withdraw with three boilers out of action 8 Nov (Operation "Terminal")

MARNE - temporarily joined assault convoy KMF1 3 Nov: stern blown off in a torpedo attack by U 515 12 Nov: vessel remained afloat

MARTIN - torpedoed by U 431 north of Algiers: blew up and sank at 0258 10 Nov: survivors were rescued by the destroyer QUENTIN (Force H)

METEOR, MILNE - (both Force H)

OFFA, ONSLOW - both left Azores 4 Nov with the cruisers CUMBERLAND and NORFOLK (Force Q)

OPPORTUNE - (Force H)

ORIBI - left Azores 4 Nov with the cruisers CUMBERLAND and NORFOLK (Force Q)

PANTHER - holed and badly flooded by a bomb near miss 1833 7 Nov: arrived Gibraltar 8 Nov (Force H)

PARTRIDGE, PATHFINDER, PENN - (all Force H)

PORCUPINE - rescued survivors from the personnel ship NIEUW ZEELAND 11 Nov (Force H)

PUCKERIDGE - left Gibraltar 7 Nov: escorted the aircraft carriers off Oran then joined follow-up convoys KMF2 and KMS2: arrived Oran 11 Nov

QUALITY - (Force H)

QUENTIN - rescued survivors from the destroyer MARTIN 10 Nov (Force H)

QUIBERON, TARTAR - (both Force H)

VANOC - left Gibraltar 4 Nov: joined assault convoy KMS1 6 Nov to the Algiers beachheads: rescued the pilot from a crashed Seafire from ARGUS 7 Nov: positioned off Bougie 11 Nov

VANSITTART - temporarily joined assault convoy KMS1 1 Nov: assigned to Arzeu Z beachhead: rescued survivors from the landing ship WARWICK CASTLE 14 Nov

VELOX - from Gibraltar, joined assault convoy KMF1 4 Nov: detached 6 Nov: stood by the US Navy transport THOMAS STONE 7 Nov

VENOMOUS - left the UK 21 Oct with advance convoy KX4A to Gibraltar

VERITY - from Gibraltar, joined assault convoy KMF1 4 Nov: detached 6 Nov: assigned to Oran Y beachhead

WESTCOTT - from Gibraltar, joined assault convoy KMF1 4 Nov: detached 6 Nov: assigned to the Oran beachheads: in action against submarines 8 Nov: joined follow-up convoys KMF2 and KMS2: arrived Oran 11 Nov

WHEATLAND - left Gibraltar 5 Nov: joined assault convoy KMF1 6 Nov: arrived Algiers B beachhead 8 Nov: landed troops at Bone 12 Nov

WILTON - left Gibraltar 5 Nov: joined assault convoy KMF1 6 Nov: arrived Algiers B beachhead 8 Nov: escorted the landing ship AWATEA towards Djidjelli 10-11 Nov but diverted and entered Bougie harbour: left there 11 Nov then assisted with the search for AWATEA's survivors same day: upper deck and ship's side superficially damaged by a bomb which failed to explode 12 Nov (Operation "Perpetual")

The destroyer VERITY was part of the Gibraltar Escort Force assigned to the North African landings.

FLEETWOOD was one of 14 sloops assigned to the operation.

WISHART - from Gibraltar, joined assault convoy KMF1 4 Nov: detached 6 Nov: towed the US Navy transport THOMAS STONE to Algiers 7-11 Nov

WIVERN - left Gibraltar 3 Nov: joined assault convoy KMF1 4 Nov: in company with the aircraft carrier FURIOUS 7 Nov: assigned to Oran beachheads: intercepted French naval vessels off Oran 9 Nov then joined follow-up convoys KMF2 and KMS2: arrived Oran 11 Nov

WRESTLER - left the UK 21 Oct with advance convoy KX4A to Gibraltar: left there 5 Nov: joined assault convoy KMS1 6 Nov for the Algiers beachheads: positioned off Bougie 11 Nov

ZETLAND - from Gibraltar, joined assault convoy KMF1 6 Nov: arrived Algiers C beachhead 8 Nov: provided bombardment support same day: took the destroyer BROKE in tow 9 Nov and embarked her crew: escorted the landing ship AWATEA towards Djidjelli 10-11 Nov but diverted to Bougie

BEACON SUBMARINES
P45 - from Gibraltar, assigned to Algiers C beachhead

P48 - from Gibraltar, assigned to Algiers B beachhead

P54 - assigned to Oran X and Y beachheads

P221 - from Gibraltar: assigned to Algiers A beachhead

URSULA - from Gibraltar, assigned to Arzeu Z beachhead

SLOOPS
ABERDEEN - left the UK 26 Oct with assault convoy KMF1: assigned to Arzeu Z beachhead

BIDEFORD - left the UK 25 Oct with follow-up convoy KMS2

DEPTFORD - joined assault convoy KMS1: led the cargo ships into Arzeu Z beachhead 8 Nov

EGRET - left the UK 1 Nov with follow-up convoy KMF2

ENCHANTRESS - left the UK 26 Oct with assault convoy KMF1: refuelled from the cruiser SHEFFIELD 3 Nov: joined assault convoy KMS1 6 Nov: arrived Algiers C beachhead 8 Nov

FLEETWOOD - left the UK 1 Nov with follow-up convoy KMF2

IBIS - left the UK 26 Oct with assault convoy KMF1: refuelled from the cruiser SHEFFIELD 3 Nov: joined assault convoy KMS1 6 Nov: assigned to Algiers C beachhead: at 1724 10 Nov, whilst acting as screen for the carrier ARGUS and cruiser SCYLLA, vessel was hit by an aerial torpedo 10 miles north of Algiers and capsized within a few minutes: survivors were rescued by SCYLLA, with the destroyers BLYSKAWICA and CLARE standing by

LEITH, LONDONDERRY - both left the UK 25 Oct with follow-up convoy KMS2

PELICAN - left the UK 1 Nov with follow-up convoy KMF2: arrived Bougie 13 Nov

ROCHESTER, SANDWICH, SCARBOROUGH - all left the UK 25 Oct with follow-up convoy KMS2

STORK - left the UK 22 Oct with assault convoy KMS1 to the Algiers beachheads: at 0315 12 Nov, hit forward by a torpedo from U 77, whilst five miles north of Algiers B beachhead: despite serious hull damage, reached Algiers under tow

CUTTERS
BANFF - left the UK 1 Nov with follow-up convoy KMF2

HARTLAND - left the UK 26 Oct with assault convoy KMF1: came under heavy fire from shore batteries on the approach and when entering Oran harbour to land troops 8 Nov: severe damage and devastating casualties resulted in the ship catching fire and being abandoned (Operation "Reservist")

LANDGUARD, LULWORTH - both left the UK 25 Oct with follow-up convoy KMS2

WALNEY - left the UK 26 Oct with assault convoy KMF1: charged the boom and entered Oran harbour to land troops 8 Nov but was disabled by withering fire from French warships, set ablaze and had to be abandoned with very few survivors: she subsequently sank (Operation "Reservist")

FRIGATES
EXE - left the UK 26 Oct with assault convoy KMF1: assigned to Arzeu Z beachhead

ROTHER - left the UK 26 Oct with assault convoy KMF1: refuelled from the cruiser SHEFFIELD 1 and 3 Nov: arrived Algiers A beachhead 8 Nov: left there for Bougie 10 Nov: rescued survivors from the landing ship AWATEA 11 Nov (Operation "Perpetual")

SPEY - left the UK 26 Oct with assault convoy KMF1: refuelled from the cruiser SHEFFIELD 1-2 Nov: stood by the US Navy transport THOMAS STONE 7 Nov, then accompanied her landing craft and finally took aboard the 700 personnel from those craft to complete their journey to the beachhead 8 Nov: left Algiers 10 Nov: swept Bougie approaches 11 Nov (Operation "Perpetual")

SWALE - left the UK 26 Oct with assault convoy KMF1: assigned to Arzeu Z beachhead

CORVETTES
ARMERIA - left Gibraltar 9 Nov: joined follow-up convoys KMF2 and KMS2: arrived Oran 11 Nov

AUBRETIA - assigned to assault convoy KMS1 to Algiers C beachhead: left Gibraltar 11 Nov for Algiers: left for Bougie 10 Nov (Operation "Perpetual")

CONVOLVULUS - joined assault convoy KMS1: assigned to Algiers A beachhead

COREOPSIS - left Gibraltar 5 Nov (Force R)

CYCLAMEN - left Gibraltar 9 Nov: joined follow-up convoys KMF2 and KMS2: arrived Oran 11 Nov

DIANELLA - left Gibraltar 11 Nov for Algiers

GARDENIA - joined assault convoy KMS1: arrived Oran X beachhead 8 Nov: at 0135 9 Nov involved in collision with the trawler FLUELLEN off Oran: abandoned and sank 0315 same day

GERANIUM - left Gibraltar 9 Nov: joined follow-up convoy KMS2

LOTUS - left Gibraltar 11 Nov for Algiers

LOUISBURG - Canadian: left the UK 25 Oct with follow-up convoy KMS2

MARIGOLD - left the UK 22 Oct with assault convoy KMS1: assigned to Algiers A beachhead: rescued survivors from the MT ship MARON 13 Nov and took the crew off the MT ship LALANDE 14 Nov

PENTSTEMON - joined assault convoy KMS1: in collision with the minesweeper ALARM 0430 5 Nov: arrived Algiers C beachhead 8 Nov: left Algiers 10 Nov: arrived Bougie 11 Nov: went alongside the landing ship AWATEA then rescued her survivors same day (Operation "Perpetual")

POPPY - left Gibraltar 11 Nov for Algiers

PRESCOTT - Canadian: left the UK 25 Oct with follow-up convoy KMS2

RHODODENDRON - joined assault convoy KMS1: assigned to Arzeu Z beachhead

SAMPHIRE - joined assault convoy KMS1 6 Nov: arrived Algiers C beachhead 8 Nov: took survivors from the US Navy transport LEEDSTOWN to Algiers 9 Nov: left there 10 Nov to bury at sea crew members killed when PALOMARES bombed the previous day: arrived Bougie 11 Nov: rescued survivors from the anti-aircraft ship TYNWALD 12 Nov (Operation "Perpetual")

SPIRAEA - left Gibraltar 9 Nov: joined follow-up convoy KMS2

STARWORT - left Gibraltar 11 Nov for Algiers

VETCH - left the UK 22 Oct with assault convoy KMS1: assigned to Oran X beachhead: stood by the trawler FLUELLEN 9 Nov

VIOLET - assigned to Arzeu Z beachhead

WOODSTOCK - Canadian: left Gibraltar 11 Nov for Oran

MINESWEEPERS
ACUTE - left the UK 22 Oct with assault convoy KMS1: joined assault convoy KMF1 6 Nov: arrived Algiers B beachhead 8 Nov: swept anchorage 9 Nov: completed an anti-submarine patrol 13 Nov

ALARM - left the UK 22 Oct with assault convoy KMS1: sustained slight bow damage above the waterline in collision with the corvette PENTSTEMON 0430 5 Nov: joined assault convoy KMF1 6 Nov: arrived Algiers B beachhead 8 Nov: swept anchorage 9 Nov: completed an anti-submarine patrol 13 Nov

ALBACORE - left the UK 22 Oct with assault convoy KMS1: joined assault convoy KMF1 6 Nov: arrived Algiers B beachhead 8 Nov: left Algiers 10 Nov: swept Bougie approaches 11 Nov: slightly damaged by a bomb near miss off Bougie, so left for Algiers 13 Nov (Operation "Perpetual")

ALGERINE - left the UK 22 Oct with assault convoy KMS1: joined assault convoy KMF1 6 Nov: arrived Algiers C beachhead 8 Nov: took the destroyer COWDRAY in tow 9 Nov: completed an anti-submarine patrol 13 Nov: at 0355 15 Nov torpedoed and sunk off Bougie by the Italian submarine ASCIANGHI: survivors rescued by the anti-aircraft ship POZARICA

BRIXHAM - unable to leave the UK with convoy KX4A to Gibraltar as planned: engaged on inshore salvage work off Bougie 12 Nov (Operation "Perpetual")

BUDE - assigned to join assault convoy KMS1 to Arzeu R and Z beachheads

CADMUS - left the UK 22 Oct with assault convoy KMS1 then joined assault convoy KMF1 6 Nov: arrived Algiers A beachhead 8 Nov: swept anchorage 9 Nov: left there 10 Nov: sustained damage port side forward in collision with the cruiser SHEFFIELD 0411 11 Nov: swept Bougie approaches same day: rescued survivors from the personnel ship NARKUNDA 14 Nov (Operation "Perpetual")

CLACTON - left Gibraltar 2 Nov: joined assault convoy KMS1: assigned to Arzeu R and Z beachheads: suffered considerable hull damage in collision with the minesweeper FELIXSTOWE north of Arzeu at 1807 9 Nov but remained operational

FELIXSTOWE - left Gibraltar 2 Nov: assigned to Arzeu R and Z beachheads: superficially damaged in collision with the minesweeper CLACTON north of Arzeu at 1807 9 Nov

HUSSAR - assigned to assault convoy KMS1: joined assault convoy KMF1 6 Nov: arrived Algiers C beachhead 8 Nov: left for Bougie 10 Nov (Operation "Perpetual")

POLRUAN - left Gibraltar 2 Nov: joined assault convoy KMS1: assigned to Arzeu R and Z beachheads: engaged on inshore salvage work 12 Nov

RHYL, ROTHESAY - both left Gibraltar 2 Nov: joined assault convoy KMS1: assigned to Arzeu R and Z beachheads

SPEEDWELL - assigned to assault convoy KMS1: joined assault convoy KMF1 6 Nov: arrived Algiers C beachhead 8 Nov: in action against submarines same day: left for Bougie 10 Nov (Operation "Perpetual")

STORNOWAY - left Gibraltar 2 Nov: joined assault convoy KMS1: assigned to Arzeu R and Z beachheads

TRAWLERS
ARCTIC RANGER - left Gibraltar 5 Nov (Force R)

CAVA - joined assault convoy KMF1 7 Nov: arrived Algiers C beachhead 8 Nov

CORIOLANUS, EDAY - both assigned to Oran Y beachhead

FLUELLEN - assigned to escort the landing ships MISOA and TASAJERA to Arzeu Z beachhead: in collision with the corvette GARDENIA off Oran X beachhead at 0135 9 Nov: the corvette VETCH stood by

FOULA - left the UK 21 Oct with advance convoy KX4A to Gibraltar: left there 9 Nov: joined follow-up convoys KMF2 and KMS2: arrived Oran 11 Nov

HORATIO - assigned to escort the landing ship BACHAQUERO to Oran X beachhead

HOY - from Gibraltar, joined assault convoy KMF1 7 Nov: arrived Algiers B beachhead 8 Nov: left there 10 Nov: arrived Bougie 11 Nov: assisted with the search for survivors from the landing ship AWATEA same day (Operation "Perpetual")

HUNDA - left the UK 21 Oct with advance convoy KX4A to Gibraltar: left there 9 Nov: joined follow-up convoys KMF2 and KMS2: arrived Oran 11 Nov

IMPERIALIST - left Gibraltar 5 Nov (Force R)

73

INCHCOLM - from Gibraltar: joined assault convoy KMF1 7 Nov: arrived Algiers B beachhead 8 Nov: left there 10 Nov: arrived Bougie 11 Nov (Operation "Perpetual")

INCHMARNOCK - assigned to Oran Y beachhead

JULIET - joined assault convoy KMF1 7 Nov: arrived Algiers A beachhead 8 Nov

JURA - left Gibraltar 9 Nov: joined follow-up convoys KMF2 and KMS2: arrived Oran 11 Nov

KERRERA - assigned to Oran Y beachhead

KINGSTON CHRYSOLITE - joined follow-up convoys KMF2 and KMS2: arrived Oran 11 Nov

KINTYRE - left the UK 21 Oct with advance convoy KX4A to Gibraltar: left there 9 Nov: joined follow-up convoys KMF2 and KMS2: arrived Oran 11 Nov

LOCH OSKAIG - left Gibraltar 5 Nov: rescued survivors from the destroyer ISAAC SWEERS 13 Nov (Force R)

LORD HOTHAM, LORD NUFFIELD - escorted the cased petrol ship COXWOLD: arrived Bougie 13 Nov

MULL - from Gibraltar, joined assault convoy KMF1 7 Nov: arrived Algiers B beachhead 8 Nov: escorted the landing ship DEWDALE from Algiers to Bougie 10-11 Nov: rescued survivors from the landing ship AWATEA 11 Nov (Operation "Perpetual")

OTHELLO - joined assault convoy KMF1 7 Nov: arrived Algiers C beachhead 8 Nov

RONALDSAY - assigned to escort the landing ships MISOA and TASAJERA to Arzeu Z beachhead

ROUSAY - left Gibraltar 9 Nov: joined follow-up convoys KMF2 and KMS2: arrived Oran 11 Nov

RUSKHOLM - left Gibraltar 9 Nov for Oran

RYSA - from Gibraltar, joined assault convoy KMF1 7 Nov: arrived Algiers A beachhead 8 Nov: left there 10 Nov: arrived Bougie 11 Nov (Operation "Perpetual")

ST NECTAN - left Gibraltar 5 Nov (Force R)

SHIANT - assigned to escort the landing ships MISOA and TASAJERA to Arzeu Z beachhead

STROMA - joined assault convoy KMF1 7 Nov: arrived Algiers A beachhead 8 Nov

STRONSAY - left Gibraltar 9 Nov for Oran

WESTRAY - left the UK 21 Oct with advance convoy KX4A to Gibraltar: left there 9 Nov: joined follow-up convoys KMF2 and KMS2: arrived Oran 11 Nov

BOOM DEFENCE VESSEL
BARDOLF - left Gibraltar 9 Nov: arrived Oran 11 Nov

ARMED YACHTS
CHARLES McIVER - as armed boarding vessel: left Gibraltar 9 Nov: arrived Oran 11 Nov

PHILANTE - left the UK 1 Nov with follow-up convoy KMF2

SAYONARA - as armed boarding vessel: left Gibraltar 7 Nov with LCTs: arrived Arzeu Z beachhead 9 Nov

TUGS
HENGIST - towed the destroyer COWDRAY to Algiers 16 Nov

RESTIVE - joined follow-up convoys KMF2 and KMS2: arrived Oran 11 Nov

ST DAY - towed the US Navy transport THOMAS STONE to Algiers 7-11 Nov: arrived Bougie 16 Nov

EXAMINATION VESSEL
MINNA - rescued survivors from the naval collier GARLINGE 10 Nov

MOTOR LAUNCHES
HDML 1091, 1127, 1128, 1130, 1131, 1134, 1139, 1142, 1146, 1152, 1162, 1210, 1221, 1225, 1237

ML 238, 273, 280, 283, 295, 307, 336, 338, 433, 444, 458, 463, 469, 471, 480, 483. MLs 480 and 483 took part in "Operation Reservist" at Oran 8 Nov

MOTOR MINESWEEPERS
MMS 5, 13, 20, 21, 33, 46, 58, 63, 65, 88, 89, 92, 116, 118, 133, 134, 135, 140, 171, 184

ALMANZORA. [MPL 8567]

Named ships carrying personnel, equipment and supplies

NAME OF SHIP Gross tonnage/Year of Build Owner or *Managers, if British, or Nationality (and owner) - *WARTIME FUNCTION [HM = His Majesty's commissioned ship: MT Ship = Cargo ship assigned primarily for carrying military vehicles: WSA = War Shipping Agency]*

ABNER NASH 7,177/42 US (WSA) - *MT/STORE SHIP*: loaded at Beirut 16-25 Jun: left there 1 Jul and Alexandria 6 Jul in follow-up convoy MWS37: arrived Acid North beachhead 13 Jul: carried 125 personnel, 118 vehicles, 643 tons cased petrol and 1,999 tons stores

ABRAHAM LINCOLN 7,191/42 US (WSA) - *MT SHIP*: loaded at Haifa 10-11 Jun: left there 16 Jun and Alexandria 6 Jul in follow-up convoy MWS37: arrived Acid North beachhead 13 Jul: carried 149 vehicles, 100 tons cased petrol and 50 tons stores

AELBERT CUYP 7,036/42 Dutch (*Oceaan) - *MT SHIP*: from Glasgow, left the Clyde 25 Jun in follow-up convoy KMS19: detached to Algiers then called forward to Augusta 16 Jul (Force Y)

AFRICAN PRINCE 4,653/39 Prince - *MT SHIP*: loaded at Beirut 10-13 Jun: left there 16 Jun and Alexandria 6 Jul in follow-up convoy MWS37: arrived Acid North beachhead 13 Jul: carried 140 personnel, 132 vehicles, 105 tons cased petrol and 55 tons stores

ALCINOUS 6,189/25 Dutch (Oceaan) - *MT SHIP*: left the Mersey 11 Jun and the Clyde 24 Jun in assault convoy KMS18B: transferred to assault convoy KMF18 9 Jul for early unloading: arrived Bark West beachhead 10 Jul

ALGORAB 4,938/21 Dutch (Goudriaan) - *MT/STORE SHIP*: loaded at Alexandria 11-15 Jun: left there 6 Jul in follow-up convoy MWS37 to arrive Acid South beachhead 13 Jul: carried 223 vehicles, 646 tons cased petrol and 1,632 tons stores

ALMANZORA 15,551/14 Royal Mail - *PERSONNEL SHIP (capacity 2,844)*: embarked personnel at Suez: left Alexandria 9 Jul in follow-up convoy MWF37: arrived Syracuse 13 Jul

ARONDA 9,031/41 British India - *PERSONNEL SHIP (capacity 1,662)*: embarked personnel at Suez: left Alexandria 9 Jul in follow-up convoy MWF37: arrived Syracuse 13 Jul

ARUNDEL CASTLE 19,118/21 Union-Castle - *PERSONNEL SHIP (capacity 2,305)*: left Glasgow 28 Jun and the Clyde 1 Jul in follow-up convoy KMF19: arrived Bark South beachhead 13 Jul (Force X)

ASCANIA 14,013/25 Cunard White Star - *LANDING SHIP, PERSONNEL (capacity 2,291)*: left the Clyde 28 Jun in assault convoy KMF18: arrived Bark West beachhead 10 Jul

ATLANTIC COAST 890/34 Coast - *CASED PETROL SHIP*: from Swansea, left the Clyde 25 Jun in follow-up convoy KMS19: arrived Bark South beachhead 13 Jul then moved to Augusta (Force X)

BAARN 5,621/27 Dutch (Koninklijke Nederlandsche) - *MT SHIP*: loaded at Alexandria 4-10 Jun and left there 3 Jul in assault convoy MWS36: arrived Acid South beachhead 10 Jul: carried 160 vehicles, 137 tons cased petrol and 428 tons stores: No 1 hold set on fire by a bomb near miss at 1235 11 Jul: as the vessel was carrying ammunition, she was sunk by the destroyer TARTAR after a towage attempt by the cruiser CARLISLE failed: survivors taken aboard the landing ship PRINS ALBERT

BANFORA 9,472/14 *Elder Dempster - *PERSONNEL SHIP (capacity 2,120)*: left Glasgow 30 Jun and the Clyde 1 Jul in follow-up convoy KMF19: detached to Algiers 9 Jul: arrived Malta 16 Jul and Augusta 19 Jul (Force Y)

BATORY 14,287/36 Polish (Gdynia-America) - *LANDING SHIP, PERSONNEL (capacity 1,663)*: left the Clyde 28 Jun in assault convoy KMF18: arrived Bark West beachhead 10 Jul: left for Alexandria same day: at 0432 13 Jul, was severely damaged above the water-line in collision with the personnel ship CHRISTIAAN HUYGENS

BENEDICT 4,949/30 Booth - *MT SHIP*: left the Mersey 10 Jun and the Clyde 24 Jun in assault convoy KMS18B: arrived Bark West beachhead 10 Jul

BENJAMIN GOODHUE 7,176/42 US (WSA) - *MT SHIP*: loaded at Alexandria 4-15 Jun: left there 3 Jul in assault convoy MWS36 to arrive Acid South beachhead 10 Jul: carried 111 vehicles, 205 tons cased petrol and 464 tons stores

BERGENSFJORD 11,015/13 Norwegian (Norske Amerika) - *PERSONNEL SHIP*: embarked personnel at Suez: left Port Said 5 Jul in assault convoy MWF36 carrying the Syracuse naval port party: arrived Acid North beachhead 10 Jul: carried 871 personnel: suffered casualties in an air attack at 1630 10 Jul

BIG FOOT WALLACE 7,196/42 US (WSA) - *MT SHIP*: loaded at Haifa 4-7 Jun: left Alexandria 3 Jul in assault convoy MWS36: arrived Acid North beachhead 10 Jul: carried 156 vehicles, 43 tons cased petrol and 85 tons stores

BOXER - *HM LANDING SHIP, TANK*: left the Clyde 28 Jun in assault convoy KMF18: arrived Bark West beachhead 10 Jul: unloaded into landing craft as unable to beach

BRUISER - *HM LANDING SHIP, TANK*: left the Clyde 28 Jun in assault convoy KMF18: arrived Bark West beachhead 10 Jul: unloaded into landing craft as unable to beach

CAMERONIA 16,297/20 Anchor - *PERSONNEL SHIP (capacity 2,975)*: left the Clyde 1 Jul in follow-up convoy KMF19: detached to Malta: arrived Syracuse 16 Jul (Force Y)

CAPE HOWE 6,999/43 *Lyle - *MT SHIP*: from Barry, left the Clyde 25 Jun in follow-up convoy KMS19: detached to Algiers: arrived Malta 18 Jul and Acid North beachhead 24 Jul (Force Y)

CHARLES GORDON CURTIS 7,176/42 US (WSA) - *MT SHIP*: loaded at Haifa 21-22 Jun: left there 2 Jul and Alexandria 6 Jul in follow-up convoy MWS37: arrived Acid North beachhead 13 Jul: carried 155 personnel, 150 vehicles, 99 tons cased petrol and 49 tons stores

CHERTSEY 5,998/43 *Watts, Watts - *MT SHIP*: from Newport, left the Clyde 25 Jun in follow-up convoy KMS19: detached to Algiers: arrived Acid North beachhead 18 Jul (Force Y): carried 5 personnel, 94 vehicles and 333 tons stores

CHRISTIAAN HUYGENS 16,287/28 Dutch (Nederland) - *PERSONNEL SHIP (capacity 2,689)*: embarked personnel at Suez: left Port Said 5 Jul in assault convoy MWF36: arrived Acid North beachhead 10 Jul: left for Alexandria same day: at 0432 13 Jul, damaged in collision with the landing ship BATORY

CIRCASSIA 11,136/37 Anchor - *LANDING SHIP, INFANTRY (LARGE) (personnel capacity 2,016)*: left the Clyde 28 Jun in assault convoy KMF18: arrived Bark West beachhead 10 Jul

CITY OF CANTERBURY 8,331/22 City - *PERSONNEL SHIP (capacity 1,371)*: embarked personnel at Suez: left Alexandria 9 Jul in follow-up convoy MWF37: arrived Syracuse 13 Jul

CITY OF DELHI 7,443/25 *City - *MT SHIP*: from the Mersey, left the Clyde 25 Jun in follow-up convoy KMS19: detached to Algiers and left there 10 Jul: from Malta, arrived Acid North beachhead 29 Jul (Force Y)

CITY OF EVANSVILLE 6,528/22 *Hall - *MT SHIP*: loaded at Alexandria 10-14 Jun and left there 6 Jul in follow-up convoy MWS37 to arrive Acid South beachhead 13 Jul: carried 192 vehicles, 100 tons cased petrol and 44 tons stores

CITY OF FLORENCE 6,862/18 *Hall - *MT/STORE SHIP*: loaded at Haifa 17-26 Jun: left there 2 Jul and Alexandria 6 Jul in follow-up convoy MWS37: arrived Acid North beachhead 13 Jul: moved to Syracuse 19 Jul: carried 153 vehicles, 730 tons cased petrol and 2,075 tons stores

CITY OF NEWCASTLE 6,921/15 Hall - *MT SHIP*: from Barry, left the Clyde 25 Jun in follow-up convoy KMS19: detached to Algiers and left there 10 Jul: from Malta, arrived Acid North beachhead 29 Jul (Force Y)

CITY OF VENICE 8,762/24 *City - *MT SHIP*: left the Mersey 12 Jun and the Clyde 24 Jun in assault convoy KMS18B for Bark West beachhead: carried vehicles and 302 personnel: at 2056 4 Jul, attacked by U 375 and hit forward on the starboard side: the ship caught

CITY OF EVANSVILLE. [Capt J F van Puyvelde]

fire, was abandoned at 2220 same day and sank at 0530 5 Jul off Cape Tenez, Algeria

COLIN P KELLY JR 7,176/42 US (WSA) - *MT SHIP*: loaded at Haifa 9-13 Jun: left Alexandria 3 Jul in assault convoy MWS36: arrived Acid North beachhead 10 Jul: carried 144 personnel, 117 vehicles, 174 tons cased petrol and 399 tons stores

COXWOLD 1,124/38 Yorkshire Dale - *CASED PETROL SHIP*: from Llanelly, left the Clyde 25 Jun in follow-up convoy KMS19: detached to Algiers then arrived Acid beachheads: moved to Augusta 17 Jul (Force Y)

DANIEL CHESTER FRENCH 7,200/42 US (WSA) - *MT/STORE SHIP*: loaded at Haifa 16-22 Jun: left there 2 Jul and Alexandria 6 Jul in follow-up convoy MWS37: arrived Acid North beachhead 13 Jul: moved to Augusta 16 Jul: carried 115 vehicles, 650 tons cased petrol and 1,910 tons stores

DEBRETT 6,244/40 Lamport & Holt - *MT SHIP*: loaded at Beirut 10-13 Jun: left Alexandria 6 Jul in follow-up convoy MWS37: arrived Acid North beachhead 13 Jul: carried 195 personnel, 184 vehicles, 100 tons cased petrol and 50 tons stores

DEFENDER 8,258/15 *T & J Harrison - *MT/STORE SHIP*: from Glasgow, left the Clyde 25 Jun in follow-up convoy KMS19: detached to Algiers and left there 10 Jul: from Malta, arrived Acid North beachhead 30 Jul (Force Y): carried 58 personnel, 140 vehicles and 1,193 tons stores

DERBYSHIRE 11,660/35 Bibby - *LANDING SHIP, INFANTRY (LARGE) (personnel capacity 2,566)*: left the Clyde 28 Jun in assault convoy KMF18: arrived Bark West beachhead 10 Jul

DERWENTHALL 4,934/40 West Hartlepool - *MT SHIP*: left the Mersey 12 Jun and Clyde 24 Jun in assault convoy KMS18B: exploded a mine with her starboard paravane 6 Jul: arrived Bark West beachhead 10 Jul

DEVIS 6,054/38 Lamport & Holt - *MT SHIP*: left Manchester 11 Jun and the Clyde 24 Jun in assault convoy KMS18B for Bark West beachhead: carried vehicles and 289 personnel: at 1545 5 Jul, was torpedoed from starboard side by U 593, whilst 50 miles east of Algiers: a fierce fire and exploding ammunition caused the ship to sink stern first in 20 minutes: survivors were picked up by the destroyer CLEVELAND

DEVONSHIRE 11,275/39 Bibby - *LANDING SHIP, INFANTRY (LARGE) (personnel capacity 1,830)*: embarked personnel at Suez: left Port Said 5 Jul in assault convoy MWF36: arrived Acid South beachhead 10 Jul

DILWARA 11,080/36 British India - *LANDING SHIP, INFANTRY (LARGE)*: embarked personnel at Suez: left Port Said 5 Jul in assault convoy MWF36: arrived Acid North beachhead 10 Jul: carried 462 personnel

DIOMED 10,374/22 *Alfred Holt - *MT/STORE SHIP*: loaded at Alexandria 17-26 Jun and left there 6 Jul in follow-up convoy MWS37: arrived Bark East beachhead 13 Jul: transferred to Bark South then back to Bark East: carried 188 vehicles, 886 tons cased petrol and 2,129 tons stores

DUCHESS OF BEDFORD 20,123/28 Canadian Pacific - *LANDING SHIP, INFANTRY (LARGE)*: embarked personnel at Suez: left Port Said 5 Jul in assault convoy MWF36: arrived Acid North beachhead 10 Jul: carried 2,837 personnel

EMPIRE PERDITA post-war as NAVARINO. [World Ship Photo Library]

DUNERA 11,162/37 British India - *LANDING SHIP, INFANTRY (LARGE)*: embarked personnel at Suez: left Port Said 5 Jul in assault convoy MWF36: arrived Acid North beachhead 10 Jul: carried 1,629 personnel

DUNKELD 4,944/37 Stanhope - *MT SHIP*: loaded at Beirut 17-22 Jun: left there 1 Jul and Alexandria 6 Jul in follow-up convoy MWS37: arrived Acid North beachhead 13 Jul: carried 125 personnel, 123 vehicles, 100 tons cased petrol and 50 tons stores

DUNNOTTAR CASTLE 15,007/36 Union-Castle - *PERSONNEL SHIP (capacity 2,240)*: left the Clyde 1 Jul in follow-up convoy KMF19: arrived Bark South beachhead 13 Jul (Force X)

DURBAN CASTLE 17,388/38 Union-Castle - *LANDING SHIP, INFANTRY (LARGE) (personnel capacity 2,022)*: left the Clyde 28 Jun in assault convoy KMF18: arrived Bark West beachhead 10 Jul

EGRA 5,108/11 British India - *PERSONNEL SHIP (capacity 1,009)*: embarked personnel at Suez: left Alexandria 9 Jul in follow-up convoy MWF37: arrived Syracuse 13 Jul

EMPIRE ARCHER 7,031/42 *Raeburn & Verel - *MT SHIP*: left Glasgow 21 Jun and the Clyde 25 Jun in follow-up convoy KMS19: arrived Bark South beachhead 13 Jul (Force X)

EMPIRE CATO 7,039/42 *Hain - *MT SHIP*: left Glasgow 13 Jun and the Clyde 24 Jun in assault convoy KMS18B: arrived Bark West beachhead 10 Jul

EMPIRE CONFIDENCE 5,023/35 *Royal Mail ex German DUSSELDORF - *MT SHIP*: left Swansea 12 Jun and the Clyde 24 Jun in assault convoy KMS18B: transferred to assault convoy KMF18 9 Jul for early unloading: arrived Bark West beachhead 10 Jul

EMPIRE FALSTAFF 7,067/43 *Gibbs - *MT SHIP*: from Glasgow, left the Clyde 25 Jun in follow-up convoy KMS19: arrived Bark South beachhead 13 Jul (Force X)

EMPIRE FARMER 7,049/43 *Lyle - *MT SHIP*: from Glasgow, left the Clyde 25 Jun in follow-up convoy KMS19: arrived Bark South beachhead 13 Jul (Force X)

EMPIRE FLORIZEL 7,056/43 *J & C Harrison - *MT SHIP*: from Glasgow, left the Clyde 25 Jun in follow-up convoy KMS19: detached to Algiers: arrived Malta 18 Jul and Augusta 19 Jul (Force Y): at 0320 21 Jul, she was hit by one or more bombs which caused a series of explosions and numerous fires: the ship rapidly settled by the bow until only the top half of her mainmast was visible

EMPIRE GRANGE 6,981/43 *Ropner - *MT SHIP*: from Manchester, left the Clyde 25 Jun in follow-up convoy KMS19: detached to Algiers: arrived Acid North beachhead 18 Jul (Force Y): carried 20 personnel, 99 vehicles and 296 tons stores

EMPIRE NERISSA 7,076/42 *Chellew - *MT SHIP*: from Newport, left the Clyde 25 Jun in follow-up convoy KMS19: detached to Algiers: arrived Acid North beachhead 18 Jul (Force Y)

EMPIRE NEWTON 7,037/42 *T & J Harrison - *MT/STORE SHIP*: from the Mersey, left the Clyde 25 Jun in follow-up convoy KMS19: detached to Algiers and left there 10 Jul: from Malta, arrived Acid North beachhead 30 Jul (Force Y): carried 55 personnel, 96 vehicles and 1,040 tons stores

EMPIRE PERDITA 7,028/43 *Morrison - *MT SHIP*: from Glasgow, left the Clyde 25 Jun in follow-up convoy KMS19: arrived Bark South beachhead 13 Jul (Force X)

EMPIRE PRIDE 9,248/41 *Bibby - *LANDING SHIP, PERSONNEL (capacity 1,836)*: left the Clyde 1 Jul in follow-up convoy KMF19: arrived Bark South beachhead 13 Jul (Force X)

EMPIRE TROOPER 13,994/22 *British India ex German CAP NORTE - *PERSONNEL SHIP (capacity 1,264)*: embarked personnel at Suez: left Alexandria 9 Jul in follow-up convoy MWF37: arrived Syracuse 13 Jul

FORT BUCKINGHAM 7,122/43 *Constantine - *MT SHIP*: left the Mersey 11 Jun and the Clyde 24 Jun in assault convoy KMS18B: arrived Bark West beachhead 10 Jul

FORT CHARNISAY 7,133/43 *Anning - *MT SHIP*: from Swansea, left the Clyde 25 Jun in follow-up convoy KMS19: arrived Bark South beachhead 13 Jul: transferred to Bark East 15 Jul (Force X)

FORT FORK 7,134/42 *Reardon Smith - *MT SHIP*: left Glasgow 23 Jun and the Clyde 25 Jun in follow-up convoy KMS19: detached to Algiers: arrived Acid North beachhead 18 Jul (Force Y)

FORT GEORGE 7,129/42 *Ropner - *MT/STORE SHIP*: loaded at Alexandria 16-25 Jun and left there 6 Jul in follow-up convoy MWS37: arrived Acid North beachhead 13 Jul: suffered casualties in bomb near misses 14 Jul: moved to Syracuse 19 Jul: carried 120 vehicles, 661 tons cased petrol and 1,781 tons stores

FORT GRAHAME 7,133/43 *Sutherland - *MT SHIP*: left the Clyde 25 Jun in follow-up convoy KMS19: arrived Bark South beachhead 13 Jul (Force X)

FORT HOWE 7,133/42 *Strick - *MT SHIP*: left the Mersey 22 Jun and the Clyde 25 Jun in follow-up convoy KMS19: arrived Bark South beachhead 13 Jul: transferred to Bark East 15 Jul (Force X)

FORT LAJOIE 7,134/42 *Lyle - *MT SHIP*: left Manchester 11 Jun and the Clyde 24 Jun in assault convoy KMS18B: arrived Bark South beachhead 10 Jul: transferred to Bark East

FORT LAWRENCE 7,134/43 *Strick - *MT SHIP*: loaded at Alexandria 11-15 Jun and left there 3 Jul in assault convoy MWS36: arrived Bark East beachhead 10 Jul: carried 98 vehicles, 215 tons cased petrol and 439 tons stores

FORT MEDUCTIC 7,134/43 *Morrison - *MT SHIP*: left Manchester 11 Jun and the Clyde 24 Jun in assault convoy KMS18B: arrived Bark South beachhead 10 Jul: transferred to Bark East

FORT NASHWAAK 7,134/43 *Dodd, Thomson - *MT SHIP*: left Manchester 12 Jun and the Clyde 24 Jun in assault convoy KMS18B: arrived Bark South beachhead 10 Jul: transferred to Bark East

FORT PELLY 7,131/42 *Ropner - *MT/STORE SHIP*: loaded at Alexandria 16-25 Jun and left there 6 Jul in follow-up convoy MWS37: arrived Acid North beachhead 13 Jul: carried 120 vehicles, 652 tons cased petrol and 2,010 tons stores: moved to Augusta where arrived 18 Jul: at 0335 20 Jul, direct bomb hits caused considerable casualties as well as demolishing the after end of the ship and the amidships accommodation: the fore part of the ship caught fire and, at 0745 same day, she blew up

FORT PEMBINA 7,134/42 *Billmeir - *MT SHIP*: from Faslane, left the Clyde 25 Jun in follow-up convoy KMS19: arrived Bark South beachhead 13 Jul (Force X)

FORT STAGER 7,132/43 *Ropner - *MT SHIP*: left Newport 12 Jun and the Clyde 24 Jun in assault convoy KMS18B: arrived Bark West beachhead 10 Jul

FORT WALSH 7,126/43 *Larrinaga - *MT SHIP*: left Glasgow 9 Jun and the Clyde 25 Jun in follow-up convoy KMS19: arrived Bark South beachhead 13 Jul (Force X)

FORT YALE 7,134/42 *Charlton, McAllum - *MT SHIP*: from Barry, left the Clyde 25 Jun in follow-up convoy KMS19: detached to Algiers: arrived Acid North beachhead 18 Jul (Force Y)

FORTHBANK 5,057/29 *Weir - *MT SHIP*: left Glasgow 10 Jun and the Clyde 25 Jun in follow-up convoy KMS19: detached to Algiers and left there 10 Jul: from Malta, arrived Acid North beachhead 31 Jul (Force Y)

FRANCONIA 20,175/23 Cunard White Star - *PERSONNEL SHIP (capacity 2,102)*: embarked personnel at Liverpool: left there 27 Jun and the Clyde 1 Jul in follow-up convoy KMF19: detached to Algiers 9 Jul: arrived Sicily 19 Jul (Force Y)

FRANK B KELLOGG 7,176/42 US (WSA) - *MT SHIP*: loaded at Beirut 5-8 Jun: left there 9 Jun and Alexandria 3 Jul in assault convoy MWS36: arrived Acid North beachhead 10 Jul: carried 140 personnel, 122 vehicles, 42 tons cased petrol and 123 tons stores

FRANS VAN MIERIS 7,170/42 Dutch (*Rotterdamsche Lloyd) - *MT SHIP*: left the Mersey 21 Jun and the Clyde 25 Jun in follow-up convoy KMS19: arrived Bark South beachhead 13 Jul (Force X)

GEORGE H DERN 7,181/43 US (WSA) - *MT SHIP*: loaded at Haifa 9-13 Jun: left Alexandria 3 Jul in assault convoy MWS36: arrived Acid North beachhead 10 Jul: carried 118 vehicles, 175 tons cased petrol and 475 tons stores

GEORGE ROGERS CLARK 7,178/43 US (WSA) - *MT SHIP*: loaded at Haifa 4-7 Jun: left there 9 Jun and Alexandria 3 Jul in assault convoy MWS36: arrived Acid North beachhead 10 Jul: suffered damage and casualties when straddled by bombs at 1600 same day: carried 136 vehicles, 41 tons cased petrol and 93 tons stores

GLENGYLE 9,919/39 Glen Line - *HM LANDING SHIP, INFANTRY (LARGE) (personnel capacity 982)*: left the Clyde 28 Jun in assault convoy KMF18: arrived Bark West beachhead 10 Jul

GREYSTOKE CASTLE 5,853/28 Lancashire - *MT/STORE SHIP*: loaded at Alexandria 17-25 Jun and left there 6 Jul in follow-up convoy MWS37 to arrive Acid South beachhead 13 Jul: carried 163 vehicles, 546 tons cased petrol and 1,734 tons stores

GUDRUN MAERSK 2,294/37 *Brocklebank ex Danish

HIGHLAND PRINCE.
[A Duncan]

- *CASED PETROL SHIP*: left the Clyde 24 Jun in assault convoy KMS18B: detached to Algiers and left there 10 Jul: from Malta, directed to Syracuse 17 Jul

HARLESDEN 7,273/43 J & C Harrison - *MT SHIP*: left the Clyde 25 Jun in follow-up convoy KMS19: arrived Bark South beachhead 13 Jul (Force X)

HARPAGUS 7,271/42 J & C Harrison - *MT SHIP*: loaded at Beirut 4-8 Jun: left Alexandria 3 Jul in assault convoy MWS36: arrived Acid North beachhead 10 Jul: carried 144 personnel, 114 vehicles, 37 tons cased petrol and 128 tons stores

HARRISON GRAY OTIS 7,176/43 US (WSA) - *MT/STORE SHIP*: loaded at Alexandria 16-25 Jun and left there 6 Jul in follow-up convoy MWS37 to arrive Acid South beachhead 13 Jul: carried 120 vehicles, 650 tons cased petrol and 1,982 tons stores

HERMELIN 1,683/40 Norwegian (Bruusgaard) - *CASED PETROL SHIP*: loaded at Alexandria 30 Jun-5 Jul and left there 6 Jul in follow-up convoy MWS37: assigned to Acid South beachhead but arrived Acid North 13 Jul: carried 1,952 tons cased petrol and 100 tons stores

HIGHLAND PRINCE 7,043/42 Prince - *MT SHIP*: loaded at Beirut 2-8 Jun: left Alexandria 3 Jul in assault convoy MWS36: arrived Acid North beachhead 10 Jul: carried 119 personnel, 103 vehicles, 234 tons cased petrol and 519 tons stores

JADE 930/38 Robertson - *CASED PETROL SHIP*: from the Mersey, left the Clyde 25 Jun in follow-up convoy KMS19: detached to Algiers: arrived Acid beachheads then moved to Augusta 17 Jul (Force Y)

JERSEY HART 7,275/43 Stanhope - *MT SHIP*: left Middlesbrough 31 May and the Clyde 25 Jun in follow-up convoy KMS19: arrived Bark South beachhead 13 Jul (Force X)

JOHN BAKKE 4,718/29 Norwegian (*Knutsen) - *MT/STORE SHIP*: from the Mersey, left the Clyde 25 Jun in follow-up convoy KMS19: detached to Algiers: arrived Malta 18 Jul and Acid North beachhead 24 Jul (Force Y): carried 54 personnel, 120 vehicles and 1,623 tons stores

JOHN HART 7,176/42 US (WSA) - *MT SHIP*: loaded at Haifa 17-18 Jun: left there 2 Jul and Alexandria 6 Jul in follow-up convoy MWS37: arrived Acid North beachhead 13 Jul: carried 144 vehicles, 99 tons cased petrol and 50 tons stores

JONATHAN GROUT 7,176/42 US (WSA) - *MT SHIP*: loaded at Alexandria 10-15 Jun and left there 3 Jul in assault convoy MWS36 to arrive Acid South beachhead 10 Jul: carried 137 vehicles, 262 tons cased petrol and 437 tons stores

JOSEPH ALSTON 7,177/42 US (WSA) - *MT SHIP*: loaded at Alexandria 9-15 Jun and left there 3 Jul in assault convoy MWS36: arrived Bark East beachhead 10 Jul: carried 134 vehicles, 269 tons cased petrol and 562 tons stores

JOSEPH G CANNON 7,181/42 US (WSA) - *MT SHIP*: loaded at Haifa 5-7 Jun: left there 9 Jun and Alexandria 3 Jul in assault convoy MWS36: arrived Acid North beachhead 10 Jul: carried 137 vehicles, 46 tons cased petrol and 91 tons stores: survived a direct bomb hit in No 5 hold 1900 11 Jul: ship's bottom penetrated but, as hold unloaded, no fire broke out and the vessel left under her own steam for Malta 13 Jul

KAIMATA 5,269/31 New Zealand Shipping - *MT/STORE SHIP*: loaded at Beirut 17-24 Jun: left there 1 Jul and Alexandria 6 Jul in follow-up convoy MWS37: arrived Acid North beachhead 13 Jul: moved to Syracuse 19 Jul: carried 170 personnel, 168 vehicles, 533 tons cased petrol and 1,597 tons stores

KAROA 7,009/15 British India - *PERSONNEL SHIP (capacity 904)*: embarked personnel at Suez: left Alexandria 9 Jul in follow-up convoy MWF37: arrived Syracuse 13 Jul

KEREN 9,890/30 British India KENYA - *HM LANDING SHIP, INFANTRY (LARGE) (personnel capacity 1,158)*: embarked personnel at Suez: left Port Said 5 Jul in assault convoy MWF36: arrived Bark East beachhead 10 Jul

KOSCIUSZKO 6,852/15 Polish (Gdynia-America) - *PERSONNEL SHIP (capacity 1,218)*: embarked personnel at Suez: left Alexandria 9 Jul in follow-up convoy MWF37: arrived Syracuse 13 Jul

LAMBROOK 7,038/42 Austin Friars - *MT SHIP*: from Glasgow, left the Clyde 25 Jun in follow-up convoy KMS19: detached to Algiers: arrived Acid North beachhead 18 Jul (Force Y): carried 50 personnel, 94 vehicles and 357 tons stores

LEOPOLDVILLE 11,439/29 Belgian (Maritime Belge) - *PERSONNEL SHIP (capacity 2,248)*: embarked personnel at Suez: left Alexandria 9 Jul in follow-up convoy MWF37: arrived Syracuse 13 Jul

LESLIE M SHAW 7,178/43 US (WSA) - *MT SHIP*: loaded at Haifa 5-7 Jun: left there 9 Jun and Alexandria 3 Jul in assault convoy MWS36: arrived Acid North beachhead 10 Jul: carried 137 vehicles, 43 tons cased petrol and 153 tons stores

LETITIA 13,595/25 Donaldson Atlantic - *PERSONNEL SHIP (capacity 2,438)*: left Glasgow 29 Jun and the Clyde 1 Jul in follow-up convoy KMF19: detached to Algiers 9 Jul: arrived Sicily 19 Jul (Force Y)

LLANGIBBY CASTLE 11,951/29 Union-Castle - *LANDING SHIP, INFANTRY (LARGE) (personnel capacity 1,736)*: left the Clyde 28 Jun in assault convoy KMF18: arrived Bark West beachhead 10 Jul

LOCHEE 964/37 Dundee, Perth & London - *CASED PETROL SHIP*: left Preston 23 Jun and the Clyde 25 Jun in follow-up convoy KMS19: arrived Bark South beachhead 13 Jul: moved to Augusta 19 Jul (Force X)

MARNIX VAN ST ALDEGONDE 19,355/30 Dutch (Nederland) - *LANDING SHIP, INFANTRY (LARGE) (personnel capacity 2,809)*: left the Clyde 28 Jun in assault convoy KMF18: arrived Bark West beachhead 10 Jul

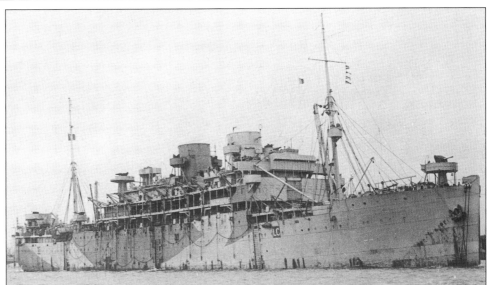

LLANGIBBY CASTLE (above) on Union-Castle passenger service and (right) when fitted out as a Landing Ship, Infantry. [A Duncan/-]

MAYO BROTHERS 7,191/42 US (WSA) - *MT SHIP*: loaded at Haifa 2-7 Jun: left there 9 Jun and Alexandria 3 Jul in assault convoy MWS36: arrived Acid North beachhead 10 Jul: carried 132 vehicles, 174 tons cased petrol and 381 tons stores

MIDDLESEX TRADER 7,241/42 Trader Navigation - *MT SHIP*: from Glasgow, left the Clyde 25 Jun in follow-up convoy KMS19: detached to Algiers then called forward to Augusta 16 Jul (Force Y)

MISOA 4,800/37 Lago - *HM LANDING SHIP, TANK*: from Tripoli, arrived at the beachhead 11 Jul

MONARCH OF BERMUDA 22,424/31 Furness, Withy - *LANDING SHIP, INFANTRY (LARGE)*: embarked personnel at Suez: left Port Said 5 Jul in assault convoy MWF36: arrived Acid North beachhead 10 Jul: carried 2,766 personnel

NARWIK 7,031/42 Polish (Gdynia-America) - *MT SHIP*: loaded at Alexandria 11-16 Jun and left there 6 Jul in follow-up convoy MWS37 to arrive Acid South beachhead 13 Jul: carried 172 vehicles, 120 tons cased petrol and 48 tons stores

NORMAN MONARCH 7,005/43 Monarch - *MT SHIP*: left the Mersey 11 Jun and the Clyde 24 Jun in assault convoy KMS18B: arrived Bark West beachhead 10 Jul

O HENRY 7,181/42 US (WSA) - *MT SHIP*: loaded at Haifa 9-13 Jun: left there 16 Jun and Alexandria 3 Jul in assault convoy MWS36: arrived Acid North beachhead 10 Jul: carried 127 vehicles, 173 tons cased petrol and 417 tons stores: was in danger from burning petrol and exploding ammunition 13 Jul but managed to get under way safely

OCEAN GLORY 7,178/42 *J & C Harrison - *MT SHIP*: loaded at Alexandria 4-9 Jun and left there 3 Jul in assault convoy MWS36 to arrive Bark East beachhead 10 Jul: carried 109 vehicles, 22 tons cased petrol and 150 tons stores

OCEAN HUNTER 7,178/42 *Robinson - *MT SHIP*: loaded at Alexandria 4-10 Jun and left there 3 Jul in assault convoy MWS36 to arrive Acid South beachhead 10 Jul: carried 123 vehicles, 114 tons cased petrol and 110 tons stores

OCEAN PEACE 7,173/42 *Hain - *MT/STORE SHIP*: loaded at Alexandria 10-16 Jun and left there 3 Jul in assault convoy MWS36: arrived Acid South beachhead 10 Jul: carried 103 vehicles, 253 tons cased petrol and 432 tons stores: cased petrol in No 1 hold caught fire, following several bomb near misses at 0455 12 Jul: when the blaze became uncontrollable, survivors transferred to the landing ship PRINS ALBERT: by 0900, the ship was ablaze fore and aft and, after a massive explosion, she settled to the bottom at 1300 same day

OCEAN PRIDE 7,173/42 *Reardon Smith - *MT SHIP*: loaded at Alexandria 4-9 Jun and left there 3 Jul in assault convoy MWS36 to arrive Acid South beachhead 10 Jul: carried 121 vehicles, 45 tons cased petrol and 106 tons stores

OCEAN STRENGTH 7,173/42 *Denholm - *MT SHIP*: loaded at Alexandria 4-9 Jun and left there 3 Jul in assault convoy MWS36 to arrive Acid South beachhead 10 Jul: carried 123 vehicles, 44 tons cased petrol and 108 tons stores

OCEAN VALLEY 7,174/42 *Capper, Alexander - *MT SHIP*: loaded at Alexandria 9-15 Jun and left there 3 Jul in assault convoy MWS36 to arrive Acid South beachhead 10 Jul: carried 98 vehicles, 183 tons cased petrol and 441 tons stores

OCEAN VENGEANCE 7,174/42 *Raeburn & Verel - *MT SHIP*: left Glasgow 9 Jun and the Clyde 25 Jun in follow-up convoy KMS19: arrived Bark South beachhead 13 Jul (Force X)

OCEAN VESPER 7,174/42 *Connell & Grace - *MT/STORE SHIP*: loaded at Alexandria 17-25 Jun and left there 6 Jul in follow-up convoy MWS37 to arrive Acid South beachhead 13 Jul: carried 96 vehicles, 680 tons cased petrol and 1,502 tons stores

OCEAN VIKING 7,174/41 *Bolton - *MT SHIP*: from Glasgow, left the Clyde 25 Jun in follow-up convoy KMS19: detached to Algiers: arrived Malta 18 Jul and Augusta 19 Jul (Force Y)

OCEAN VIRTUE 7,174/42 *Prince - *MT SHIP*: from Swansea, left the Clyde 25 Jun in follow-up convoy KMS19: detached to Algiers: called Malta 18 Jul and arrived Augusta 19 Jul (Force Y): at 0340 21 Jul, two bomb hits in No 5 hold caused fires on board: further bombs split the shell plating and caused the vessel to settle by the head with her two forward holds flooded: attempts to sink her with gunfire proved unsuccessful

OCEAN VISION 7,174/42 *Haldin & Philipps - *MT SHIP*: loaded at Alexandria 4-9 Jun and left there 3 Jul in assault convoy MWS36 to arrive Bark East beachhead 10 Jul: carried 111 vehicles, 129 tons cased petrol and 123 tons stores

OCEAN VULCAN 7,174/42 *Idwal Williams - *MT SHIP*: loaded at Alexandria 4-9 Jun and left there 3 Jul in assault convoy MWS36 to arrive Acid South beachhead 10 Jul: carried 124 vehicles, 45 tons cased petrol and 110 tons stores

ORBITA 15,495/15 Pacific Steam - *PERSONNEL SHIP (capacity 2,901)*: embarked personnel at Suez: left Alexandria 9 Jul in follow-up convoy MWF37: arrived Syracuse 13 Jul

ORESTES 7,748/26 *Alfred Holt - *MT SHIP*: left the Mersey 11 Jun and the Clyde 24 Jun in assault convoy

OTRANTO.

KMS18B: transferred to assault convoy KMF18 9 Jul for early unloading: arrived Bark West beachhead 10 Jul

ORMONDE 14,982/17 Orient - *PERSONNEL SHIP (capacity 3,580)*: embarked personnel at Liverpool: left there 26 Jun and the Clyde 1 Jul in follow-up convoy KMF19: detached to Malta: arrived Sicily 19 Jul (Force Y)

ORNA 6,779/38 British India - *MT SHIP*: loaded at Beirut 10-12 Jun: left there 1 Jul and Alexandria 6 Jul in follow-up convoy MWS37: arrived Acid North beachhead 13 Jul: carried 170 personnel, 163 vehicles, 89 tons cased petrol and 51 tons stores

ORONTES 20,097/29 Orient - *LANDING SHIP, INFANTRY (LARGE) (personnel capacity 3,440)*: embarked troops at Suez: left Port Said 5 Jul in assault convoy MWF36: arrived Acid South beachhead 10 Jul

OTRANTO 20,026/25 Orient - *LANDING SHIP, INFANTRY (LARGE)*: embarked personnel at Suez: left Port Said 5 Jul in assault convoy MWF36: arrived Bark East beachhead 10 Jul: carried 3,200 personnel

OZARDA 6,895/40 British India - *MT SHIP*: loaded at Beirut 4-8 Jun: left there 9 Jun and Alexandria 3 Jul in assault convoy MWS36: arrived Acid North beachhead 10 Jul: carried 144 personnel, 146 vehicles, 40 tons cased petrol and 120 tons stores

PACIFIC EXPORTER 6,734/28 *Furness, Withy - *MT SHIP*: left the Clyde 25 Jun in follow-up convoy KMS19: arrived Bark South beachhead 13 Jul (Force X)

PIO PICO 7,176/43 US (WSA) - *MT SHIP*: loaded at Beirut 9-15 Jun: left Alexandria 3 Jul in assault convoy MWS36: arrived Acid North beachhead 10 Jul: carried 129 personnel, 115 vehicles, 232 tons cased petrol and 542 tons stores

POCAHONTAS 7,177/42 US (WSA) - *MT SHIP*: loaded at Beirut 9-15 Jun: left Alexandria 3 Jul in assault convoy MWS36: arrived Acid North beachhead 10 Jul: carried 129 personnel, 123 vehicles, 243 tons cased petrol and 543 tons stores

PRINCE CHARLES 2,950/30 Belgian - *HM LANDING SHIP, INFANTRY (SMALL) (personnel capacity 250)*: left Bizerta 7 Jul: joined assault convoy NCF1: arrived Dime beachhead 10 Jul (US Western Task Force)

PRINCE CHARLES.

PRINCE LEOPOLD 2,950/30 Belgian - *HM LANDING SHIP, INFANTRY (SMALL) (personnel capacity 250)*: left Bizerta 7 Jul: joined assault convoy NCF1: arrived Dime beachhead 10 Jul (US Western Task Force)

PRINCESS BEATRIX 4,135/39 Dutch (Zeeland) PRINSES BEATRIX - *HM LANDING SHIP, INFANTRY (MEDIUM) (personnel capacity 400)*: left Sfax 8 Jul in assault convoy SBF1: arrived Bark South beachhead 10 Jul

PRINS ALBERT 2,938/37 Belgian - *HM LANDING SHIP, INFANTRY (SMALL)*: embarked personnel at Suez: left Port Said 5 Jul in assault convoy MWF36: arrived Acid North beachhead 10 Jul: carried 272 personnel: rescued survivors from the MT ships BAARN 11 Jul and OCEAN PEACE 12 Jul: landed commandos at the southern end of Catania Bay 13 Jul

PRINSES ASTRID 2,950/30 Belgian - *HM LANDING SHIP, INFANTRY (SMALL) (personnel capacity 250)*: left Bizerta 7 Jul: joined assault convoy NCF1: arrived Joss beachhead 10 Jul (US Western Task Force)

PRINSES JOSEPHINE CHARLOTTE 2,950/31 Belgian - *HM LANDING SHIP, INFANTRY (SMALL) (personnel capacity 250)*: left Bizerta 7 Jul: joined assault convoy NCF1: arrived Joss beachhead 10 Jul (US Western Task Force)

PROMETHEUS 6,095/25 *Alfred Holt - *MT SHIP*: left the Mersey 12 Jun and the Clyde 24 Jun in assault convoy KMS18B: transferred to assault convoy KMF18

9 Jul for early unloading: arrived Bark West beachhead 10 Jul

QUEEN EMMA 4,135/39 Dutch (Zeeland) KONINGIN EMMA - *HM LANDING SHIP, INFANTRY (MEDIUM) (personnel capacity 400)*: left Sfax 8 Jul in assault convoy SBF1: arrived Bark South beachhead 10 Jul

RAJULA 8,478/26 British India - *PERSONNEL SHIP (capacity 1,800)*: embarked personnel at Suez: left Alexandria 9 Jul in follow-up convoy MWF37: arrived Syracuse 13 Jul

RALPH IZARD 7,191/42 US (WSA) - *MT SHIP*: loaded at Haifa 10-12 Jun: left there 16 Jun and Alexandria 6 Jul in follow-up convoy MWS37: arrived Acid North beachhead 13 Jul: carried 147 vehicles, 100 tons cased petrol and 50 tons stores

REINA DEL PACIFICO 17,702/31 Pacific Steam - *LANDING SHIP, INFANTRY (LARGE) (personnel capacity 2,520)*: embarked personnel at Suez: left Port Said 5 Jul in assault convoy MWF36: arrived Acid North beachhead 10 Jul

ROHNA 8,602/26 British India - *PERSONNEL SHIP (capacity 1,950)*: embarked personnel at Suez: left Alexandria 9 Jul in follow-up convoy MWF37: arrived Syracuse 13 Jul

ROYAL SCOTSMAN 3,244/36 Burns & Laird - *HM LANDING SHIP, INFANTRY (HAND HOISTING) (personnel capacity 450)*: left Sfax 8 Jul in assault convoy SBF1: arrived Bark South beachhead 10 Jul

REINA DEL PACIFICO. [World Ship Photo Library]

ROYAL ULSTERMAN 3,244/36 Burns & Laird - *HM LANDING SHIP, INFANTRY (HAND HOISTING) (personnel capacity 450)*: left Sfax 8 Jul in assault convoy SBF1: arrived Bark South beachhead 10 Jul

RUYS 14,155/37 Dutch (KPM) - *LANDING SHIP, INFANTRY (LARGE) (personnel capacity 2,180)*: embarked personnel at Suez: left Port Said 5 Jul in assault convoy MWF36: arrived Acid South beachhead 10 Jul

ST ESSYLT 5,634/41 South American Saint - *MT SHIP*: left Swansea 12 Jun and the Clyde 24 Jun in assault convoy KMS18B for Bark West beachhead: carried vehicles and 322 personnel: at 2145 4 Jul, she was torpedoed on the starboard side by U 375, causing petrol and explosives to catch fire and, at 0545 5 Jul, the ship blew up and sank off Cape Tenez, Algeria

SAMUEL PARKER 7,176/42 US (WSA) - *MT/STORE SHIP*: loaded at Haifa 17-24 Jun: left there 2 Jul and Alexandria 6 Jul in follow-up convoy MWS37: arrived Acid North beachhead 13 Jul: carried 107 vehicles, 650 tons cased petrol and 2,022 tons stores: near missed off the beachhead in an air attack 22 Jul

SHAHJEHAN 5,454/42 Asiatic - *MT SHIP*: loaded at Alexandria 4-9 Jun: left there 3 Jul in assault convoy MWS36 for Bark East beachhead: carried 230 (including dock operating) personnel, 118 vehicles, 23 tons cased petrol and 121 tons stores: at 1110 6 Jul, she was attacked by U 453: the torpedo struck on the starboard side and possibly exited on the port side of No 2 hold: the ship sank at 0220 7 Jul, 70 miles north-east of Benghazi, after fire engulfed the ship from her funnel forward, whilst she was being towed by the tug ST MONANCE: survivors were rescued by the corvette SAKHTOURIS

SOBIESKI 11,030/39 Polish (Gdynia-America) - *LANDING SHIP, INFANTRY (LARGE)*: embarked personnel at Suez: left Port Said 5 Jul in assault convoy MWF36: arrived Acid North beachhead 10 Jul: carried 1,369 personnel

STANHILL 5,969/42 Stanhope - *MT SHIP*: left the Mersey 11 Jun and the Clyde 24 Jun in assault convoy KMS18B: arrived Bark West beachhead 10 Jul

STRATHNAVER 22,283/31 P & O - *LANDING SHIP, INFANTRY (LARGE) (personnel capacity 3,488)*: embarked personnel at Suez: left Port Said 5 Jul in assault convoy MWF36: arrived Bark East beachhead 10 Jul

TAKLIWA 7,936/24 British India - *PERSONNEL SHIP (capacity 1,068)*: embarked personnel at Suez: left Alexandria 9 Jul in follow-up convoy MWF37: arrived Syracuse 13 Jul

TARANTIA 7,268/42 Anchor - *MT SHIP*: loaded at Beirut 5-8 Jun: left there 9 Jun and Alexandria 3 Jul in

assault convoy MWS36: arrived Acid North beachhead 10 Jul: carried 155 personnel, 120 vehicles, 38 tons cased petrol and 128 tons stores

TEGELBERG 14,150/37 Dutch (KPM) - *LANDING SHIP, INFANTRY (LARGE) (personnel capacity 2,179)*: embarked personnel at Suez: left Port Said 5 Jul in assault convoy MWF36: arrived Acid North beachhead 10 Jul

TEUCER 9,079/06 *Alfred Holt - *MT/STORE SHIP*: loaded at Alexandria 12-28 Jun and left there 6 Jul in follow-up convoy MWS37 to arrive Acid South beachhead 13 Jul then moved to Syracuse: carried 213 vehicles, 268 tons cased petrol and 1,704 tons stores: hastily moved out of danger from a fuelling point fire 17 Jul

THISTLEMUIR 7,237/42 *Allan, Black - *MT SHIP*: loaded at Alexandria 4-14 Jun and left there 3 Jul in assault convoy MWS36: arrived Bark East beachhead 10 Jul: carried 104 vehicles, 148 tons cased petrol and 421 tons stores

THRUSTER - *HM LANDING SHIP, TANK*: left the Clyde 28 Jun in assault convoy KMF18: arrived Bark West beachhead 10 Jul: unloaded into landing craft as unable to beach

TIMOTHY PICKERING 7,181/42 US (WSA) - *MT/STORE SHIP*: loaded at Alexandria 16-25 Jun and left there 6 Jul in follow-up convoy MWS37 to arrive Acid South beachhead 13 Jul: carried 122 vehicles, 651 tons cased petrol and 1,707 tons stores: at 1144 13 Jul, an attack by two aircraft caused the vessel's after hold to blow up and the ship to become a total loss

TORONTO 5,018/28 Norwegian (Wilhelmsen) - *MT SHIP*: loaded at Alexandria 17-20 Jun and left there 6 Jul in follow-up convoy MWS37 to arrive Acid South beachhead 13 Jul: carried 174 vehicles, 100 tons cased petrol and 39 tons stores

TOWER HILL 7,268/42 Tower - *MT/STORE SHIP*: loaded at Beirut 16-28 Jun: left there 1 Jul and Alexandria 6 Jul in follow-up convoy MWS37: arrived Acid North beachhead 13 Jul: carried 145 personnel, 121 vehicles, 730 tons cased petrol and 1,911 tons stores: after suffering casualties from bomb near misses 14 Jul, moved to Syracuse 19 Jul

ULSTER MONARCH 3,791/29 Belfast - *HM LANDING SHIP, INFANTRY (HAND HOISTING) (personnel capacity 780)*: embarked personnel at Suez: left Port Said 5 Jul in assault convoy MWF36: arrived Acid North beachhead 10 Jul: landed 300 commandos at Augusta 12 Jul

WILL ROGERS 7,200/42 US (WSA) - *MT SHIP*: loaded at Alexandria 11-16 and 23 Jun and left there 6 Jul in follow-up convoy MWS37: arrived Acid North beachhead 13 Jul: carried 128 vehicles, 100 tons cased petrol and 82 tons stores

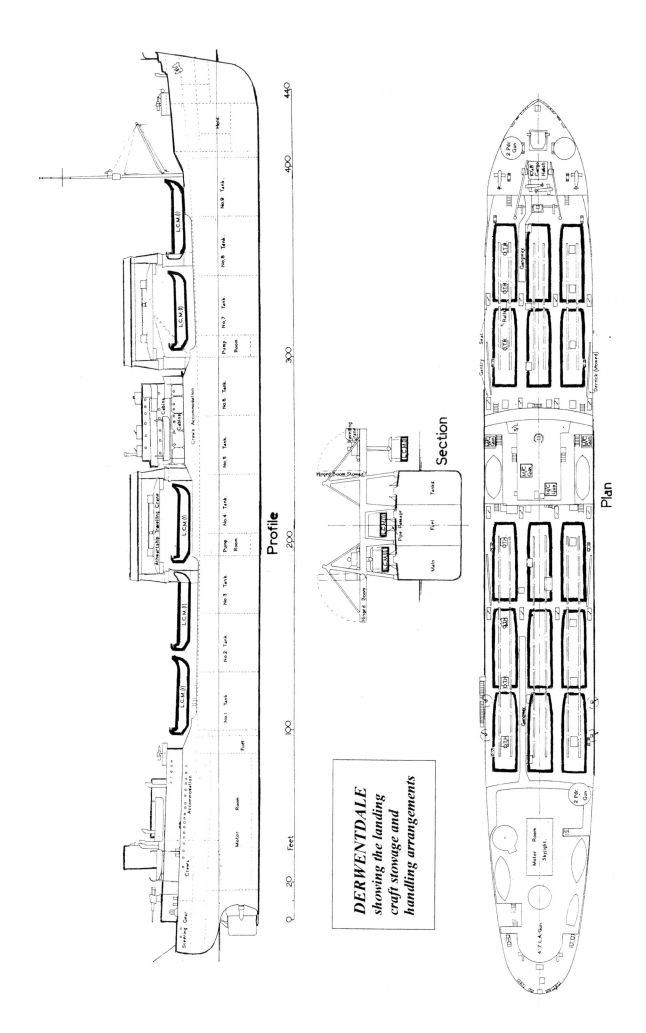

Profile

No.9 Tank. | No.8 Tank. | No.7 Tank. | Pump Room | No.6 Tank. | No.5 Tank. | No.4 Tank. | Pump Room | No.3 Tank. | No.2 Tank. | No.1 Tank | Fuel

L.C.M.(1) L.C.M.(1) L.C.M.(1) L.C.M.(1) L.C.M.(1) L.C.M.(1)

Hold

Crew's Accommodation

Cabin Cabin

Athwartship Travelling Crane

Motor Room

Accommodation

Crew

Steering Gear

440 400 300 200 100 20 0
Feet

DERWENTDALE
showing the landing
craft stowage and
handling arrangements

Section

Travelling Crane

L.C.M.(1)

Hinged Boom Stowed

L.C.M.(1) L.C.M.(1)

Hinged Boom

Pipe Passage

Main Fuel Tanks

Plan

2 Pdr. Gun

LC.A.8 Cargo Hatch

Gangway

Gantry Seat

Derrick (stowed)

M/C Gun M/C Gun

M/C Gun

M/C Gun

Gantry

Railing

2 Pdr. Gun

Motor Room Skylight.

4·7 L.A. Gun

86

WILLIAM PATTERSON 7,191/42 US (WSA) - *MT/STORE SHIP*: loaded at Beirut 17-26 Jun: left there 1 Jul and Alexandria 6 Jul in follow-up convoy MWS37: arrived Acid North beachhead 13 Jul: landed 125 personnel, 124 vehicles, 667 tons cased petrol and 1,955 tons stores: discharge delayed owing to bad stowage

WILLIAM T COLEMAN 7,187/42 US (WSA) - *MT/STORE SHIP*: loaded at Alexandria 16-26 Jun and left there 6 Jul in follow-up convoy MWS37 to arrive Acid South beachhead 13 Jul then moved to Syracuse: damaged in a heavy air attack 17 Jul: carried 125 vehicles, 651 tons cased petrol and 665 tons stores

WINCHESTER CASTLE 20,012/30 Union-Castle - *LANDING SHIP, INFANTRY (LARGE) (personnel capacity 1,158)*: embarked personnel at Suez: left Port Said 5 Jul in assault convoy MWF36: arrived Acid South beachhead 10 Jul

ZANE GREY 7,176/43 US (WSA) - *MT/STORE SHIP*: loaded at Haifa 17-23 Jun: left there 2 Jul and Alexandria 6 Jul in follow-up convoy MWS37: arrived Acid North beachhead 13 Jul: carried 113 vehicles, 650 tons cased petrol and 2,018 tons stores

Other merchant ships including Royal Fleet Auxiliaries

ABA 7,938/18 Elder Dempster - *HOSPITAL SHIP*: left Tripoli 9 Jul: arrived Sicily 10 Jul: undamaged in an air attack same day: embarked 157 survivors from the hospital ship TALAMBA 11 Jul

AMRA 8,314/38 British India - *HOSPITAL SHIP*: from Tripoli, at Bark East beachhead 11 Jul: moved to Acid North 13 Jul

CEDARDALE 8,132/39 Admiralty - *OILER*: left Benghazi 8 Jul: refuelled 24 destroyers 9 Jul (Force R)

DERWENTDALE 8,398/41 Admiralty - *LANDING SHIP, GANTRY*: carrying 15 landing craft, left Glasgow 11 Jun and the Clyde 24 Jun in assault convoy KMS18B: transferred to assault convoy KMF18 9 Jul for early unloading: arrived Bark West beachhead 10 Jul

DINARD 2,313/24 Southern Railway - *HOSPITAL CARRIER*: left Bizerta 10 Jul: arrived Bark West beachhead 11 Jul: with 219 patients aboard, left Bark East beachhead for Tripoli 15 Jul

DORSETSHIRE 9,717/20 Bibby - *HOSPITAL SHIP*: left Tripoli 9 Jul and Malta 10 Jul: arrived Bark South beachhead same day: moved to Bark East beachhead 11 Jul: suffered damage and casualties from two bombs at 0502 12 Jul

EMPIRE CHARMIAN 7,513/43 *British India - *LANDING SHIP, CARRIER*: embarked 21 landing craft at Port Said: left there 29 Jun and Alexandria 3 Jul in assault convoy MWS36: arrived Acid North beachhead 10 Jul

EMPIRE ELAINE 7,513/42 *Cayzer, Irvine - *LANDING SHIP, CARRIER*: carrying 21 landing craft, left the Clyde 24 Jun in assault convoy KMS18B: arrived Bark West beachhead 10 Jul

EMPIRE LASS 813/41 *Rowbotham - *WATER CARRIER*: from Malta, assigned to arrive Acid North beachhead 10 Jul: damaged in an air attack at 0445 12 Jul

ENNERDALE 8,219/41 Admiralty - *LANDING SHIP, GANTRY*: embarked landing craft at Port Said: left there 29 Jun and Alexandria 3 Jul in assault convoy MWS36: arrived Acid South beachhead 10 Jul

LLANDOVERY CASTLE 10,640/25 Union-Castle - *HOSPITAL SHIP*: delayed at Alexandria for repairs: left there 7 Jul and Tripoli 13 Jul: arrived Acid North beachhead then moved to Syracuse 15 Jul: with 607 patients aboard, left for Tripoli 16 Jul

MORAY COAST 687/40 Coast - *PETROL CARRIER*: from Malta, assigned to arrive Acid South beachhead 10 Jul

NASPRITE 965/41 Admiralty - *PETROL CARRIER*: from Malta, assigned to arrive Acid North beachhead 10 Jul

NEWFOUNDLAND 6,791/25 Johnston Warren - *HOSPITAL SHIP*: at Bougie under orders but not required

OPHIR 4,115/28 Dutch (KPM) - *HOSPITAL SHIP*: left Port Said 5 Jul: assigned to arrive at the beachhead 11 Jul

PEARLEAF 5,993/17 Admiralty - *OILER*: detached from follow-up convoy MWS37 to Benghazi 9 Jul (Force R)

ST DAVID 2,702/32 *G W Railway - *HOSPITAL CARRIER*: from Philippeville, left Malta 10 Jul: arrived beachhead 10 Jul: landed medical supplies 12 Jul

ST JULIEN 1,952/25 G W Railway - *HOSPITAL CARRIER*: left Philippeville 8 Jul via Malta: arrived Bark West beachhead 10 Jul: landed medical supplies 12 Jul: with 130 patients aboard, left Bark East beachhead for Sousse 17 Jul

SOMERSETSHIRE 9,716/21 Bibby - *HOSPITAL SHIP*: left Tripoli 16 Jul: arrived Syracuse 17 Jul: with 743 patients aboard, left for Tripoli 18 Jul

TALAMBA. [MPL 7686]

TALAMBA 8,018/24 British India - *HOSPITAL SHIP*: from Tripoli, arrived at the beachhead 10 Jul: whilst lying fully floodlit, was dive bombed and sunk off the Acid beachheads at 2200 same day: survivors rescued by the cruisers CARLISLE and UGANDA and destroyers ESKIMO and TARTAR

Unnamed naval vessels carrying personnel and equipment

LANDING SHIPS, TANK
LST 323, 364, 367, 368, 404, 405, 407, 409, 411, 413, 414, 415, 416, 417, 425 - all left Alexandria 24 Jun and Tripoli 8 Jul in assault convoy MWS36: arrived Acid and Bark beachheads 10 Jul: **LST 162, 422** - both detached to Malta as spare ships. LST 407 - suffered casualties from an air attack 10 Jul: she became stranded 11 Jul until refloated by the tug RESTIVE 15 Jul

LST 301, 305, 319, 321, 365, 366, 406, 424 - from the UK, all (except 406) arrived Algiers 2 Jul in advance convoy KMS18A: LST 406 followed in assault convoy KMS18B, after loading machinery parts at Londonderry: all left Algiers 5 Jul in assault convoy KMS18 to arrive Bark West beachhead 10 Jul

LST 63, 64, 164, 198, 200, 418 - all left the UK in follow-up convoy KMS19 (Force Y)

27 LSTs loaded vehicles at Sousse, embarked personnel at Sfax and left there 8 Jul in assault convoys SBM1/SBS1 to arrive Bark South beachhead 10 Jul. These included **LST 62, 302, 304, 320, 361, 363, 402, 419** and probably also **LST 8, 9, 65, 159, 199, 303, 322, 324, 362, 401, 403, 408, 410, 420, 423, 426, 427, 428, 430**. LST 361 - became stranded at the beachhead until towed clear by the tug HENGIST. **LST 429** - lost by fire between Sousse and Sfax 3 Jul

LANDING CRAFT, INFANTRY (LARGE)
Participating craft included -
LCI(L) 99, 103, 106, 112, 117, 118, 123, 124, 125, 126, 127, 131, 132, 134, 163, 169, 171, 172, 177, 179, 181, 182, 183, 185, 241, 248, 249, 250, 252, 256, 258, 260, 263, 266, 269, 275, 277, 281, 282, 284, 287, 290, 291, 295, 298, 299, 300, 302, 305, 307, 309, 310, 312, 317, 318

LANDING CRAFT, TANK
LCT 302, 303, 332, 399, 535, 536, 538, 580, 614 - all left Malta 9 Jul to arrive Bark West beachhead 10 Jul. LCT 614 put back with defects 10 Jul

LCT 306, 307, 308, 311, 314, 317, 318, 324, 325, 329, 333, 339, 341, 354, 355, 356, 361, 364, 372, 375, 377, 385, 390, 410, 416, 420, 445, 446, 537, 554, 556, 570, 583, 615, 850 - all left Libya 7 Jul: joined assault convoy MWS36 to arrive Acid and Bark beachheads 10 Jul. LCT 311 - damaged whilst under tow 10 Jul: LCT 410 - lost 12 Jul

LCT 397, 413, 547, 549, 550, 551, 552, 559, 578, 584, 585 - were amongst those craft which loaded vehicles at Sousse, embarked personnel at Sfax and left there 7 Jul in assault convoy SBS1 to arrive Bark South beachhead 10 Jul. LCT 547 - foundered en route to the beachhead 8 Jul

LCT 540, 563, 589, 591, 592, 594, 617, 625 - all arrived Joss beachhead 10 Jul (US Western Task Force)

Other participating craft included - **LCT 169, 343, 417**

Naval vessels in support

BATTLESHIPS
HOWE, KING GEORGE V - both left Algiers 9 Jul:

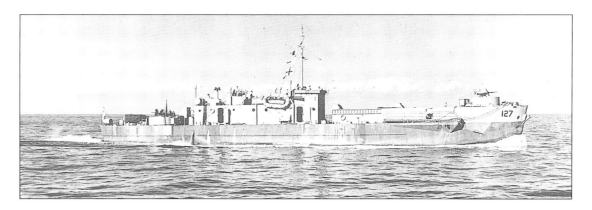

Landing Craft, Infantry (Large) 127. [IWM A20825]

provided bombardment support off the west coast of Sicily 11-12 Jul (Operation "Fracture") (Force Z)

NELSON, **RODNEY** - both left Algiers 6 Jul: positioned south-east of Sicily 10-11 Jul (Force H)

VALIANT, **WARSPITE** - both left Alexandria 7 Jul: both positioned south-east of Sicily 10 Jul (Force H)

AIRCRAFT CARRIERS
FORMIDABLE - left Alexandria 7 Jul: positioned south-east of Sicily 10-11 Jul (Force H)

INDOMITABLE - left Algiers 6 Jul: positioned south-east of Sicily 10-11 Jul (Force H): damaged in an aerial torpedo attack 0020 16 Jul

CRUISERS
AURORA - left Bone 6 Jul: in assault convoy KMS18 6-7 Jul: joined Force H 8 Jul: detached 9 Jul: provided bombardment support at Catania and Taormina 10 Jul (Operation "Arsenal") and on northern flank of beachhead area 11 Jul

CARLISLE - left Alexandria 6 Jul: joined assault convoy MWF36 to Acid beachheads: served as anti-aircraft, fighter direction, radar guard and stand-by

headquarters ship: rescued survivors from the hospital ship TALAMBA 10 Jul: attempted to tow the MT ship BAARN 11 Jul

CLEOPATRA - left Algiers 6 Jul: joined Force H: detached to cover the northern flank of beachhead area 11 Jul: damaged by a torpedo, at 0617 16 Jul, originally thought to have been fired by the Italian submarine DANDOLO but now credited to ALAGI

COLOMBO - left the UK 28 Jun with assault convoy KMF18: detached to Algiers: left there 6 Jul: joined assault convoy KMS18: arrived Bark West beachhead 10 Jul to provide anti-aircraft support

DELHI - left Algiers 6 Jul: joined assault convoy KMF18 to Bark West beachhead to provide anti-aircraft support

DIDO - left Bone 10 Jul: provided bombardment support at Marsala, on the west coast of Sicily 11-12 Jul (Operation "Fracture") (Force Z)

EMERALD - left the UK 1 Jul with assault convoy KMF19: detached at Gibraltar (en route via the Cape to join the Eastern Fleet)

EURYALUS - left Algiers 6 Jul: joined Force H:

The battleship NELSON. [MPL 512]

detached to cover the northern flank of the beachhead area 11 Jul

MAURITIUS - left Malta 9 Jul: joined assault convoy MWF36: arrived Acid beachheads 10 Jul: provided bombardment support 10-12 Jul (Force K)

NEWFOUNDLAND, **ORION** - both left Malta 9 Jul: joined assault convoy KMF18 for Bark beachheads: provided bombardment support 10-12 Jul (Force K)

PENELOPE - left Bone 6 Jul: joined assault convoy KMS18 6-7 Jul: joined Force H 8 Jul: detached 9 Jul: provided bombardment support at Catania 10 Jul (Operation "Arsenal") and on the northern flank of the beachhead area 11 Jul

SIRIUS - left Bone 10 Jul: provided bombardment support at Marsala on the west coast of Sicily 11-12 Jul (Operation "Fracture") (Force Z)

UGANDA - left Malta 9 Jul: joined assault convoy MWF36: arrived Acid beachheads 10 Jul: provided bombardment support north of Syracuse same day: narrowly missed in a fighter-bomber attack 1909 same day, then rescued survivors from the hospital ship TALAMBA: provided further bombardment support 11-12 Jul (Force K)

MONITORS
ABERCROMBIE - left Tunis 8 Jul (Force Q): arrived Cent beachhead 10 Jul (US Western Task Force)

EREBUS - left Alexandria 3 Jul in assault convoy MWS36: was unable to transfer to assault convoy MWF36 owing to lack of speed: arrived Acid beachheads 10 Jul: provided bombardment support 11-12 Jul and bombarded Catania airfield 13 Jul (Force A)

ROBERTS - left Algiers 5 Jul: joined assault convoy KMS18: transferred to assault convoy KMF18 9 Jul: provided bombardment support 10 Jul onwards (Force Q)

GUNBOATS
APHIS, **COCKCHAFER** - both left Malta 9 Jul: joined assault convoy MWF36: arrived Acid beachheads 10 Jul (Force A)

FLORES - Dutch: left Malta 9 Jul: joined assault convoy MWF36 to Bark East beachhead: provided bombardment support (Force A)

SCARAB - left Malta 9 Jul: joined assault convoy MWF36: arrived Acid beachheads 10 Jul (Force A)

SOEMBA - Dutch: left Alexandria 3 Jul in assault convoy MWS36: joined assault convoy MWF36 9 Jul: arrived Bark East beachhead 10 Jul: provided bombardment support (Force A)

LANDING SHIPS, HEADQUARTERS
ANTWERP - forward operations ship: as flagship of Naval Commander, Eastern Task Force: left Malta 9 Jul: arrived Bark beachheads 10 Jul: carried the British

Army commander and his staff from Malta to Sicily, arrived 11 Jul

BULOLO - left Port Said 5 Jul in assault convoy MWF36: arrived Acid North beachhead 10 Jul (Force A)

HILARY - left the Clyde 28 Jun in assault convoy KMF18: arrived Bark West beachhead 10 Jul (Force V)

LARGS - ex French CHARLES PLUMIER: left Sfax 8 Jul in assault convoy SBF1: arrived Bark South beachhead 10 Jul (Force B)

AUXILIARY ANTI-AIRCRAFT SHIPS

ALYNBANK - left Alexandria 3 Jul in assault convoy MWS36: arrived Bark beachheads 10 Jul: suffered casualties in a near miss during a dive-bombing attack same day (Force A)

ULSTER QUEEN - left the UK 28 Jun: joined assault convoy KMF18: detached to Algiers 7 Jul: joined assault convoy SBF1 9 Jul: arrived Bark South beachhead 10 Jul (Force B)

MINELAYER

ABDIEL - left Alexandria 8 Jul: carried the Commander-in-Chief Mediterranean Fleet on a tour of inspection of the beachheads 10 Jul

DESTROYERS

ADRIAS - Greek: left Port Said 5 Jul with assault convoy MWF36: detached 7 Jul: left Alexandria 9 Jul with follow-up convoy MWF37 to Syracuse (Escort Group R)

ALDENHAM - left Port Said 5 Jul with assault convoy MWF36: detached to refuel 8 Jul: rejoined 9 Jul to arrive at the beachhead 10 Jul (Escort Group P)

ANTHONY - left Bone 7 Jul: joined assault convoy KMF18 (Escort Group V): joined assault convoy KMS18 9 Jul to arrive at the beachhead 10 Jul (Escort Group S): on anti-submarine patrol 10 Jul

ARROW - left Algiers 9 Jul in place of the destroyer PETARD (Force Z)

ATHERSTONE - left Bizerta 7 Jul: joined assault convoy KMS18: detached 8 Jul: joined assault convoy KMF18 9 Jul: detached to Tunis same day (Escort Group T)

BEAUFORT - left Port Said 5 Jul with assault convoy MWF36: detached to refuel 8 Jul: rejoined 9 Jul to arrive at the beachhead 10 Jul (Escort Group P)

BELVOIR - left Alexandria 3 Jul with assault convoy MWS36: temporarily detached for anti-submarine hunt 6 Jul: detached to Benghazi: left there 8 Jul: joined assault convoy MWF36 to arrive at the beachhead 10 Jul (Escort Group Q)

BLANKNEY - left Bone 7 Jul: joined assault convoy KMF18: detached to refuel 9 Jul: rejoined to arrive Bark West beachhead (Escort Group V): provided bombardment support 10 Jul: whilst on anti-submarine patrol, suffered a crumpled stem in collision with the destroyer BRISSENDEN 0100 12 Jul but remained operational

BLENCATHRA - left Bone 7 Jul: joined assault convoy KMF18: detached to refuel 9 Jul: rejoined to arrive Bark West beachhead 10 Jul (Escort Group V): on anti-submarine patrol 10 Jul

BRECON - assigned to join assault convoy KMF18 7 Jul but delayed at Oran until 9 Jul (Escort Group V)

BRISSENDEN - left Bone 7 Jul: joined assault convoy KMF18: detached to refuel 9 Jul: rejoined to arrive Bark West beachhead 10 Jul (Escort Group V): provided bombardment support 10 Jul: after a brief bombardment, took the surrender of the town of Pazzallo 11 Jul: whilst on anti-submarine patrol, seriously damaged in collision with the destroyer BLANKNEY 0100 12 Jul and left for Malta

BROCKLESBY - left Algiers 7 Jul: joined assault convoy KMF18: detached 8 Jul: left Malta 9 Jul in assault convoy SBF2 to arrive Bark South beachhead 10 Jul (Escort Group U)

CALPE - left Algiers 5 Jul: joined assault convoy KMS18: detached to refuel 8 Jul: rejoined same day to arrive Bark West beachhead 10 Jul (Escort Group S): on anti-submarine patrol 10 Jul

CLARE - left the UK 25 Jun with follow-up convoy KMS19: detached to Bone 9 Jul (Escort Group D)

CLEVELAND - left Algiers 5 Jul: joined assault convoy KMS18: rescued survivors from the MT ship DEVIS same day: detached to refuel 8 Jul: rejoined same day to arrive Bark West beachhead 10 Jul (Escort Group S)

DULVERTON - left Alexandria 3 Jul with assault convoy MWS36: detached to Benghazi: left there 7 Jul: joined assault convoy MWF36 to arrive Bark East beachhead 10 Jul (Escort Group Q)

EASTON - left Port Said 5 Jul with assault convoy MWF36: detached 7 Jul: left Alexandria 9 Jul with follow-up convoy MWF37 to arrive Syracuse 13 Jul (Escort Group R)

ECHO - left Alexandria 7 Jul (Force H): on patrol off Sicily with the cruisers AURORA and PENELOPE 11 Jul

ECLIPSE - delayed at Alexandria: rejoined the fleet 8 Jul (Force H)

EGGESFORD - left Sfax 7 Jul with assault convoy

The destroyer FURY. [IWM A10309]

SBS1 to arrive Bark South beachhead 10 Jul (Escort Group W)

ESKIMO - left Malta 8 Jul: joined assault convoy MWF36: arrived Acid beachheads 10 Jul: rescued survivors from the hospital ship TALAMBA same day: hit by a bomb 12 Jul and towed to Malta (Force K)

EXMOOR - left Port Said 5 Jul with assault convoy MWF36: detached to refuel 8 Jul: rejoined 9 Jul to arrive Acid beachheads 10 Jul (Escort Group P)

FARNDALE - left Algiers 5 Jul: joined assault convoy KMS18: detached to refuel 8 Jul: rejoined same day to arrive Bark West beachhead 10 Jul (Escort Group S): on anti-submarine patrol 10 Jul

FAULKNOR, FURY - both left Alexandria 7 Jul (Force H)

HAMBLEDON - left Bone 7 Jul: joined assault convoy KMF18: detached to refuel 9 Jul: rejoined to arrive Bark West beachhead 10 Jul (Escort Group V): provided anti-aircraft support 10 Jul

HAYDON - left Algiers 5 Jul: joined assault convoy KMS18: detached to refuel 8 Jul: rejoined same day to arrive Bark West beachhead 10 Jul (Escort Group S): on anti-submarine patrol 10 Jul

HOLCOMBE - left Bizerta 7 Jul: joined assault convoy KMS18: detached 8 Jul: joined assault convoy KMF18 9 Jul: detached to Tunis same day (Escort Group T)

HURSLEY - left Alexandria 6 Jul: joined assault convoy MWF36: detached 7 Jul: left Alexandria 9 Jul with follow-up convoy MWF37 to arrive Syracuse 13 Jul (Escort Group R)

HURWORTH - left Port Said 5 Jul with assault convoy MWF36: detached 7 Jul: assigned to follow-up convoy MWF37 but delayed two days by boiler trouble (Escort Group R)

ILEX - left Alexandria 7 Jul (Force H): on patrol off Sicily with the cruisers AURORA and PENELOPE 10-11 Jul

INCONSTANT - left the UK 1 Jul with follow-up convoy KMF19: detached 9 Jul (Escort Group C)

INGLEFIELD - left Alexandria 7 Jul (Force H): detached with the cruisers AURORA and PENELOPE 9 Jul to provide bombardment support at Catania 10 Jul (Operation "Arsenal")

INTREPID - left Alexandria 7 Jul (Force H)

ISIS - left Bone with the cruisers DIDO and SIRIUS 10 Jul (Force Z)

JERVIS - left Algiers 9 Jul (Force Z)

KANARIS - Greek: left Port Said 5 Jul with assault convoy MWF36: detached to refuel 8 Jul: rejoined 9 Jul to arrive at the beachhead 10 Jul (Escort Group P)

KRAKOWIAK - Polish: left Algiers 5 Jul: joined assault convoy KMS18: detached to refuel 8 Jul: rejoined same day to arrive Bark West beachhead 10 Jul (Escort Group S)

LAFOREY - left Malta 8 Jul: joined assault convoys MWF36 then KMF18 to arrive Bark beachheads 10 Jul (Force K)

LAMERTON - left Algiers 6 Jul: joined assault convoy KMF18 7 Jul: detached to refuel at Sousse 8 Jul: joined assault convoy SBF1 9 Jul to arrive Bark South beachhead 10 Jul (Escort Group U)

LAUDERDALE - left Sfax 8 Jul with assault convoy SBM1 to arrive Bark South beachhead 10 Jul (Escort Group W)

LEDBURY - left Gibraltar 5 Jul: joined assault convoy KMF18: detached to Algiers 7 Jul: left there same day: joined assault convoy KMS18: detached to Sousse 8 Jul: joined assault convoy SBF1 9 Jul to arrive Bark West beachhead 10 Jul (Escort Group S)

LIDDESDALE - left Bizerta 7 Jul: joined assault convoy KMS18: detached 8 Jul: joined assault convoy KMF18 9 Jul: detached to Tunis same day (Escort Group T)

LOOKOUT, **LOYAL** - both left Malta 8 Jul: joined assault convoys MWF36 then KMF18: arrived Bark beachheads 10 Jul (Force K)

MENDIP - left Bone 7 Jul: joined assault convoy KMF18: detached to refuel 9 Jul: rejoined to arrive Bark West beachhead 10 Jul (Escort Group V): on anti-submarine patrol 10 Jul

MIAOULIS - Greek: left Port Said 5 Jul with assault convoy MWF36: detached to refuel 8 Jul: rejoined 9 Jul to arrive at the beachhead 10 Jul (Escort Group P)

NUBIAN - left Malta 8 Jul: joined assault convoy MWF36 9 Jul to arrive Acid North beachhead 10 Jul: re-opened the port of Syracuse 11 Jul (Force K)

OAKLEY - left Sfax 8 Jul with assault convoy SBM1 to arrive Bark South beachhead 10 Jul (Escort Group W)

OFFA - left Malta 8 Jul: detached with the cruisers AURORA and PENELOPE 9 Jul to provide bombardment support at Catania 10 Jul (Operation "Arsenal") (Force H)

The Hunt class destroyer OAKLEY. [IWM A15628]

PALADIN, **PANTHER**, **PATHFINDER**, **PENN** - all left Algiers 9 Jul (Force Z)

PETARD - left Malta 8 Jul (Force H)

PINDOS - Greek: left Alexandria 3 Jul with assault convoy MWS36: detached to Benghazi: left there 7 Jul: joined assault convoy MWF36 to arrive Bark East beachhead 10 Jul (Escort Group Q)

PIORUN - Polish: left Malta 8 Jul (Force H)

PUCKERIDGE - left Bone 5 Jul: joined assault convoy KMS18: detached to refuel 8 Jul: rejoined same day to arrive Bark West beachhead 10 Jul (Escort Group S)

QUAIL - left Malta 8 Jul (Force H)

QUANTOCK - left Algiers: joined assault convoy KMF18 7 Jul: detached to Malta: left there 8 Jul in assault convoy SBF2 to arrive Bark South beachhead 10 Jul (Escort Group U)

QUEEN OLGA - see VASILISSA OLGA

QUEENBOROUGH, **QUILLIAM** - both left Malta 8 Jul (Force H)

RAIDER - left Alexandria 7 Jul (Force H): on patrol off Sicily with the cruisers AURORA and PENELOPE 10 Jul

ROCKWOOD - left Port Said 5 Jul with assault convoy MWF36: detached to refuel 8 Jul: rejoined 9 Jul to arrive Acid beachheads 10 Jul (Escort Group P)

SLAZAK - Polish: left Bizerta 7 Jul: joined assault convoy KMS18: detached 8 Jul: joined assault convoy KMF18 9 Jul: detached to Tunis same day (Escort Group T)

TARTAR - left Malta 8 Jul: joined assault convoy MWF36 to arrive Acid beachheads 10 Jul: rescued survivors from the hospital ship TALAMBA same day: sank the MT ship BAARN 11 Jul (Force K)

TETCOTT - left Alexandria 3 Jul with assault convoy MWS36: temporarily detached for anti-submarine hunt 6 Jul: detached to Benghazi: left there 8 Jul: joined assault convoy MWF36 to arrive Acid beachheads 10 Jul (Escort Group Q)

TROUBRIDGE, **TUMULT** - both left Malta 8 Jul (Force H)

TYNEDALE - left Algiers 5 Jul: joined assault convoy KMS18: detached to refuel 8 Jul: rejoined same day to arrive Bark West beachhead 10 Jul (Escort Group S): on anti-submarine patrol 10 Jul

TYRIAN - left Malta 8 Jul (Force H)

VASILISSA OLGA (QUEEN OLGA) - Greek: left Alexandria 7 Jul (Force H)

VENOMOUS - left Alexandria 9 Jul with follow-up convoy MWF37 to arrive Syracuse 13 Jul (Escort Group X)

VICEROY - left Algiers 5 Jul: joined assault convoy KMS18: detached to Malta for repairs 9 Jul (Escort Group S): left for the beachhead (Escort Group V): provided anti-aircraft protection 10 Jul

WALLACE - left Bone 7 Jul: joined assault convoy KMF18: detached to refuel 9 Jul: rejoined to arrive Bark West beachhead 10 Jul (Escort Group V): provided anti-aircraft protection 10 Jul

WANDERER - left the UK 1 Jul with follow-up convoy KMF19: detached 9 Jul (Escort Group C)

WHADDON - left Sfax 7 Jul with assault convoy SBS1 to arrive Bark South beachhead 10 Jul (Escort Group W)

WHEATLAND, **WILTON** - both left Algiers 7 Jul: joined assault convoy KMF18: detached to Sousse 8 Jul: joined assault convoy SBF1 9 Jul to arrive Bark South beachhead 10 Jul (Escort Group U)

WISHART, **WITHERINGTON** - both left Alexandria 9 Jul with follow-up convoy MWF37 to arrive Syracuse 13 Jul (Escort Group X)

WOOLSTON - left Bone 7 Jul: joined assault convoy KMF18: detached to refuel 9 Jul: rejoined to arrive Bark West beachhead 10 Jul (Escort Group V): provided anti-aircraft protection 10 Jul

WRESTLER - left the UK 1 Jul with follow-up convoy KMF19: detached 9 Jul (Escort Group C)

BEACON SUBMARINES
SAFARI - left Bizerta: assigned to Joss beachhead (US Western Task Force)

SERAPH - left Algiers 30 Jun: assigned to Cent beachhead (US Western Task Force)

SHAKESPEARE - left Algiers 1 Jul: assigned to Dime beachhead (US Western Task Force)

UNISON - left Malta 6 Jul: assigned to Bark South beachhead

UNRIVALLED - left Malta 6 Jul: assigned to Bark West beachhead

UNRUFFLED - left Malta 6 Jul: assigned to Acid beachhead

UNSEEN - left Malta 6 Jul: assigned to Bark East beachhead

HM sloop CRANE.

SUBMARINES ON PATROL

DZIK - Polish: left Malta 3 Jul: helped to seal off the Gulf of Taranto

SOKOL - Polish: left Malta 1 Jul: guarded the Straits of Messina from the north

TACTICIAN - left Malta 3 Jul: helped to seal off the Gulf of Taranto

ULTOR - left Malta 3 Jul: guarded the Straits of Messina from the north

UNBROKEN - left Malta 3 Jul: helped to seal off the Gulf of Taranto

UNITED - left Malta 7 Jul: helped to seal off the Gulf of Taranto

UNRULY - left Malta 1 Jul: guarded the Straits of Messina from the north

UNSHAKEN, **UPROAR** - both left Malta 3 Jul: helped to seal off the Gulf of Taranto

SLOOPS

CHANTICLEER, **CRANE** - both left the UK 28 Jun with assault convoy KMF18: detached to Bone 7 Jul: assigned to join follow-up convoy KMS19 9 Jul to arrive at the beachhead 13 Jul (Escort Group A)

CYGNET - left the UK 28 Jun with assault convoy KMF18: sustained minor damage in collision with the yacht CASSANDRA off Europa Point 0433 5 Jul: detached to Bone 7 Jul: assigned to join follow-up convoy KMS19 9 Jul to arrive at the beachhead 13 Jul (Escort Group A)

ERNE - left the UK 26 Jun with assault convoy KMS18B: detached 5 Jul (Escort Group B)

JUMNA - Indian: left Alexandria 3 Jul with assault convoy MWS36 to arrive at the beachhead 10 Jul (Escort Group X)

PHEASANT - left the UK 28 Jun with assault convoy KMF18: detached to Bone 7 Jul: assigned to join follow-up convoy KMS19 9 Jul to arrive at the beachhead 13 Jul (Escort Group A)

SHOREHAM - left Alexandria 3 Jul with assault convoy MWS36 to arrive Bark beachheads 10 Jul (Escort Group X)

SUTLEJ - Indian: left Alexandria 3 Jul with assault convoy MWS36: joined assault convoy MWF36 9 Jul to arrive at the beachhead 10 Jul (Escort Group X)

WHIMBREL - left the UK 28 Jun with assault convoy KMF18: detached to Bone 7 Jul: assigned to join follow-up convoy KMS19 9 Jul to arrive at the beachhead 13 Jul (Escort Group A)

CUTTERS

BANFF - left the UK 24 Jun with assault convoy KMS18B: detached 5 Jul (Escort Group B)

FISHGUARD - left the UK 25 Jun with follow-up convoy KMS19: detached to Bone 9 Jul (Escort Group D)

FRIGATES
BANN - left the UK 1 Jul with follow-up convoy KMF19: detached 9 Jul (Escort Group C)

DART - left the UK 24 Jun with follow-up convoy KMS19: detached to Bone 9 Jul (Escort Group D)

PLYM - left the UK 1 Jul with follow-up convoy KMF19: detached 9 Jul (Escort Group C)

SWALE - left the UK 1 Jul with follow-up convoy KMF19: detached at Gibraltar

TEST - left the UK 28 Jun with assault convoy KMF18: detached to Bone 7 Jul: assigned to join follow-up convoy KMS19 9 Jul to arrive at the beachhead 13 Jul (Escort Group A)

TEVIOT - left the UK 24 Jun with assault convoy KMS18B: detached 5 Jul (Escort Group B)

TRENT - left the UK 28 Jun with assault convoy KMF18: detached to Bone 7 Jul: assigned to join follow-up convoy KMS19 9 Jul to arrive at the beachhead 13 Jul (Escort Group A)

CORVETTES
BERGAMOT - left the UK 25 Jun with assault convoy KMS18B: detached 5 Jul (Escort Group B)

BLUEBELL - left the UK 25 Jun with follow-up convoy KMS19: detached to Bone 9 Jul (Escort Group D)

BRYONY - left the UK 24 Jun with assault convoy KMS18B: detached 5 Jul (Escort Group B)

CAMELLIA - left the UK 24 Jun with follow-up convoy KMS19: detached 5 Jul (Escort Group D)

CONVOLVULUS - left Alexandria 6 Jul with follow-up convoy MWS37 to arrive Acid North beachhead 13 Jul (Escort Group X)

The Flower class corvette DIANELLA. [IWM A14030]

DELPHINIUM - left Benghazi 8 Jul (Force R)

DIANELLA - left the UK 25 Jun with follow-up convoy KMS19: detached 9 Jul (Escort Group D)

HONEYSUCKLE - left the UK 24 Jun with assault convoy KMS18B: stood by the MT ship ST ESSYLT 4-5 Jul: detached 5 Jul (Escort Group B)

HYACINTH - left Alexandria 3 Jul with assault convoy MWS36 to arrive at the beachhead 10 Jul (Escort Group X)

HYDERABAD - left the UK 24 Jun with assault convoy KMS18B: detached 5 Jul (Escort Group B)

LOTUS - left the UK 25 Jun with follow-up convoy KMS19: detached 9 Jul (Escort Group D)

OXLIP - left the UK 24 Jun with assault convoy KMS18B: detached 5 Jul (Escort Group B)

PENTSTEMON - left Alexandria 6 Jul with follow-up convoy MWS37 to arrive Acid North beachhead 13 Jul (Escort Group X)

POPPY - left the UK 25 Jun with follow-up convoy KMS19: detached 9 Jul (Escort Group D)

PRIMULA - left Alexandria 3 Jul with assault convoy MWS36 to arrive at the beachhead 10 Jul (Escort Group X)

RHODODENDRON - left the UK 24 Jun with assault convoy KMS18B: rescued survivors from the MT ship ST ESSYLT 5 Jul: detached same day (Escort Group B)

SAKHTOURIS - Greek: left Alexandria 3 Jul with assault convoy MWS36: rescued survivors from the cargo ship SHAHJEHAN 6 Jul and landed them at Benghazi: rejoined the convoy to arrive at the beachhead 10 Jul (Escort Group X)

STARWORT - left the UK 25 Jun with follow-up convoy KMS19: detached 9 Jul (Escort Group D)

VETCH - left Alexandria 6 Jul with follow-up convoy MWS37 to arrive Acid North beachhead 13 Jul (Escort Group X)

MINESWEEPERS
ACUTE, **ALBACORE** - both left Tunis 9 Jul (War Channel Maintenance Force)

BOSTON - left Malta 9 Jul astern of assault convoy MWF 36 to arrive at the beachhead 10 Jul

BRIXHAM - left Sfax 7 Jul with assault convoy SBS1 to arrive Bark South beachhead 10 Jul

BUDE - left Tunis 9 Jul (War Channel Maintenance Force)

Thirty-four Royal Naval minesweepers were allocated to the Sicily invasion, including SHARPSHOOTER seen here. [MPL 2602]

CADMUS - left Bizerta 7 Jul: joined assault convoy KMS18: joined assault convoy KMF18 9 Jul to arrive at the beachhead 10 Jul

CAIRNS, CESSNOCK - both Australian: left Alexandria 6 Jul with follow-up convoy MWS37 to arrive at the beachhead 13 Jul (Escort Group X)

CIRCE - left Bizerta 7 Jul: joined assault convoy KMS18: joined assault convoy KMF18 9 Jul to arrive at the beachhead 10 Jul

CLACTON - left Tunis 9 Jul (War Channel Maintenance Force)

CROMARTY - left Malta 9 Jul astern of assault convoy MWF36 to arrive at the beachhead 10 Jul

ESPIEGLE - left Bizerta 7 Jul: joined assault convoy KMS18: joined assault convoy KMF18 9 Jul to arrive at the beachhead 10 Jul

FELIXSTOWE - left Bizerta 6 Jul: joined assault convoy SBS1 to arrive Bark South beachhead 10 Jul

FLY - left Bizerta 7 Jul: joined assault convoy KMS18: joined assault convoy KMF18 9 Jul to arrive at the beachhead 10 Jul

GAWLER - Australian: left Benghazi 7 Jul: joined assault convoy MWS36 to arrive at the beachhead 10 Jul (Escort Group X)

GERALDTON - Australian: left Alexandria 6 Jul in follow-up convoy MWS37 to arrive at the beachhead 13 Jul (Escort Group X)

HAZARD, HEBE - both left Malta 9 Jul: joined assault convoy KMS18 to arrive at the beachhead 10 Jul

HYTHE - left Tripoli 8 Jul: joined assault convoy MWS36: joined assault convoy MWF36 9 Jul to arrive Bark East beachhead 10 Jul

IPSWICH, LISMORE, MARYBOROUGH - all Australian: left Benghazi 7 Jul: joined assault convoy MWS36 to arrive Bark East beachhead 10 Jul (Escort Group X)

MUTINE - left Malta 9 Jul: joined assault convoy KMS18 to arrive Bark West beachhead 10 Jul

POLRUAN - left Bizerta 6 Jul: joined assault convoy SBS1 to arrive Bark South beachhead 10 Jul

POOLE - left Malta 9 Jul astern of assault convoy MWF36 to arrive at the beachhead 10 Jul

RHYL - left Bizerta 6 Jul: joined assault convoy SBS1 to arrive Bark South beachhead 10 Jul

ROMNEY - left Tripoli 8 Jul: joined assault convoy MWS36: joined assault convoy MWF36 9 Jul to arrive Bark East beachhead 10 Jul

ROTHESAY - left Tunis 9 Jul (War Channel Maintenance Force)

RYE - left Tripoli 8 Jul: joined assault convoy MWS36: joined assault convoy MWF36 9 Jul to Bark East beachhead

SEAHAM - left Malta 9 Jul astern of assault convoy MWF36 to arrive at the beachhead 10 Jul: captured the Italian submarine BRONZO off Augusta and brought her into Syracuse 12 Jul

SHARPSHOOTER - left Malta 9 Jul: joined assault convoy KMS18 to arrive at the beachhead 10 Jul

STORNOWAY - left Tunis 9 Jul (War Channel Maintenance Force)

WHITEHAVEN - left Tripoli 8 Jul: joined assault convoy MWS36: joined assault convoy MWF36 9 Jul to arrive Bark East beachhead 10 Jul: attempted to assist LST 407 11 Jul

WOLLONGONG - Australian: left Alexandria 6 Jul with follow-up convoy MWS37 to arrive at the beachhead 13 Jul (Escort Group X)

AUXILIARY NETLAYER
BRITTANY - loaded with light net for use against circling torpedoes, left Port Said 5 Jul in assault convoy MWF36 as rescue ship: arrived Acid North beachhead 10 Jul: landed port party and heavy stores at Syracuse 11 Jul: served as headquarters ship (Force A)

TRAWLERS & WHALERS

BONITO - left Sfax 8 Jul with assault convoy SBM1 to arrive Bark South beachhead 10 Jul

BURRA - left Alexandria 6 Jul with follow-up convoy MWS37 to arrive Acid North beachhead 13 Jul (Escort Group X)

CAVA - left Malta 9 Jul: joined assault convoy MWS36 to arrive at the beachhead 10 Jul

CORIOLANUS - failed to leave Bizerta to arrive at the beachhead 10 Jul as assigned

FOXTROT - left Sfax 8 Jul to arrive Bark South beachhead 10 Jul

GAVOTTE - left Sfax 7 Jul with assault convoy SBS1: arrived Bark South beachhead 10 Jul

GRAYLING - left Sfax 8 Jul with assault convoy SBM1 to arrive Bark South beachhead 10 Jul

GRENADIER - left the UK 24 Jun with assault convoy KMS18B

HOY - left Sfax 8 Jul with assault convoy SBM1 but put back same day with engine trouble

INCHMARNOCK - from Malta, arrived at the beachhead 10 Jul

ISLAY - left Alexandria 6 Jul with follow-up convoy MWS37 to arrive Acid North beachhead 13 Jul (Escort Group X)

JULIET, KERRERA - both from Malta, joined assault convoy MWS36: arrived at the beachhead 10 Jul

KING SOL - left Sfax 8 Jul with assault convoy SBM1 to arrive Bark South beachhead 10 Jul

MULL - failed to leave Bizerta to arrive at the beachhead 10 Jul as assigned: left Tripoli 9 Jul

MULLET - left Sfax 8 Jul with assault convoy SBM1 to arrive Bark South beachhead 10 Jul

PROTEA - South African: left Benghazi 8 Jul (Force R)

REIGHTON WYKE - left Sfax 8 Jul with assault convoy SBM1 to arrive Bark South beachhead 10 Jul

ROMEO - left Benghazi 8 Jul (Force R)

SAHRA - left Malta 9 Jul: joined assault convoy KMS18 to arrive Bark West beachhead 10 Jul

SHIANT - from Malta, arrived at the beachhead 10 Jul

SOUTHERN ISLE, SOUTHERN SEA - both South African: left Benghazi 8 Jul (Force R)

STELLA CARINA - left Alexandria 6 Jul with follow-up convoy MWS37 to arrive Acid North beachhead 13 Jul (Escort Group X)

TANGO - left Sfax 7 Jul with assault convoy SBS1: arrived Bark South beachhead 10 Jul

VIDONIA, VINDELICIA - both for fuelling: left Malta 9 Jul: joined assault convoy KMS18 to arrive Bark West beachhead 10 Jul

VISENDA, WHITING - both left Sfax 8 Jul with assault convoy SBM1 to arrive Bark South beachhead 10 Jul

WOLBOROUGH - left Benghazi 8 Jul (Force R)

RESCUE TUGS

HENGIST - from Gibraltar, towed LST 361 off the beach 11 Jul

ORIANA - left Tripoli 8 Jul: assisted LST 407 at the beachhead 11 Jul

RESTIVE - from Gibraltar: joined assault convoy KMS18B: stood by the cargo ship CITY OF VENICE 4 Jul: refloated LST 407 at the beachhead 15 Jul

ST MONANCE - from Port Said, took in tow the cargo ship SHAHJEHAN 6 Jul until she sank 7 Jul

MOTOR TORPEDO BOATS
MTB 57, 63, 65, 66, 75, 77, 78, 81, 82, 84, 242, 260, 265, 288, 289, 295, 297, 313, 315, 316, 635, 637, 640, 655, 656, 665, 670

MOTOR GUNBOATS
MGB 641, 643, 645, 646, 657, 660, 661

MOTOR LAUNCHES
HDML 1128, 1158, 1221, 1234, 1257, 1270, 1301

ML 121, 126, 134, 135, 168, 338, 462, 480, 554, 555, 559, 560, 561, 564, 565, 575

MOTOR MINESWEEPERS
MMS 4, 9, 10, 32, 33, 34, 47, 50, 65, 80, 81, 92, 116, 118, 171, 184, 185

LANDING CRAFT, FLAK
LCF 3, 4, 5, 6, 7, 8, 9, 10, 12, 14, 15, 16, 17, 18 - divided between Eastern and Western Task Forces

LANDING CRAFT, GUN (LARGE)
LCG(L) 1, 2, 3, 4, 5, 6, 7, 8, 9, 10, 11, 12, 13, 14, 17, 18, 19, 20 - divided between Eastern and Western Task Forces

LANDING CRAFT, TANK (ROCKET)
LCT(R) 136, 140, 141, 147, 167, 171 - all left Sfax 7 Jul in assault convoy SBS1 to arrive Bark South beachhead 10 Jul

B6. SALERNO, ITALY: 9 SEPTEMBER 1943

DEVONSHIRE. [World Ship Photo Library]

Named ships carrying personnel, equipment and supplies

NAME OF SHIP   Gross tonnage/Year of Build   Owner or Managers, if British, or Nationality (and owner or *managers) - WARTIME FUNCTION [HM = His Majesty's commissioned ship: MT Ship = Cargo ship assigned primarily for carrying military vehicles]

AFRICAN PRINCE 4,653/39 Prince - MT SHIP: left Alexandria 5 Sep for Malta and onward routing in follow-up convoy TSS4 to arrive Salerno 11 Sep

ALCINOUS 6,189/25 Dutch (Oceaan) - MT SHIP: loaded at Bougie: left there 2 Sep and Bizerta 7 Sep in assault convoy FSS2 to arrive Salerno 9 Sep

BENEDICT 4,949/30 Booth - MT SHIP: left Philippeville 5 Sep for Malta and onward routing in follow-up convoy TSS4 to arrive Salerno 11 Sep

BOLLSTA 1,832/24 Norwegian (*Olsen) - STORE SHIP: left Bizerta 7 Sep in assault convoy FSS2 to arrive Salerno 9 Sep

BOXER - HM LANDING SHIP, TANK: left Oran 5 Sep in assault convoy NSF1: arrived Salerno 9 Sep (US Southern Attack Force): carried 416 personnel, 45 amphibious and land vehicles, 14 guns and 2 trailers

BRUISER - HM LANDING SHIP, TANK: left Oran 5 Sep in assault convoy NSF1: arrived Salerno 9 Sep (US Southern Attack Force): carried 17 amphibious vehicles

CERION 2,588/38 Anglo-Saxon - CASED PETROL SHIP: left Tripoli 6 Sep in assault convoy TSS2: arrived Salerno 9 Sep

CITY OF EVANSVILLE 6,528/22 *Hall - MT SHIP: left Tripoli 6 Sep in assault convoy TSS2 to arrive Salerno 9 Sep

DEVONSHIRE 11,275/39 Bibby - LANDING SHIP, INFANTRY (LARGE) (personnel capacity 1,830): left Tripoli 6 Sep in assault convoy TSF1: arrived Salerno 9 Sep

DUCHESS OF BEDFORD 20,123/28 Canadian Pacific - LANDING SHIP, INFANTRY (LARGE) (personnel capacity 3,160): left Oran 5 Sep in assault convoy NSF1: arrived Salerno 9 Sep (US Southern Attack Force)

EMPIRE CATO 7,039/42 *Hain - MT SHIP: left Philippeville 5 Sep for Malta for onward routing in follow-up convoy TSS4 to arrive Salerno 11 Sep

FORT PEMBINA 7,134/42 *Billmeir - MT SHIP: from Tripoli, arrived Malta 6 Sep for onward routing in follow-up convoy TSS4 to arrive Salerno 11 Sep

GLENGYLE 9,919/39 Glen Line - HM LANDING SHIP, INFANTRY (LARGE) (personnel capacity 982): left Tripoli 6 Sep in assault convoy TSF1: arrived Salerno 9 Sep

MIDDLESEX TRADER. [Capt J F van Puyvelde]

JERSEY HART 7,275/43 Stanhope - *MT SHIP*: from Tripoli, left Malta 11 Sep in follow-up convoy TSS4 to arrive Salerno 11 Sep

LOCHEE 964/37 Dundee, Perth & London - *CASED PETROL SHIP*: left Tripoli 6 Sep in assault convoy TSS2 to arrive Salerno 9 Sep

LYMINGE 2,499/19 Constants - *STORE SHIP*: left Bizerta 9 Sep in convoy FSS4 to arrive Salerno 11 Sep: damaged by fire after a bomb near miss at Salerno at 1340 12 Sep

MARNIX VAN ST ALDEGONDE 19,355/30 Dutch (Nederland) - *LANDING SHIP, INFANTRY (LARGE)*: left Oran 5 Sep in assault convoy NSF1: arrived Salerno 9 Sep (US Southern Attack Force): carried 1,800 personnel, 45 vehicles, 2 cranes and 13 trailers: slightly damaged in an air attack 10 Sep

MIDDLESEX TRADER 7,241/42 Trader Navigation - *MT SHIP*: left Tripoli 6 Sep in assault convoy TSS2 to arrive Salerno 9 Sep

NARWIK 7,031/42 Polish (Gdynia-America) - *MT SHIP*: left Tripoli 6 Sep in assault convoy TSS2 to arrive Salerno 9 Sep

NORMAN MONARCH 7,005/43 Monarch - *MT SHIP*: left Tripoli 6 Sep in assault convoy TSS2 to arrive Salerno 9 Sep

OCEAN VENGEANCE 7,174/42 *Raeburn & Verel - *MT SHIP*: left Tripoli 5 Sep and Malta 11 Sep in follow-up convoy TSS4 to arrive Salerno 11 Sep

ORONTES 20,097/29 Orient - *LANDING SHIP, INFANTRY (LARGE) (personnel capacity 3,440)*: left Oran 5 Sep in assault convoy NSF1: arrived Salerno 9 Sep (US Southern Attack Force)

PRINCE CHARLES 2,950/30 Belgian - *HM LANDING SHIP, INFANTRY (SMALL) (personnel capacity 250)*: left Palermo 8 Sep in assault convoy TSF1X: arrived Salerno 9 Sep

PRINCE LEOPOLD 2,950/30 Belgian - *HM LANDING SHIP, INFANTRY (SMALL) (personnel capacity 250)*: left Palermo 8 Sep in assault convoy TSF1X: arrived Salerno 9 Sep

PRINCESS BEATRIX 4,135/39 Dutch (Zeeland) PRINSES BEATRIX - *HM LANDING SHIP, INFANTRY (MEDIUM) (personnel capacity 400)*: left Tripoli 6 Sep in assault convoy TSF1: arrived Salerno 9 Sep

PRINS ALBERT 2,938/37 Belgian - *HM LANDING SHIP, INFANTRY (SMALL) (personnel capacity 380)*: left

ORONTES.

Palermo 8 Sep in assault convoy TSF1X: arrived Salerno 9 Sep

PRINSES ASTRID 2,950/30 Belgian - *HM LANDING SHIP, INFANTRY (SMALL) (personnel capacity 250)*: left Tripoli 6 Sep in assault convoy TSF1: arrived Salerno 9 Sep

PRINSES JOSEPHINE CHARLOTTE 2,950/31 Belgian - *HM LANDING SHIP, INFANTRY (SMALL) (personnel capacity 250)*: left Tripoli 6 Sep in assault convoy TSF1: arrived Salerno 9 Sep

PROMETHEUS 6,095/25 *Alfred Holt - *MT SHIP*: loaded at Bougie: left there 2 Sep and Bizerta 7 Sep in assault convoy FSS2 to arrive Salerno 9 Sep

ROYAL SCOTSMAN 3,244/36 Burns & Laird - *HM LANDING SHIP, INFANTRY (HAND HOISTING) (personnel capacity 450)*: left Tripoli 6 Sep in assault convoy TSF1: arrived Salerno 9 Sep

ROYAL ULSTERMAN 3,244/36 Burns & Laird - *HM LANDING SHIP, INFANTRY (HAND HOISTING) (personnel capacity 450)*: left Tripoli 6 Sep in assault convoy TSF1: arrived Salerno 9 Sep

SOBIESKI 11,030/39 Polish (Gdynia-America) - *LANDING SHIP, INFANTRY (LARGE) (personnel capacity 1,684)*: left Tripoli 6 Sep in assault convoy TSF1: arrived Salerno 9 Sep

TEUCER 9,079/06 *Alfred Holt - *MT SHIP*: left Alexandria 5 Sep and Malta 11 Sep in follow-up convoy TSS4 to arrive Salerno 11 Sep

THRUSTER - *HM LANDING SHIP, TANK*: left Oran 5 Sep in assault convoy NSF1: arrived Salerno 9 Sep (US Southern Attack Force): carried 17 amphibious vehicles

ULSTER MONARCH 3,791/29 Belfast - *HM LANDING SHIP, INFANTRY (HAND HOISTING) (personnel capacity 780)*: left Tripoli 6 Sep in assault convoy TSF1: arrived Salerno 9 Sep

WELSH COAST 646/38 Coast - *CASED PETROL SHIP*: left Bizerta 7 Sep in assault convoy FSS2 to arrive Salerno 9 Sep

Other merchant ships including Royal Fleet Auxiliaries

ABA 7,938/18 Elder Dempster - *HOSPITAL SHIP*: left Bizerta 9 Sep: arrived Salerno 10 Sep (US Southern Attack Force): moved to northern beachhead 12 Sep: with 147 patients aboard, left for Bizerta same day

ALETTA 3,085/27 Dutch (Nederlandsch-Indische) - *WATER CARRIER*: left Bizerta 7 Sep in follow-up convoy FSS3 to arrive Salerno 9 Sep

ALEXANDRE ANDRE 5,322/28 Belgian (Gulf Oil) - *TANKER*: left Tripoli 6 Sep in assault convoy TSS2 to arrive Salerno 9 Sep

DERWENTDALE 8,398/41 Admiralty - *LANDING SHIP, GANTRY*: left Bizerta 7 Sep in assault convoy FSS2: arrived Salerno 9 Sep (US Southern Attack Force): carried 15 landing craft: suffered engine room damage by a bomb near miss 1215 15 Sep: towed to Malta

EMPIRE CHARMIAN 7,513/43 *British India - *LANDING SHIP, CARRIER*: left Bizerta 7 Sep in assault convoy FSS2: arrived Salerno 9 Sep (US Southern Attack Force): carried 30 landing craft: left for passage to Messina 18 Sep during which the ship's Master was killed in an air attack

EMPIRE COPPICE 814/43 *Coastal Tankers - *WATER CARRIER*: left Bizerta 7 Sep in assault convoy FSS2 to arrive Salerno 9 Sep

EMPIRE SPEY 4,292/29 *Nisbet - *NAVAL COLLIER*: entered Salerno harbour 11 Sep

LEINSTER 4,303/37 Coast - *HOSPITAL SHIP*: left Palermo 10 Sep: arrived Salerno 12 Sep: attacked by aircraft but undamaged same day and 13 Sep, then embarked casualties from the hospital ship NEWFOUNDLAND

NEWFOUNDLAND 6,791/25 Johnston Warren - *HOSPITAL SHIP*: left Bizerta 10 Sep: arrived Salerno 12 Sep: at 0510 13 Sep, a bomb explosion between her bridge and funnel caused a serious outbreak of fire: attempts to fight the blaze were made by the US destroyers MAYO and PLUNKETT and later by the US tug MORENO: these vessels were urgently required for other duties and, with no rescue tug available and the ship constituting a hazard to navigation, she had to be sunk and went down at 2300 14 Sep, as a result of PLUNKETT firing 70 shells at her: survivors boarded LEINSTER, ST ANDREW and TAIREA

ST ANDREW 2,702/32 *G W Railway - *HOSPITAL CARRIER*: left Bizerta 10 Sep: arrived Salerno 12 Sep: assisted the hospital ship NEWFOUNDLAND and carried survivors to Bizerta 13 Sep

ST DAVID 2,702/32 *G W Railway - *HOSPITAL CARRIER*: left Philippeville 7 Sep via Palermo: arrived Salerno 9 Sep: left for Philippeville 10 Sep with 283 patients aboard, 20 of whom died during the passage: rescued five British airmen from the sea same day

ST JULIEN 1,952/25 G W Railway - *HOSPITAL CARRIER*: left Palermo 9 Sep: arrived Salerno 10 Sep: left for Bone with 219 patients

SOMERSETSHIRE 9,716/21 Bibby - *HOSPITAL SHIP*: left Palermo 10 Sep: arrived Salerno 11 Sep: with 441 patients aboard, left for Philippeville same day

The cruiser ORION off Salerno during the operation. [IWM A19149]

TAIREA 7,933/24 British India - *HOSPITAL SHIP*: at Salerno 12 Sep: assisted the hospital ship NEWFOUNDLAND 13 Sep

Unnamed naval vessels carrying personnel and equipment

LANDING SHIPS, TANK
LST 11, 63, 64, 162, 165, 198, 200, 301, 302, 303, 304, 319, 320, 321, 322, 323, 324, 361, 362, 363, 364, 365, 366, 367, 368, 402, 403, 406, 408, 410, 411, 412, 417, 418, 419, 420, 421, 426, 427, 428, 430 - all left Tripoli/Sousse 6 Sep in assault/follow-up convoys TSS2/TSS3: arrived Salerno 9 Sep. LST 417 - beached and withdrawn after stern severely damaged in an aerial torpedo attack at Termini 2303 8 Sep: LST 304, 363, 365, 412, 430 - all hit by shore gunfire 9 Sep. **LST 8, 423** - did not sail

LST 12, 160, 161, 199, 404, 405, 409, 413, 415, 416, 422, 425 - all left Termini 8 Sep in assault convoy FSS2X: arrived Salerno 9 Sep (US Southern Attack Force)

LANDING CRAFT, INFANTRY (LARGE)
Participating craft included -
LCI(L) 177, 249, 299, 309. LCI(L) 299 - damaged by gunfire 9 Sep

LANDING CRAFT, TANK
Participating craft included -
LCT 154, 164, 169, 195, 219, 221, 244, 277, 320, 329, 344, 346, 364, 383, 548, 549, 550, 551, 552, 553, 554, 556, 559, 561, 578, 583, 584, 585, 586, 601, 615, 624. LCT 154 - sunk by mine 9 Sep: LCT 219, 221, 551 - damaged by shore gunfire 9 Sep: LCT 550 damaged by shore gunfire 12 Sep: LCT 601 - sunk by shore gunfire 9 Sep: LCT 624 - sunk by a bomb in convoy at 1650 8 Sep

Naval vessels in support

BATTLESHIPS
NELSON, RODNEY - both left Malta 7 Sep for the Tyrrhenian Sea (Force H)

VALIANT - left Malta 7 Sep for the Tyrrhenian Sea: detached to meet the surrendering Italian battle fleet 9 Sep (Force H)

WARSPITE - left Malta 7 Sep for the Tyrrhenian Sea: narrowly missed in an aerial torpedo attack 8 Sep: detached to meet the surrendering Italian battle fleet 9 Sep: subsequently, off Salerno, suffered casualties and serious damage when hit by a glider bomb 16 Sep (Force H)

AIRCRAFT CARRIERS
FORMIDABLE - left Malta 7 Sep for the Tyrrhenian Sea: narrowly missed in an aerial torpedo attack 8 Sep: provided air support for Forces H and V 9-11 Sep (Force H)

ILLUSTRIOUS - left Malta 7 Sep for the Tyrrhenian Sea: provided air support for Forces H and V 9-11 Sep (Force H)

UNICORN - left Malta 8 Sep: arrived Salerno 9 Sep: provided air cover for the landings 9-12 Sep and for the protection of Force V 11-12 Sep (Force V)

ESCORT CARRIERS
ATTACKER, BATTLER, HUNTER, STALKER - all left Malta 8 Sep: arrived Salerno 9 Sep: provided air cover for the landings 9-12 Sep (Force V)

CRUISERS
CHARYBDIS - left Malta 8 Sep: arrived Salerno 9 Sep (Force V)

DELHI - left Tripoli 6 Sep with assault convoy TSF1: arrived Salerno 9 Sep and provided anti-aircraft protection: in collision with the cruiser UGANDA in a smoke screen 2153 same day

EURYALUS - left Malta 8 Sep: arrived Salerno 9 Sep (Force V)

MAURITIUS, ORION - both left Augusta 7 Sep: arrived Salerno 9 Sep: provided bombardment support same day

SCYLLA - left Malta 8 Sep: arrived Salerno 9 Sep (Force V)

UGANDA - left Augusta 7 Sep: arrived Salerno 9 Sep and provided bombardment support: in collision with the cruiser DELHI in a smokescreen 2153 same day: hit aft by a remote-controlled bomb at 1450 13 Sep, causing casualties and severe damage in her after engine room on the starboard side: left for Malta in tow of US tug NARRAGANSETT 14 Sep, using her undamaged port engine to assist

AURORA, **DIDO**, **PENELOPE**, **SHEFFIELD** and **SIRIUS** were not involved in the early stages of the invasion, although they provided bombardment support from 14 Sep onwards

MONITORS

ABERCROMBIE - left Bizerta 7 Sep in assault convoy FSS2: arrived Salerno 9 Sep: provided bombardment support same day: struck a mine 1710 same day (US Southern Attack Force)

ROBERTS - left Bizerta 7 Sep in assault convoy FSS2: arrived Salerno 9 Sep: provided bombardment support same day

GUNBOAT

FLORES - Dutch: left Palermo 8 Sep: arrived Salerno 9 Sep: provided bombardment support same day: damaged by a near miss in an air attack 0805 11 Sep (US Southern Attack Force)

LANDING SHIP, HEADQUARTERS

HILARY - left Tripoli 6 Sep in assault convoy TSF1: experienced difficulty in maintaining convoy speed owing to poor quality bunker coal: arrived Salerno 9 Sep

AUXILIARY ANTI-AIRCRAFT SHIP

ALYNBANK - left Tripoli 6 Sep in assault convoy TSS2: arrived Salerno 9 Sep: suffered damage and casualties when hit by shore gunfire 1410 same day

FIGHTER DIRECTION SHIPS

PALOMARES - left Algiers 6 Sep in assault convoy NSF1X: arrived Salerno 9 Sep: directed fighters of Force V

ULSTER QUEEN - left Oran 5 Sep in assault convoy NSF1: arrived Salerno 9 Sep: served as stand-by ship for PALOMARES

ULSTER QUEEN as a Royal Navy ship (above) [IWM FL12413] and (below), in total contrast, in pre-war days as a passenger ship. [NMM N37893]

DESTROYERS

ATHERSTONE - (Force V)

BEAUFORT - left Tripoli 6 Sep with assault convoy TSF1: arrived Salerno 9 Sep

BELVOIR - left Tripoli 6 Sep with assault convoy TSF1 to arrive Salerno 9 Sep

BLACKMORE - left Palermo 8 Sep: joined assault convoy TSF1X: arrived Salerno 9 Sep: provided bombardment support same day

BLANKNEY - left Bizerta 4 Sep and Castellamare 7 Sep with assault convoy FSS1: arrived Salerno 9 Sep: provided bombardment support same day

BLENCATHRA - left Oran 6 Sep with convoy NSM1: assigned to US Southern Attack Force as minelaying escort but not required

BRECON - left Bizerta 6 Sep: joined assault convoy FSS2 8 Sep: arrived Salerno 9 Sep: provided bombardment support same day

BROCKLESBY - left Tripoli 5 Sep and Termini 8 Sep with assault convoy TSM1 to arrive Salerno 9 Sep

CALPE, CATTERICK, CLEVELAND - (all Force V)

DULVERTON - left Tripoli 6 Sep with assault convoy TSF1 to arrive Salerno 9 Sep

ECHO - (Force H)

ECLIPSE - detached 8 Sep to act as an aircraft marker but not required (Force H)

EXMOOR - left Tripoli 6 Sep with assault convoy TSF1: arrived Salerno 9 Sep

FARNDALE - (Force V)

FAULKNOR, FURY - (both Force H)

HAMBLEDON - left Oran 6 Sep with convoy NSM1: assigned to US Southern Attack Force as minelaying escort but not required: arrived Salerno 12 Sep

HAYDON, HOLCOMBE - (both Force V)

ILEX, INGLEFIELD, INTREPID - (all Force H)

KRAKOWIAK - Polish (Force V)

LAFOREY - left Augusta 7 Sep: arrived Salerno 9 Sep and provided bombardment support: damaged by shore gunfire same day

The destroyer LAFOREY. [IWM A17367]

The Hunt class destroyer MENDIP. [Wright & Logan]

LAMERTON - left Malta 9 Sep: joined follow-up convoy NSS1: arrived Salerno 11 Sep (US Southern Attack Force)

LE FANTASQUE - Free French: joined Force H 8 Sep

LEDBURY - left Palermo 8 Sep: joined assault convoy TSF1X: arrived Salerno 9 Sep and provided bombardment support: subjected to shore gunfire 0213 same day

LIDDESDALE - (Force V)

LOOKOUT - left Augusta 7 Sep: arrived Salerno 9 Sep: provided bombardment support same day

LOYAL - left Augusta 7 Sep: arrived Salerno 9 Sep and provided bombardment support: No 2 boiler put out of action by shore gunfire same day

MENDIP - left Bizerta 7 Sep with assault convoy FSS2: suffered damage in a bomb near miss 8 Sep: arrived Salerno 9 Sep: provided bombardment support same day

NUBIAN - left Augusta 7 Sep: arrived Salerno 9 Sep: provided bombardment support same day

OAKLEY - left Oran 6 Sep with convoy NSM1: assigned to US Southern Attack Force as minelaying escort but not required

OFFA, PETARD - (both Force H)

PINDOS - Greek: left Tripoli 6 Sep with assault convoy TSF1 to arrive Salerno 9 Sep

PIORUN - Polish (Force H)

QUAIL - (Force H)

QUANTOCK - left Tripoli 6 Sep with assault convoy TSS2 to arrive Salerno 9 Sep: provided bombardment support 12 Sep

QUEEN OLGA - see VASILISSA OLGA

QUEENBOROUGH, QUILLIAM, RAIDER - (all Force H)

SLAZAK - Polish (Force V)

TARTAR - left Augusta 7 Sep: arrived Salerno 9 Sep: provided bombardment support same day

TETCOTT - left Tripoli 6 Sep with assault convoy TSF1 to arrive Salerno 9 Sep

VASILISSA OLGA (QUEEN OLGA) - Greek (Force H)

JERVIS, PANTHER, PATHFINDER and **PENN** were not involved in the early stages of the invasion, although they formed part of the battleship screen from 14 Sep onwards

BEACON SUBMARINE
SHAKESPEARE

MINESWEEPERS
ACUTE - left Tripoli 6 Sep with assault convoy TSF1: arrived Salerno 9 Sep

ALBACORE - left Palermo 8 Sep in assault convoy TSF1X: arrived Salerno 9 Sep

BRIXHAM, **BUDE** - both left Bizerta 7 Sep in assault convoy FSS2: arrived Salerno 9 Sep

CADMUS - left Tripoli 6 Sep with assault convoy TSF1: arrived Salerno 9 Sep: damaged by a bomb near miss 0510 same day

CIRCE - left Tripoli 6 Sep with assault convoy TSF1: arrived Salerno 9 Sep

CLACTON - left Bizerta 7 Sep in assault convoy FSS2: arrived Salerno 9 Sep

ESPIEGLE - left Tripoli 6 Sep with assault convoy TSF1: arrived Salerno 9 Sep

FELIXSTOWE - left Tripoli 3 Sep and Termini 7 Sep in assault convoy TSS1 to arrive Salerno 9 Sep

FLY - left Tripoli 6 Sep with assault convoy TSF1: arrived Salerno 9 Sep

MUTINE - left Palermo 8 Sep in assault convoy TSF1X: arrived Salerno 9 Sep

POLRUAN, **RHYL** - both left Bizerta 7 Sep in assault convoy FSS2: arrived Salerno 9 Sep

ROTHESAY - left Tripoli 6 Sep with assault convoy TSF1: arrived Salerno 9 Sep

STORNOWAY - left Bizerta 7 Sep in assault convoy FSS2: arrived Salerno 9 Sep

AIR-SEA RESCUE SHIP
ANTWERP - left Bizerta: positioned midway between Sicily and Salerno but no rescue operations were required

AUXILIARY NETLAYER
BRITTANY - left Bizerta 7 Sep in assault convoy FSS2: arrived Salerno 9 Sep: carried the Naval Officer in Charge, Salerno

TRAWLERS
COVERLEY, **ENSAY**, **GAVOTTE**, **MINUET**, **MOUSA**, **PIROUETTE**, **REIGHTON WYKE**, **ST KILDA**, **SHEPPEY**, **STELLA CARINA**, **TANGO**, **VISENDA** - all left Tripoli 6 Sep with assault convoy TSS2 to arrive Salerno 9 Sep

BOOM DEFENCE VESSEL
BARNDALE - entered Salerno harbour 11 Sep

TUGS
FAVOURITE - left Tripoli 6 Sep: entered Salerno harbour 11 Sep

HENGIST - left Tripoli 6 Sep in assault convoy TSS2: arrived Salerno 9 Sep

MOTOR LAUNCHES
HDML 1242, **1246**, **1247**, **1253**, **1254**, **1258**, **1270**, **1271**, **1297**, **1301**

ML 121, **126**, **134**, **135** - all for minesweeping, left Palermo in assault convoy TSM1X to arrive Salerno 9 Sep

ML 238, **273**, **280**, **283**, **336** - all left Tripoli 5 Sep in assault convoy TSM1 to arrive Salerno 9 Sep

ML 554, **555**, **556**, **557**, **559**, **560** - all left Bizerta as part of a diversion group

ML 561, **562**, **564**, **566** - all left Tripoli 6 Sep with follow-up convoy TSS3 to arrive Salerno 9 Sep

MOTOR MINESWEEPERS
MMS 5, **133**, **134** - all left in assault convoy TSS1 to arrive Salerno 9 Sep

BYMS 11, **14**, **24**, **209** - all left Tripoli 3 Sep and Termini 7 Sep with assault convoy TSS1 to arrive Salerno 9 Sep

LANDING CRAFT, FLAK
LCF 3, **5**, **8** - all left Bizerta 4 Sep and Castellamare 7 Sep in assault convoy FSS1 to arrive Salerno 9 Sep

LCF 10, **12**, **15**, **16** - all left Tripoli 3 Sep and Termini 7 Sep in assault convoy TSS1 to arrive Salerno 9 Sep

LANDING CRAFT, GUN
LCG(L) 1, **5**, **6**, **7**, **20** - all left Bizerta 4 Sep and Castellamare 7 Sep in assault convoy FSS1 to arrive Salerno 9 Sep

LCG(L) 2, **4**, **8**, **19** - all left Tripoli 3 Sep and Termini 7 Sep in assault convoy TSS1 to arrive Salerno 9 Sep. LCG 2, 8 - both damaged by shore gunfire 9 Sep

LANDING CRAFT, TANK (ROCKET)
LCT(R) 136, **140**, **147** - all left Tripoli 3 Sep and Termini 7 Sep in assault convoy TSS1 to arrive Salerno 9 Sep

LCT(R) 141, **167**, **171** - all left Bizerta 4 Sep and Castellamare 7 Sep in assault convoy FSS1 to arrive Salerno 9 Sep

WINCHESTER CASTLE. [A Duncan]

Named ships carrying personnel, equipment and supplies

NAME OF SHIP Gross tonnage/Year of Build   Owner or *Managers, if British, or Nationality (and owner) - *WARTIME FUNCTION [HM = His Majesty's commissioned ship: MT Ship = Cargo ship assigned primarily for carrying military vehicles: WSA = War Shipping Administration]*

ALEXANDER MARTIN 7,177/42 US (WSA) - *MT/STORE SHIP*: left Naples 28 Jan in the follow-up convoy for Anzio, carrying British and American stores

ASCANIA 14,013/25 Cunard White Star - *LANDING SHIP, PERSONNEL (capacity 2,291)*: left Naples 21 Jan in TG 81.4: arrived X beachhead 22 Jan (US Force X)

BOXER - *HM LANDING SHIP, TANK*: left Naples 21 Jan in assault group D: arrived P beachhead 22 Jan: carried 213 personnel and 65 vehicles

BRET HARTE 7,176/42 US (WSA) - *MT/STORE SHIP*: from Naples, at Anzio 23 Jan discharging British and American stores

BRUISER - *HM LANDING SHIP, TANK*: left Naples 21 Jan in assault group D: arrived P beachhead 22 Jan: carried 172 personnel, 43 vehicles, 16 guns and 12 motor cycles

CIRCASSIA 11,136/37 Anchor - *LANDING SHIP, INFANTRY (LARGE) (personnel capacity 2,016)*: left Naples 21 Jan in TG 81.4: arrived X beachhead 22 Jan (US Force X)

DERBYSHIRE 11,660/35 Bibby - *LANDING SHIP, INFANTRY (LARGE) (personnel capacity 2,566)*: left Naples 21 Jan in assault group D: arrived P beachhead 22 Jan

EMPIRE AUSTEN 7,057/42 *Honeyman - *MT/STORE SHIP*: left Naples 26 Jan in the follow-up convoy for Anzio, carrying British and American stores

FORT MEDUCTIC 7,134/43 *Morrison - *MT/STORE SHIP*: left Naples 26 Jan in the follow-up convoy for Anzio, carrying British and American stores

GLENGYLE 9,919/39 Glen Line - *HM LANDING SHIP, INFANTRY (LARGE) (personnel capacity 982)*: left Naples 21 Jan in assault group D: arrived P beachhead 22 Jan

HILARY A HERBERT 7,176/43 US (WSA) - *MT/STORE SHIP*: from Naples, listed to arrive Anzio 22 Jan, carrying British and American stores: suffered damage at Anzio, when an aircraft crashed into her starboard side at 1645 26 Jan and from a bomb explosion later the same day: subsequently towed to Naples by the tug PROSPEROUS

JOHN BANVARD 7,191/43 US (WSA) - *MT/STORE SHIP*: from Naples, listed to arrive Anzio 22 Jan, carrying British and American stores

LAWTON B EVANS 7,197/43 US (WSA) - *MT/STORE SHIP*: from Naples, listed to arrive Anzio 22 Jan, carrying British and American stores

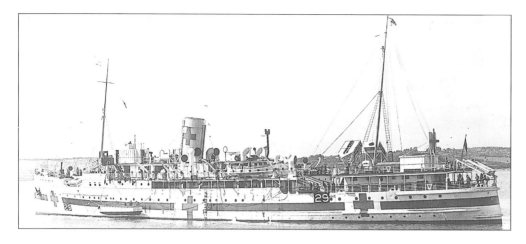

The hospital carrier ST JULIEN with a landing craft converted into a water ambulance.

PRINCESS BEATRIX 4,135/39 Dutch (Zeeland) PRINSES BEATRIX - *HM LANDING SHIP, INFANTRY (MEDIUM) (personnel capacity 400)*: left Naples 21 Jan in TG 81.2: arrived X beachhead 22 Jan: carried US Rangers (US Force X)

ROYAL ULSTERMAN 3,244/36 Burns & Laird - *HM LANDING SHIP, INFANTRY (HAND HOISTING) (personnel capacity 450)*: left Naples 21 Jan in TG 81.2: arrived X beachhead 22 Jan: carried US Rangers (US Force X)

SAMUEL HUNTINGTON 7,181/42 US (WSA) - *MT/STORE SHIP*: left Naples 28 Jan in the follow-up convoy for Anzio, carrying British and American stores: extensively damaged by bombs at Anzio 29 Jan and blew up early the following day

SOBIESKI 11,030/39 Polish (Gdynia-America) - *LANDING SHIP, INFANTRY (LARGE) (personnel capacity 1,684)*: left Naples 21 Jan in assault group D: arrived P beachhead 22 Jan

THRUSTER - *HM LANDING SHIP, TANK*: left Naples 21 Jan: arrived P beachhead 22 Jan: embarked a further 368 personnel from LST 301 off the beachhead to make a total of 720 personnel and 39 vehicles

WINCHESTER CASTLE 20,012/30 Union-Castle - *LANDING SHIP, INFANTRY (LARGE) (personnel capacity 1,100)*: left Naples 21 Jan in TG 81.2: arrived X beachhead 22 Jan: carried US Rangers (US Force X)

Hospital Carriers

DINARD 2,313/24 Southern Railway - left Naples 25 Jan: arrived Anzio 27 Jan

LEINSTER 4,303/37 Coast - left Naples 23 Jan: arrived Anzio 24 Jan: forward davit on starboard side hit during a bombing attack at 1810 same day: water ambulance, which caught fire, was set adrift: left for Naples same day with 100 survivors from the hospital carrier ST DAVID aboard

ST ANDREW 2,702/32 *G W Railway - left Naples 23 Jan: arrived Anzio, where near missed during three air attacks 24 Jan: rescued 60 survivors from the hospital carrier ST DAVID and left for Naples same day

ST DAVID 2,702/32 *G W Railway - left Naples 22 Jan: arrived Anzio 23 Jan: whilst fully illuminated, hit by a bomb aft at 1922 24 Jan: with vessel's bottom thought to have been holed and her engine room shattered, she sank by the stern in five minutes: survivors were rescued by the hospital carriers LEINSTER and ST ANDREW

ST JULIEN 1,952/25 G W Railway - left Naples 22 Jan: arrived Anzio 23 Jan and landed supplies of blankets and stretchers: with 41 patients aboard, left for Naples same day

Unnamed naval vessels carrying personnel and equipment

LANDING SHIPS, TANK
LST 11, 303, 304, 320, 324, 326, *327, 351, 361, 381, 404, 430 [*US] - all left Salerno 21 Jan in assault group B: arrived P beachhead 22 Jan. LST 11, 320 - both damaged 22 Jan

LST *33, *36, 63, 65, 362, 363, 368, 401, 402, 403, 405, 407, 409, 413, 416, 421, 422, 425 [*Greek] - all left Naples 21 Jan in assault group C: arrived P beachhead 22 Jan but, owing to delays and shelling at P beachhead, some moved to X beachhead for discharge. LST 363 - suffered casualties from cannon fire and a bomb near miss 1638 22 Jan: LST 422 - mined and gutted by fire 26 Jan

LST 410 - left Naples 21 Jan in TG 81.2: entered Anzio harbour 22 Jan (US Force X)

Other participants included -
LST 8, 9, 12, 62, 159, 160, 161, 162, 163, 164, 199, 301, 302, 305, 319, 321, 322, 364, 365, 366, 367, 406, 408, 412, 415, 418, 419, 420, 423, 426, 428

LANDING CRAFT, INFANTRY (LARGE)
LCI(L) 6, 99, 108, 111, 116, 119, 122, 163, 170, 174, 176, 184, 186, 210, 243, 244, 248, 251, 254, 273, 278, 283, 290, 316 - all left Naples 21 Jan in assault group C: arrived P beachhead 22 Jan: owing to delays and shelling at P beachhead, some moved to X beachhead for discharge

LCI(L) 147, 175, 303, 307, 308 (and two more craft: numbers unknown) - all left Naples 21 Jan in assault group D: arrived P beachhead 22 Jan

LANDING CRAFT, TANK
LCT 16, 24, 26, 31, 125, 136, 137, 152, 217, 219 - all left Salerno 20 Jan in assault group A: arrived P beachhead 22 Jan

LCT 140, 148, 210, 224, 237, 277, 340 (and two more craft: numbers unknown) - all left Salerno 21 Jan in assault group E: arrived P beachhead 22 Jan

Other participating craft included -
LCT 344, 579, 607, 615 - all left Naples 21 Jan: arrived Anzio 22 Jan

Naval vessels in support

CRUISERS
DIDO - left Naples 21 Jan: carried out a diversionary bombardment near Civitavecchia that night: provided bombardment support at X beachhead 29 Jan

ORION - left Naples 21 Jan: arrived P beachhead 22 Jan: provided bombardment support 22-23 Jan

PENELOPE - left Naples 21 Jan in TG 81.8: arrived X beachhead 22 Jan (US Force X)

SPARTAN - left Naples 21 Jan: arrived P beachhead 22 Jan: provided bombardment support 22-23 Jan: after arriving Anzio on 27 Jan on a second visit, vessel was hit by a glider bomb at 1756 29 Jan and sank at 1905 same day, with massive casualties: survivors were taken to Naples in the cruiser DIDO

GUNBOATS
FLORES, SOEMBA - both Dutch: left Naples 22 Jan: arrived X beachhead same day (US Force X)

LANDING SHIP, HEADQUARTERS
BULOLO - left Naples 21 Jan in assault group D: arrived P beachhead 22 Jan: served as stand-by fighter direction ship

FIGHTER DIRECTION SHIPS
PALOMARES - left Naples 21 Jan in assault group D: arrived P beachhead 22 Jan: served as stand-by fighter direction ship: at 0830 same day, struck a mine and began to settle by the stern, with her propeller and rudder out of action: left for Naples same day in tow of the tugs EDENSHAW AND EVEA

ULSTER QUEEN - left Naples 21 Jan: arrived at the beachhead 22 Jan: served as the main fighter direction ship

DESTROYERS
BEAUFORT - from Naples, listed for assault group C to arrive P beachhead 22 Jan

BRECON - left Naples 21 Jan with assault group C: arrived P beachhead 22 Jan

CRETE - see KRITI

CROOME - left Naples 21 Jan in TG 81.6 to arrive X beachhead 22 Jan (US Force X)

FAULKNOR, GRENVILLE - both from Naples, listed for assault group D to arrive P beachhead 22 Jan

INGLEFIELD - left Naples 21 Jan: carried out a diversionary bombardment near Civitavecchia that night

JANUS - left Naples 21 Jan with assault group B: arrived P beachhead 22 Jan: provided bombardment support 22-23 Jan: at 1746 23 Jan, a hit by an aerial torpedo caused her forward magazines to explode and the ship to sink at 1819 same day: survivors were rescued by the destroyer JERVIS and small craft

JERVIS - left Naples 21 Jan with assault group B: arrived P beachhead 22 Jan: provided bombardment support 22-23 Jan: at 1750 23 Jan, hit right forward by a glider bomb with removed a few feet of her bow: rescued survivors from JANUS same day

KEMPENFELT - left Naples 21 Jan: carried out a diversionary bombardment near Civitavecchia that night

KRITI (CRETE) - Greek ex HMS HURSLEY: left Naples 21 Jan to arrive X beachhead 22 Jan (US Force X)

LAFOREY - left Naples 21 Jan with assault group D: arrived P beachhead 22 Jan: provided bombardment support 22-24 Jan

LE FANTASQUE - Free French: from Naples, carried out a diversionary bombardment near Civitavecchia night of 21-22 Jan

LOYAL - left Naples 21 Jan with assault group D to arrive P beachhead 22 Jan

TETCOTT - left Naples 21 Jan with assault group C: arrived P beachhead 22 Jan

THEMISTOKLIS - Greek ex HMS BRAMHAM: left Naples 21 Jan in TG 81.6 to arrive X beachhead 22 Jan (US Force X)

ULSTER - left Naples 21 Jan with assault group C to arrive P beachhead 22 Jan

URCHIN - from Naples, listed for assault group C to arrive P beachhead 22 Jan

BEACON SUBMARINES
ULTOR - left Naples 20 Jan for P beachhead

The minesweeper FLY. [MPL 2654]

UPROAR - left Naples 20 Jan for X beachhead (US Force X)

MINESWEEPERS
ACUTE, **ALBACORE** - both from Salerno, listed for assault group B to arrive P beachhead 22 Jan

BRAVE - from Naples, replacing STORNOWAY, listed for assault group A to arrive P beachhead 22 Jan

BUDE - left Salerno 21 Jan to arrive P beachhead 22 Jan

CADMUS, **CIRCE**, **ESPIEGLE**, **FLY**, **MUTINE** - all from Salerno, listed for assault group B to arrive P beachhead 22 Jan

RINALDO - from Salerno, replacing BRIXHAM, listed for assault group A to arrive P beachhead 22 Jan

ROTHESAY - from Salerno, listed for assault group A to arrive P beachhead 22 Jan

WATERWITCH - from Salerno, replacing POLRUAN, listed for assault group A to arrive P beachhead 22 Jan

TRAWLERS
HORNPIPE - left Naples 21 Jan with assault group C: arrived P beachhead 22 Jan

ST KILDA, **SHEPPEY** - both from Salerno, listed for assault group A to arrive P beachhead 22 Jan

TWO STEP - from Salerno, listed for assault group E to arrive P beachhead 22 Jan

BOOM DEFENCE VESSEL
BARNDALE - left Naples 21 Jan: entered Anzio harbour 22 Jan: went alongside the sinking cruiser SPARTAN 29 Jan

TUGS
EDENSHAW, **EVEA** - both US: left Naples 21 Jan: arrived P beachhead 22 Jan: both left for Naples same day with the fighter direction ship PALOMARES in tow

PROSPEROUS - assigned to X beachhead (US Force X): towed the cargo ship HILARY A HERBERT to Naples

WEAZEL - towed a pontoon from Naples: arrived Anzio 22 Jan

LANDING CRAFT, INFANTRY (HEADQUARTERS)
LCI(H) 97, **232** - both left Naples 21 Jan in assault group B to arrive P beachhead 22 Jan

MOTOR LAUNCHES
ML 121, **134**, **462**, **554** - all from Salerno, listed for assault group A to arrive P beachhead 22 Jan

ML 338, **558**, **569** - all from Salerno, listed for assault group B to arrive P beachhead 22 Jan

ML 295, **307**, **443**, **565**, **567**, **573**, **575**, **581**

LANDING CRAFT, FLAK
Participating craft included -
LCF 14, **16** - both left Salerno 20 Jan with assault group A: arrived P beachhead 22 Jan

LANDING CRAFT, GUN
Participating craft included -
LCG 14, **19** - both left Salerno 20 Jan with assault group A: arrived P beachhead 22 Jan

LANDING CRAFT, TANK (ROCKET)
Participating craft included -
LCT(R) 167 - left Salerno 20 Jan with assault group A: arrived P beachhead 22 Jan and provided bombardment support same day

LANDING CRAFT, INFANTRY (REPAIR)
LCI 219 - from Naples, listed for assault group D to arrive P beachhead 22 Jan

LANDING CRAFT, TANK (BEACH REPAIR)
LCT 160, **170** - both from Salerno, listed for assault group E to arrive P beachhead 22 Jan

LANDING CRAFT, TANK (SALVAGE)
LCT 288 - from Salerno, listed for assault group A to arrive P beachhead 22 Jan

BALLOON TENDER
FT 6 - left Salerno 21 Jan in assault group E to arrive P beachhead 22 Jan

B8. THE SOUTH OF FRANCE: 15 AUGUST 1944

CAMERONIA. [Wright & Logan]

Named vessels carrying personnel, equipment and supplies

NAME OF SHIP Gross tonnage/Year of build Owner of *Managers, if British or Nationality (and owner or *managers) - *WARTIME FUNCTION* [HM = His Majesty's commissioned ship: MT Ship = Cargo ship assigned primarily for carrying military vehicles]

ASCANIA 14,013/25 Cunard White Star - *LANDING SHIP, INFANTRY (LARGE)*: left Naples 13 Aug in assault convoy SF1A: arrived Delta beachhead 15 Aug: carried 2,067 personnel

BATORY 14,287/36 Polish (Gdynia-America) - *LANDING SHIP, PERSONNEL*: left Taranto 12 Aug in follow-up convoy TF1: arrived Delta beachhead 16 Aug: carried 1,638 personnel

BRUISER - *HM LANDING SHIP, TANK*: left Oran 11 Aug in Special No 2 assault convoy: arrived Delta beachhead 15 Aug: carried 350 personnel and 50 vehicles

CAMERONIA 16,297/20 Anchor - *PERSONNEL SHIP*: left Taranto 12 Aug in follow-up convoy TF1: arrived Delta beachhead 16 Aug: carried 3,060 personnel

CHERTSEY 5,998/43 *Watts, Watts - *MT SHIP*: loaded at Taranto 3-4 Aug and left there 10 Aug in follow-up convoy TM1: arrived Delta beachhead 16 Aug: carried 294 personnel and 124 vehicles

CHISWICK 6,006/43 *Watts, Watts - *MT SHIP*: left

Naples 17 Aug in follow-up convoy SM3 to arrive Camel beachhead 20 Aug

CIRCASSIA 11,136/37 Anchor - *LANDING SHIP, INFANTRY (LARGE)*: left Taranto 12 Aug in follow-up convoy TF1: arrived Delta beachhead 16 Aug: carried 1,983 personnel

COULGORM 6,997/42 Dornoch - *MT SHIP*: loaded at Brindisi 1-4 Aug: left Taranto 10 Aug in follow-up convoy TM1: arrived Delta beachhead 16 Aug: carried 255 personnel and 127 vehicles

DERBYSHIRE 11,660/35 Bibby - *LANDING SHIP, INFANTRY (LARGE)*: left Naples 13 Aug in assault convoy SF1B: arrived Alpha beachhead 15 Aug: carried 2,237 personnel

DILWARA 11,080/36 British India - *LANDING SHIP, INFANTRY (LARGE)*: left Naples 13 Aug in assault convoy SF1A: arrived Delta beachhead 15 Aug: carried 1,770 personnel

DUNERA 11,162/37 British India - *LANDING SHIP, INFANTRY (LARGE)*: left Naples 13 Aug in assault convoy SF1B: arrived Alpha beachhead 15 Aug: carried 1,563 personnel

DURBAN CASTLE 17,388/38 Union-Castle - *PERSONNEL SHIP*: left Taranto 12 Aug in follow-up convoy TF1: arrived Alpha beachhead 16 Aug: carried 2,570 personnel

EASTERN PRINCE 10,926/29 Prince - *PERSONNEL SHIP*: left Taranto 12 Aug in follow-up convoy TF1: arrived Delta beachhead 16 Aug: carried 1,213 personnel

EMPIRE CLARION 7,031/42 *Ropner - *MT SHIP*: loaded at Brindisi 28-29 Jul: left Taranto 10 Aug in follow-up convoy TM1: arrived Alpha beachhead 16 Aug: carried 281 personnel and 117 vehicles

EMPIRE LORD 7,359/44 *Runciman - *MT SHIP*: left Naples 17 Aug in follow-up convoy SM3 to arrive Delta beachhead 20 Aug

EMPIRE NOBLE 7,125/44 *Langdon Rees - *MT SHIP*: loaded at Taranto 25-27 Jul and left there 10 Aug in follow-up convoy TM1: arrived Alpha beachhead 16 Aug: carried 278 personnel, 127 vehicles and 36 tons stores

EMPIRE OUTPOST 6,978/43 *Ropner - *MT SHIP*: loaded at Brindisi 28-29 Jul: left Taranto 10 Aug in follow-up convoy TM1: arrived Alpha beachhead 16 Aug: carried 286 personnel and 129 vehicles

EMPIRE PRIDE 9,248/41 *Bibby - *LANDING SHIP, PERSONNEL*: left Taranto 12 Aug in follow-up convoy TF1: arrived Alpha beachhead 16 Aug: carried 2,322 personnel

EMPIRE ROSALIND 7,290/43 *Runciman - *MT/STORE SHIP*: loaded at Taranto 25-30 Jul and left there 10 Aug in follow-up convoy TM1: arrived Alpha beachhead 16 Aug: carried 279 personnel, 106 vehicles and 1,225 tons stores

EMPIRE UNICORN 7,067/43 *Maclay & McIntyre - *MT SHIP*: loaded at Taranto 25-26 Jul and left there 10 Aug in follow-up convoy TM1: arrived Alpha beachhead 16 Aug: carried 303 personnel, 95 vehicles and 45 tons stores

ESSEX TRADER 7,237/43 *Trader Navigation - *MT SHIP*: loaded at Taranto 4-6 Aug and left there 10 Aug in follow-up convoy TM1: arrived Delta beachhead 16 Aug: carried 295 personnel, 120 vehicles and 53 tons stores: suffered many casualties when ship hit by at least 15 anti-personnel bombs 1830 same day

FORT AKLAVIK 7,132/43 *Dodd, Thomson - *MT/STORE SHIP*: loaded at Taranto 25-30 Jul and left there 10 Aug in follow-up convoy TM1: arrived Alpha beachhead 16 Aug: carried 293 personnel, 120 vehicles and 1,200 tons stores

FORT BEAUSEJOUR 7,151/43 *Ropner - *MT/STORE SHIP*: loaded at Taranto 25-29 Jul and left there 10 Aug in follow-up convoy TM1: arrived Alpha beachhead 16 Aug: carried 270 personnel, 117 vehicles and 1,213 tons stores

FORT CHESTERFIELD 7,127/43 *Hain - *MT SHIP*: loaded at Taranto 3-4 Aug and left there 10 Aug in follow-up convoy TM1: arrived Alpha beachhead 16 Aug: carried 303 personnel, 114 vehicles and 57 tons stores

FORT CUMBERLAND 7,134/43 *Lyle - *MT SHIP*: loaded at Taranto 1-3 Aug and left there 10 Aug in follow-up convoy TM1: arrived Alpha beachhead 16 Aug: carried 271 personnel, 118 vehicles and 46 tons stores

FORT FROBISHER 7,134/43 *Maclay & McIntyre - *MT SHIP*: loaded at Brindisi 25-27 Jul and left Taranto 10 Aug in follow-up convoy TM1: arrived Alpha beachhead 16 Aug: carried 297 personnel and 121 vehicles

FORT FRONTENAC 7,148/43 *J & C Harrison - *MT/STORE SHIP*: loaded at Taranto 25-30 Jul and left there 10 Aug in follow-up convoy TM1: arrived Alpha beachhead 16 Aug: carried 266 personnel, 127 vehicles and 1,173 tons stores

FORT GASPEREAU 7,134/43 *Watts, Watts - *MT SHIP*: loaded at Brindisi 2-4 Aug: left Taranto 10 Aug in follow-up convoy TM1: arrived Delta beachhead 16 Aug: carried 297 personnel and 127 vehicles: grounded 17 Aug but refloated the following day

FORT GRAHAME 7,133/43 *Sutherland - *MT SHIP*: loaded at Brindisi 2-4 Aug: left Taranto 10 Aug in follow-up convoy TM1: arrived Delta beachhead 16 Aug: carried 281 personnel and 112 vehicles

FORT HALL 7,157/43 *E R Management - *MT SHIP*: left Naples 17 Aug in follow-up convoy SM3 to arrive Delta beachhead 20 Aug

FORT MAISONNEUVE 7,128/42 *Chellew - *MT/STORE SHIP*: loaded at Taranto 31 Jul-4 Aug and left there 10 Aug in follow-up convoy TM1: arrived Delta beachhead 16 Aug: carried 168 personnel, 124 vehicles and 1,080 tons stores: hit by anti-personnel bombs 1830 same day

FORT MARIN 7,159/43 *E R Management - *MT SHIP*: loaded at Brindisi 25-27 Jul and left Taranto 10 Aug in follow-up convoy TM1: arrived Alpha beachhead 16 Aug: carried 292 personnel and 124 vehicles

FORT MICHIPICOTEN 7,152/43 *Maclay & McIntyre - *MT SHIP*: loaded at Taranto 6-8 Aug and left there 10 Aug in follow-up convoy TM1: arrived Delta beachhead 16 Aug: carried 289 personnel, 126 vehicles and 46 tons stores

FORT PEMBINA 7,134/42 *Billmeir - *MT SHIP*: loaded at Taranto 4-7 Aug and left there 10 Aug in follow-up convoy TM1: arrived Delta beachhead 16 Aug: carried 260 personnel, 126 vehicles and 109 tons stores

FORT RICHELIEU 7,150/43 *Radcliffe - *MT SHIP*:

KEREN as KENYA. [A Duncan]

loaded at Brindisi 31 Jul-2 Aug and left Taranto 10 Aug in follow-up convoy TM1: arrived Delta beachhead 16 Aug: carried 299 personnel and 130 vehicles

FORT STAGER 7,132/43 *Ropner - *MT SHIP*: loaded at Taranto 31 Jul-2 Aug and left there 10 Aug in follow-up convoy TM1: arrived Delta beachhead 16 Aug: carried 227 personnel, 112 vehicles and 57 tons stores

HARLESDEN 7,273/43 Hain - *MT SHIP*: loaded at Brindisi 28-29 Jul and left Taranto 10 Aug in follow-up convoy TM1: arrived Alpha beachhead 16 Aug: carried 226 personnel and 108 vehicles

JAN LIEVENS 7,178/42 Dutch (Koninklijke Nederlandsche) ex British OCEAN MERCHANT - *MT SHIP*: loaded at Naples 5-8 Aug and left there 13 Aug in follow-up convoy SM2: arrived Camel beachhead 15 Aug: carried 206 personnel and 88 land and amphibious vehicles

JERSEY HART 7,275/43 Stanhope - *MT SHIP*: loaded at Brindisi 28-31 Jul: left Taranto 10 Aug in follow-up convoy TM1: arrived Alpha beachhead 16 Aug: carried 266 personnel and 128 vehicles

KEREN 9,890/30 British India KENYA - *HM LANDING SHIP, INFANTRY (LARGE)*: left Naples 13 Aug in assault convoy SF1: arrived Camel beachhead 15 Aug: carried 1,114 personnel

NORMAN MONARCH 7,005/43 Monarch - *MT SHIP*: loaded at Taranto 1-3 Aug and left there 10 Aug in follow-up convoy TM1: arrived Alpha beachhead 16 Aug: carried 269 personnel, 118 vehicles and 37 tons stores

OCEAN GALLANT 7,178/42 *Turnbull, Scott - *MT SHIP*: loaded at Brindisi 25-26 Jul: left Taranto 10 Aug in follow-up convoy TM1: arrived Alpha beachhead 16 Aug: carried 268 personnel and 117 vehicles

OCEAN GLORY 7,178/42 *J & C Harrison - *MT SHIP*: loaded at Taranto 6-8 Aug and left there 10 Aug in follow-up convoy TM1: arrived Delta beachhead 16 Aug: carried 289 personnel, 113 vehicles and 29 tons stores

OCEAN GYPSY 7,178/42 *J & C Harrison - *MT SHIP*: loaded at Taranto 5-7 Aug and left there 10 Aug in follow-up convoy TM1: arrived Delta beachhead 16 Aug: carried 315 personnel and 124 vehicles

OCEAN MESSENGER 7,178/42 *Watts, Watts - *MT/STORE SHIP*: loaded at Taranto 31 Jul-4 Aug and left there 10 Aug in follow-up convoy TM1: arrived Delta beachhead 16 Aug: carried 291 personnel, 118 vehicles and 1,189 tons stores

OCEAN PRIDE 7,173/42 *Reardon Smith - *MT SHIP*: loaded at Brindisi 31 Jul-3 Aug: left Taranto 10 Aug in follow-up convoy TM1: arrived Delta beachhead 16 Aug: carried 248 personnel and 110 vehicles

OCEAN RIDER 7,178/42 *Larrinaga - *MT/STORE SHIP*: loaded at Taranto 1-6 Aug, during which time cargo in No 5 lower hold became fire damaged and was replaced: left Taranto 10 Aug in follow-up convoy TM1:

arrived Delta beachhead 16 Aug: carried 295 personnel, 119 vehicles and 1,287 tons stores

OCEAN TRAVELLER 7,178/42 *Lyle - *MT/STORE SHIP*: loaded at Taranto 31 Jul-4 Aug and left there 10 Aug in follow-up convoy TM1: arrived Delta beachhead 16 Aug: carried 304 personnel, 116 vehicles and 1,142 tons stores

OCEAN VESPER 7,174/42 *Connell & Grace - *MT SHIP*: loaded at Taranto 28 Jul-1 Aug and left there 10 Aug in follow-up convoy TM1: arrived Alpha beachhead 16 Aug: carried 300 personnel, 102 vehicles and 103 tons stores

PRINCE BAUDOUIN 3,219/34 Belgian - *HM LANDING SHIP, INFANTRY (SMALL) (personnel capacity 384)*: left Naples 11 Aug and Propriano 14 Aug in assault convoy SY1: arrived Sitka area same day

PRINCE DAVID 6,892/30 Canadian - *HM Canadian LANDING SHIP, INFANTRY (MEDIUM)*: left Naples 11 Aug and Propriano 14 Aug in assault convoy SY1: arrived Sitka area same day: carried 248 personnel

PRINCE HENRY 6,893/30 Canadian NORTH STAR - *HM Canadian LANDING SHIP, INFANTRY (MEDIUM)*: left Naples 10 Aug, Castellabate 11 Aug and Propriano

14 Aug in assault convoy SY1: arrived Sitka area same day: carried 279 personnel

PRINCESS BEATRIX 4,135/39 Dutch (Zeeland) PRINSES BEATRIX - *HM LANDING SHIP, INFANTRY (MEDIUM) (personnel capacity 400)*: left Naples 11 Aug and Propriano 14 Aug in assault convoy SY1: arrived Sitka area same day

PRINS ALBERT 2,938/37 Belgian - *HM LANDING SHIP, INFANTRY (SMALL) (personnel capacity 507)*: left Naples 11 Aug and Propriano 14 Aug in assault convoy SY1: arrived Sitka area same day

SAMBLADE 7,219/43 *Port - *MT SHIP*: left Naples 17 Aug in follow-up convoy SM3 to arrive Alpha beachhead 20 Aug

SAMBRE 7,219/43 *Cunard White Star - *MT SHIP*: loaded at Brindisi 25-27 Jul: left Taranto 10 Aug in follow-up convoy TM1: arrived Alpha beachhead 16 Aug: carried 280 personnel and 135 vehicles

SAMDAK 7,219/43 *Moss Hutchison - *MT SHIP*: left Naples 17 Aug in follow-up convoy SM3 to arrive Delta beachhead 20 Aug

SAMFLEET 7,219/44 *Weir - *MT SHIP*: late replacement for THISTLEMUIR, which withdrawn after

PRINSES BEATRIX post-war (above) and (below) as the Landing Ship, Infantry PRINCESS BEATRIX. [A Duncan/NMM N31947]

SOBIESKI. [A Duncan]

a bunker fire: loaded at Taranto 7-8 Aug and left there 10 Aug in follow-up convoy TM1: arrived Alpha beachhead 16 Aug: carried 325 personnel, 140 vehicles and 63 tons stores

SAMGLORY 7,210/44 *Dodd, Thomson - *MT SHIP*: left Naples 17 Aug in follow-up convoy SM3 to arrive Alpha beachhead 20 Aug

SAMINGOY 7,255/44 *New Zealand Shipping - *MT SHIP*: left Naples 17 Aug in follow-up convoy SM3 to arrive Camel beachhead 20 Aug

SAMKEY 7,219/43 *New Zealand Shipping - *MT SHIP*: left Naples 17 Aug in follow-up convoy SM3 to arrive Alpha beachhead 20 Aug

SAMOA 7,219/43 *Alfred Holt - *MT SHIP*: loaded at Brindisi 25-26 Jul: left Taranto 10 Aug in follow-up convoy TM1: arrived Alpha beachhead 16 Aug: carried 289 personnel and 140 vehicles

SAMPAN 7,219/43 *Union-Castle - *MT SHIP*: loaded at Brindisi 28-29 Jul: left Taranto 10 Aug in follow-up convoy TM1: arrived Alpha beachhead 16 Aug: carried 251 personnel and 123 vehicles

SAMPFORD 7,219/43 *Weir - *MT SHIP*: left Naples 17 Aug in follow-up convoy SM3 to arrive Delta beachhead 20 Aug

SAMSTEEL 7,219/43 *Union-Castle - *MT SHIP*: loaded at Taranto 1-3 Aug and left there 10 Aug in

follow-up convoy TM1: arrived Delta beachhead 16 Aug: carried 245 personnel and 129 vehicles

SAMTRUTH 7,210/44 *Haldin & Philipps - *MT SHIP*: left Naples 17 Aug in follow-up convoy SM3 to arrive Camel beachhead 20 Aug

SAMWASH 7,219/43 *Weir - *MT SHIP*: loaded at Naples 3-6 Aug and left there 13 Aug in follow-up convoy SM2: arrived Camel beachhead 15 Aug: carried 243 personnel and 80 land and amphibious vehicles

SOBIESKI 11,030/39 Polish (Gdynia America) - *LANDING SHIP, INFANTRY (LARGE)*: left Taranto 12 Aug in follow-up convoy TF1: arrived Alpha beachhead 16 Aug: carried 1,795 personnel

STAFFORDSHIRE 10,701/29 Bibby - *PERSONNEL SHIP*: left Taranto 12 Aug in follow-up convoy TF1: arrived Alpha beachhead 16 Aug: carried 2,227 personnel

TAKLIWA 7,936/24 British India - *PERSONNEL SHIP (capacity 1,334)*: left Taranto 12 Aug in follow-up convoy TF1: arrived Delta beachhead 16 Aug

THISTLEDALE 7,241/42 *Allan, Black - *MT SHIP*: loaded at Brindisi 31 Jul-2 Aug: left Taranto 10 Aug in follow-up convoy TM1: arrived Delta beachhead 16 Aug: carried 292 personnel, 123 vehicles and 34 tons stores

THRUSTER - *HM LANDING SHIP, TANK*: left Oran 11 Aug in Special No 2 assault convoy: arrived Delta beachhead 15 Aug: landed 423 personnel and 53 vehicles

VAN DER CAPELLE 7,037/42 Dutch (*Holland-Amerika) ex British EMPIRE RUSKIN - *MT SHIP*: loaded at Taranto 28-30 Jul and left there 10 Aug in follow-up convoy TM1: arrived Delta beachhead 16 Aug: carried 280 personnel, 118 vehicles and 68 tons stores: grounded 17 Aug but refloated following day

VOLENDAM 15,434/22 Dutch (Holland-Amerika) - *PERSONNEL SHIP*: left Taranto 12 Aug in follow-up convoy TF1: arrived Alpha beachhead 16 Aug: carried 2,803 personnel

WINCHESTER CASTLE 20,012/30 Union-Castle - *LANDING SHIP, INFANTRY (LARGE)*: left Oran 11 Aug in Special No 2 assault convoy: arrived Camel beachhead 15 Aug: carried 617 personnel

WORCESTERSHIRE 11,402/31 Bibby - *PERSONNEL SHIP*: left Taranto 12 Aug in follow-up convoy TF1: arrived Delta beachhead 16 Aug: carried 2,894 personnel

Other merchant ships including Royal Fleet Auxiliaries and British-controlled French and Italian naval tankers

CARA 1,760/29 *Glen & Co - *NAVAL COLLIER*: from Taranto, left Ajaccio 15 Aug for Delta beachhead

CELEROL 2,649/17 Admiralty - *OILER*: carrying diesel and lubricants, left Maddalena 14 Aug: failed to locate assigned assault convoy SM2 so sailed unescorted: arrived Delta beachhead 15 Aug

DEWDALE 8,265/41 Admiralty - *LANDING SHIP, GANTRY*: carrying 14 landing craft, fuel oil, diesel and water, left Naples 12 Aug in assault convoy SM1: arrived Camel beachhead 15 Aug: near missed by a rocket bomb 2100 same day

ELISE 7,910/31 Norwegian (*Bech) - *TANKER*: carrying fuel oil, listed to leave Naples 12 Aug for Camel beachhead

ELORN French Navy (British-controlled) - *TANKER*: carrying fuel oil, listed to leave Naples 12 Aug in assault convoy SM1 to arrive Alpha beachhead 15 Aug

EMPIRE ANN 232/43 *Townsend - *TUG*: listed to leave Naples 12 Aug: arrived Alpha beachhead to provide berthing assistance: towed LCT 552 to Calvi

EMPIRE DAMSEL 784/42 *Rowbotham - *TANKER*: carrying high octane fuel, listed to leave Maddalena 12 Aug to join assault convoy SM1 to arrive Camel beachhead 15 Aug

EMPIRE ELAINE 7,513/42 *Cayzer, Irvine - *LANDING SHIP, CARRIER*: loaded 20 landing craft in the Middle East: left Naples 12 Aug in assault convoy SM1B: arrived Alpha beachhead 15 Aug

EMPIRE FAUN 846/43 *Coastal Tankers - *WATER CARRIER*: from Naples, left Ajaccio 15 Aug for Alpha beachhead

EMPIRE FAY 814/43 *Hemsley Bell - *TANKER*: carrying high octane fuel, left Bizerta 4 Aug for Maddalena: from there, listed to join assault convoy SM1A: arrived Delta beachhead

EMPIRE GAWAIN 784/42 *Bulk Oil - *TANKER*: carrying diesel, left Naples 8 Aug for Maddalena: from there, listed to join assault convoy SM1B to arrive Alpha beachhead 15 Aug

EMPIRE HARP 861/42 *Coastal Tankers - *WATER CARRIER*: arrived Naples 6 Aug: listed to leave there 13 Aug: arrived Delta beachhead

EMPIRE LASS 813/41 *Rowbotham - *TANKER*: carrying high octane fuel, left Ajaccio 15 Aug for Alpha beachhead

EMPIRE SPITFIRE 232/43 *Townsend - *TUG*: listed to leave Naples 12 Aug for Alpha beachhead

ENNERDALE 8,219/41 Admiralty - *LANDING SHIP, GANTRY*: carrying 14 landing craft, 4,000 tons fuel oil, 1,035 tons diesel and 2,500 tons water, left Naples 12 Aug in assault convoy SM1A: arrived Delta beachhead 15 Aug

LE MEKONG French Navy (British-controlled) - *TANKER*: carrying fuel oil, arrived Naples 11 Aug: from there, listed to arrive Delta beachhead 19 Aug

MYRIEL 3,560/13 Euxine - *WATER CARRIER*: arrived Naples 11 Aug: listed to leave there 12 Aug in assault convoy SM1B: arrived at the beachhead only part loaded

PO Italian Navy (British-controlled) - *WATER CARRIER*: from Naples, left Ajaccio 15 Aug for Camel beachhead

SPINDLETOP 1,155/43 *Anglo-Saxon - *TANKER*: carrying diesel, left Ajaccio 15 Aug to arrive Camel beachhead 16 Aug

THELMA 1,593/35 *Glen & Co - *NAVAL COLLIER*: replacing AMSTEL, left Ajaccio 15 Aug for the beachhead

VAR French Navy (British-controlled) - *TANKER*: carrying fuel oil, arrived Naples 11 Aug: from there, listed to arrive Alpha beachhead 19 Aug

The cruiser ROYALIST.

Unnamed naval vessels carrying personnel and equipment

LANDING SHIP, TANK
LST 12

LANDING CRAFT, INFANTRY (LARGE)
LCI(L) 133, 247, 258, 259, 260, 264, 274, 278, 280, 283, 284, 289, 290, 292, 294, 297, 303, 314, 316, 318

LANDING CRAFT, TANK
LCT 307, 316, 321, 322, 325, 328, 330, 339, 344, 347, 356, 357, 361, 364, 377, 379, 380, 386, 388, 389, 396, 397, 401, 412, 420, 421, 445, 446, 535, 538, 540, 542, 548, 552, 554, 556, 560, 561, 563, 578, 581, 582, 585, 591, 592, 594, 595, 601, 607, 614, 615, 617, 620, 625, 702, 849. LCT 307 - damaged by shore gunfire and abandoned 15 Aug: LCT 339, 625 - damaged by shore gunfire 15 Aug: LCT 552 - engine room badly damaged by shore gunfire 15 Aug: LCT 591 - damaged in collision with the minesweeper BRAVE 16 Aug

Naval vessels in support

BATTLESHIP
RAMILLIES - left Algiers 13 Aug: arrived Alpha beachhead 15 Aug: provided bombardment support same day

ESCORT CARRIERS
ATTACKER, EMPEROR, HUNTER, KHEDIVE, PURSUER, SEARCHER, STALKER - all left Malta 12 Aug: arrived 30 miles off the beachhead 15 Aug, to provide spotting, strafing and bombing support

CRUISERS
AJAX - left Malta 13 Aug: arrived Alpha beachhead 15 Aug: provided bombardment support same day

ARGONAUT - from Palermo, arrived Camel beachhead 15 Aug: provided bombardment support same day

AURORA, BLACK PRINCE - both left Malta 13 Aug: arrived Alpha beachhead 15 Aug: provided bombardment support same day

CALEDON, COLOMBO, DELHI - all for anti-aircraft defence, left Malta 12 Aug with the carrier force: arrived at the beachhead 15 Aug

DIDO - left Naples 12 Aug and Propriano 14 Aug: arrived Sitka area same day: provided bombardment support 15-18 Aug

ORION - left Malta 13 Aug: arrived Alpha beachhead 15 Aug: provided bombardment support same day

ROYALIST - left Malta 12 Aug as carrier force flagship: arrived at the beachhead 15 Aug

SIRIUS - held at Naples as reserve ship and not used until 25 Aug

GUNBOATS
APHIS, SCARAB - both left Malta 5 Aug and Ajaccio 14 Aug with the Special Operations Group: carried out a diversionary bombardment east of the assault area 15 Aug

AIR-SEA RESCUE & FIGHTER DIRECTION SHIPS
ANTWERP - left Naples 12 Aug via Ajaccio in assault convoy SF2: detached just prior to the Straits of Bonifacio to act as beacon for the airborne assault and as air-sea rescue ship between Corsica and the beachhead area

STUART PRINCE - left Ajaccio 14 Aug: served as beacon for the airborne assault and as air-sea rescue ship, then assigned as a fighter direction and radar ship

ULSTER QUEEN - left Naples 12 Aug via Ajaccio in assault convoy SF2B: arrived Alpha beachhead 15 Aug as stand-by fighter direction ship

LANDING SHIPS, DOCK
EASTWAY - listed to leave Naples 13 Aug in assault convoy SF1 to arrive Camel beachhead 15 Aug

HIGHWAY - left Naples 13 Aug in assault convoy SF1B to arrive Alpha beachhead 15 Aug

DESTROYERS
ALDENHAM - left Naples 13 Aug with follow-up convoy SM2: arrived at the beachhead 15 Aug

ATHERSTONE - left Taranto 11 Aug: listed to leave Naples 17 Aug with follow-up convoy SM3 for the beachhead

BEAUFORT, **BELVOIR** - both left Naples 13 Aug with follow-up convoy SM2 to arrive at the beachhead 15 Aug

BICESTER - from Naples, listed for assault convoy SM1 to arrive Camel beachhead 15 Aug

BLACKMORE - left Naples 13 Aug with follow-up convoy SM2 to arrive at the beachhead 15 Aug

BRECON - from Naples, listed for follow-up convoy SM3 to arrive at the beachhead 20 Aug

CALPE - left Oran 10 Aug and Algiers 12 Aug with assault convoy AM1 to arrive at the beachhead 15 Aug

CATTERICK, **CLEVELAND** - both left Oran 10 Aug with assault convoy AM1: detached 13 Aug: rejoined 14 Aug to arrive at the beachhead 15 Aug

CRETE - see KRITI

EGGESFORD - left Naples 13 Aug with follow-up convoy SM2: arrived at the beachhead 15 Aug

FARNDALE - left Taranto 10 Aug and Ajaccio 15 Aug with follow-up convoy TM1 to arrive at the beachhead 16 Aug

HAYDON - listed for the operation: left Malta 13 Aug

KRITI (CRETE) - Greek ex HMS HURSLEY: from Naples, listed for assault convoy SF2A to arrive Delta beachhead 15 Aug

LAUDERDALE - left Naples 13 Aug with follow-up convoy SM2 to arrive at the beachhead 15 Aug

LIDDESDALE - from Naples, listed for assault convoy SM1A to arrive Delta beachhead 15 Aug

LOOKOUT - left Naples 12 Aug and Propriano 14 Aug with assault convoy SY1: arrived Sitka area same day: provided bombardment support 15 Aug

NAVARINON - Greek ex HMS ECHO: left Malta 12 Aug with the carrier force to arrive at the beachhead 15 Aug

OAKLEY - from Naples, listed for assault convoy SF2B to arrive Alpha beachhead 15 Aug

PINDOS - Greek: left Naples 13 Aug with follow-up convoy SM2 to arrive at the beachhead 15 Aug

The Hunt class destroyer WHEATLAND. [IWM A17366]

TEAZER, TENACIOUS - both left Malta 12 Aug with the carrier force to arrive at the beachhead 15 Aug

TERMAGENT, TERPISHORE - both left Malta 13 Aug: joined the battleship RAMILLIES 14 Aug: arrived Alpha beachhead 15 Aug: provided bombardment support same day

THEMISTOKLIS - Greek ex HMS BRAMHAM: left Naples 11 Aug with assault convoy SY1 to arrive Sitka area 14 Aug

TROUBRIDGE - left Malta 12 Aug with the carrier force to arrive at the beachhead 15 Aug

TUMULT - left Malta 12 Aug with the carrier force: detached 14 Aug

TUSCAN, TYRIAN - both left Malta 12 Aug with the carrier force to arrive at the beachhead 15 Aug

WHADDON - left Naples 13 Aug with follow-up convoy SM2 to arrive at the beachhead 15 Aug

WHEATLAND - left Algiers 10 Aug: replaced the destroyer TUMULT with the carrier force on 15 Aug

ZETLAND - from Naples, listed for assault convoy SS1 to arrive Camel beachhead 15 Aug

CORVETTES
AUBRETIA, COLUMBINE - both left Taranto 10 Aug with follow-up convoy TM1 to arrive at the beachhead 16 Aug

MINESWEEPERS
ANTARES, ARCTURUS - both left Naples 11 Aug for Salerno and assault convoy SF2A to arrive Delta beachhead 15 Aug

ARIES - replacing RHYL, left Naples 9 Aug with assault convoy SS1B: arrived beachhead 15 Aug: part of the flotilla which sank five small patrol vessels same day

BRAVE - left Naples 11 Aug for Salerno and assault convoy SF2A to arrive at the beachhead 15 Aug: damaged in collision with LCT 591 16 Aug

BRIXHAM - left Naples 9 Aug with assault convoy SS1B: arrived Alpha beachhead 15 Aug: part of the flotilla which sank five small patrol vessels same day

BUDE - left Naples 9 Aug with assault convoy SS1B: arrived Alpha beachhead 15 Aug

CLINTON, LARNE, OCTAVIA - all from Naples, left Propriano 13 Aug: arrived Sitka area 14 Aug

POLRUAN - left Naples 9 Aug with assault convoy SS1B: arrived Alpha beachhead 15 Aug: part of the flotilla which sank five small patrol vessels same day

RINALDO - joined assault convoy SF2A off Naples 12 Aug to arrive Delta beachhead 15 Aug

ROSARIO - left Naples 11 Aug for Salerno and assault convoy SF2A to arrive Delta beachhead 15 Aug

ROTHESAY - left Naples 9 Aug with assault convoy SS1B: arrived Alpha beachhead 15 Aug: part of the flotilla which sank five small patrol vessels same day

SPANKER - left Naples 11 Aug for Salerno and assault convoy SF2A to arrive Delta beachhead 15 Aug

SPEEDY - from Naples, listed for assault convoy SF2 to arrive at the beachhead 15 Aug

STORMCLOUD - from Naples, left Propriano 13 Aug: arrived Sitka area 14 Aug

STORNOWAY - left Naples 9 Aug with assault convoy SS1B: arrived Alpha beachhead 15 Aug: part of the flotilla which sank five small patrol vessels same day

WELFARE - from Naples, left Propriano 13 Aug: arrived Sitka area 14 Aug

TRAWLERS & WHALERS
AILSA CRAIG - from Naples, listed for assault convoy SM1 to arrive Camel beachhead 15 Aug

BOREALIS - as danlayer, from Maddalena, joined assault convoy SS1B: arrived Alpha beachhead 15 Aug

CALM - as danlayer, from Naples, listed for assault convoy SS1A to arrive Delta beachhead 15 Aug

CROWLIN - from Naples, listed for assault convoy SM1 to arrive Camel beachhead 15 Aug

FOULA, HASCOSAY - as danlayers, both from Naples, listed for assault convoy SS1 to arrive Camel beachhead 15 Aug

KINTYRE - as danlayer, from Naples, left Propriano 13 Aug: arrived Sitka area 14 Aug

MEWSTONE - for minesweeping, from Naples, listed for assault convoy SM1 to arrive Camel beachhead 15 Aug

NEBB - as danlayer, from Maddalena, joined assault convoy SS1B: arrived Alpha beachhead 15 Aug

PRODUCT - as repair ship, from Naples, listed to leave 12 Aug for the beachhead

SATSA - as danlayer, from Naples, listed for assault convoy SF1A to arrive Delta beachhead 15 Aug

SKOKHOLM - from Naples, listed for assault convoy SM1 to arrive Camel beachhead 15 Aug

BOOM DEFENCE VESSELS

BARDOLF - from Naples, listed for assault convoy SS1 to arrive Camel beachhead 15 Aug

BARHILL - from Naples, listed for assault convoy SS1A to arrive at the beachhead 15 Aug

BARHOLM - from Naples, listed for assault convoy SS1B to arrive Alpha beachhead 15 Aug

BARMOND - from Naples, listed for assault convoy SS1A to arrive Delta beachhead 15 Aug

BARRICADE - from Naples, listed for assault convoy SM1B to arrive Alpha beachhead 15 Aug

TUGS

ASPIRANT, **ATHLETE**, **CHARON** - all from Naples, listed for assault convoy SS1A to arrive Delta beachhead 15 Aug

MINDFUL, **VAGRANT** - both from Naples, listed for assault convoy SS1 to arrive Camel beachhead 15 Aug

LANDING CRAFT, HEADQUARTERS

LCH 240, **315** - both from Naples, listed for assault convoy SM1 to arrive at the beachhead 15 Aug. LCH 240 - return convoy control ship

FIGHTER DIRECTION TENDER

FDT 13 - from Naples, listed for assault convoy SM1A to arrive Delta beachhead 15 Aug

LANDING SHIP, EMERGENCY REPAIR

LSE 2 - from Naples, listed for assault convoy SM1 to arrive at the beachhead 15 Aug

MOTOR LAUNCHES

ML 121, **338**, **462**, **554**, **563**, **565** - all listed for assault convoy SS1 to arrive at the beachhead 15 Aug. ML 563 mined and lost 16 Aug

ML 273, **336**, **463** - all from Oran, listed to leave 15 Aug with US follow-up convoy AM2

ML 308, **337**, **451**, **456**, **461**, **478**, **576** - all from Ajaccio, listed to leave 14 Aug on special operations

ML 555, **556**, **557**, **559**, **560**, **564**, **567** - all from Naples, listed for assault convoy SS1A to arrive at the beachhead 14-15 Aug. ML 559 - arrived Sitka area 14 Aug: damaged by mine 15 Aug

ML 562 - from Naples, listed for assault convoy SS1B: arrived Sitka area 14 Aug: damaged by shore gunfire 19 Aug

ML 566, **568** - both arrived Delta beachhead 15 Aug

ML 299, **458**, **469**, **471**, **581**

MOTOR MINESWEEPERS

BYMS 2009, **2013**, **2014**, **2022**, **2024**, **2026**, **2027**, **2028**, **2171**, **2172** - all from Naples, listed for assault convoy SS1 to arrive at the beachhead 15 Aug. BYMS 2022 - damaged by mine 17 Aug

MMS 1, **3**, **8**, **13**, **17**, **18**, **23**, **24** - all arrived Delta beachhead 15 Aug

MOTOR FISHING VESSELS

MFV 47, **68**, **90**, **105**, **129**, **132** - all French-manned: from Ajaccio, listed to leave 13 Aug: MFV 47, 68 with assault convoy SS1B; 90, 105 with SS1A and 129, 132 with SS1. MFV 90 - carried petrol, diesel and lubricants

LANDING CRAFT, FLAK

LCF 4, **8**, **10**, **14**, **16**, **17** - all left Naples 9 Aug and Ajaccio 12 Aug: LCF 4, 8 in assault convoy SS1B; 10, 14 in SS1A and 16, 17 in SS1: arrived at the beachhead 15 Aug

LANDING CRAFT, GUN (LARGE)

LCG(L) 4, **8**, **12**, **14**, **20** - all from Naples, listed to leave 9 Aug: LCG(L) 4, 8 in assault convoy SS1B; 12, 14 in SS1A and 20 in SS1

LANDING CRAFT, INFANTRY (STORES)

LCI(L) 113, **161**, **253**, **257** - all from Naples via Salerno. LCI(L) 113 - assisted LCT 552 15 Aug; 161 - carried the LCT maintenance parties

LANDING CRAFT, TANK (ROCKET)

LCT(R) 140, **359**, **367**, **405**, **437**, **440** - all listed to leave Naples 9 Aug and Ajaccio 12 Aug in assault convoy SS1A to arrive at the beachhead 15 Aug

LCT(R) 136, **141**, **147**, **167**, **171**, **362**, **434**, **435**, **436**, **459** - all listed to leave Naples 9 Aug and Ajaccio 12 Aug in assault convoy SS1B to arrive at the beachhead 15 Aug

LCT(R) 366, **368**, **423**, **425**, **439**, **447**, **448**, **450**, **452**, **464**, **473**, **481**, **482**, **483** - all US-manned: from Naples, listed to leave Ajaccio 12 Aug in assault convoy SS1 to arrive at the beachhead 15 Aug

OTHER LANDING CRAFT, TANK

LCT (Balloon) 135, **164**, **169** - all listed to leave Naples 9 Aug: 135 in assault convoy SS1B; 164 in SS1A and 169 in SS1

LCT(RU) 160, **170** - both for salvage, listed to leave Naples 9 Aug, via Ajaccio: 160 in assault convoy SS1B and 170 in SS1A to arrive at the beachhead 15 Aug

LCT(Smoke) 9, **17** - both listed to leave Naples 9 Aug: 9 in assault convoy SS1B and 17 in SS1A to arrive at the beachhead 15 Aug

BALLOON TENDERS

FT 6, **30** - both listed to leave Naples 9 Aug: 6 in assault convoy SS1A and 30 in SS1B to arrive at the beachhead 15 Aug

B9. RANGOON, BURMA: 2 MAY 1945

GLENROY. [World Ship Photo Library]

Named ships carrying personnel, equipment and supplies

NAME OF SHIP Gross tonnage/Year of Build Owner or *Managers, if British, or Nationality (and *managers) - *WARTIME FUNCTION [HM = His Majesty's commissioned ship: MT Ship = Cargo ship assigned primarily for carrying military vehicles]*

BARPETA 3,194/14 British India - *LANDING SHIP, INFANTRY (LARGE) AND LANDING CRAFT DEPOT SHIP (personnel capacity 460)*: left Kyaukpyu 29 Apr in assault convoy Charlie: arrived Rangoon River 2 May, then served as depot ship

BELPAREIL 7,203/26 Norwegian (*Christen Smith) - *MT SHIP*: carrying 30 landing craft, left Bombay 24 Apr, Colombo 29 Apr and Kyaukpyu 8 May in build-up convoy KRS2: arrived Rangoon

CITY OF AUCKLAND 8,336/14 *Hall - *MT SHIP*: left Madras 6 May and Akyab 11 May in build-up convoy KRS4 to arrive Rangoon 14 May

DERBYSHIRE 11,660/35 Bibby - *PERSONNEL SHIP (capacity 2,613)*: left Madras 1 May and Kyaukpyu 9 May in build-up convoy KRF2: arrived Rangoon 11 May

DILWARA 11,080/36 British India - *PERSONNEL SHIP (capacity 2,186)*: from Calcutta, left Kyaukpyu 9 May in build-up convoy KRF2A: arrived Rangoon 11 May

DRAMATIST 5,443/20 *T & J Harrison - *STORE SHIP*: left Calcutta 30 Apr and Kyaukpyu 4 May in follow-up convoy KRS1A: arrived Rangoon

DUNERA 11,162/37 British India - *PERSONNEL SHIP (capacity 2,276)*: left Kyaukpyu 30 Apr in assault convoy Baker: arrived Rangoon River 2 May

EGRA 5,108/11 British India - *PERSONNEL SHIP (capacity 1,017)*: left Calcutta 2 May and Kyaukpyu 9 May in build-up convoy KRF2: arrived Rangoon 10 May

EKMA 5,108/11 British India - *PERSONNEL SHIP (capacity 1,183)*: left Calcutta 2 May and Kyaukpyu 9 May in build-up convoy KRF2: arrived Rangoon 11 May

ELLENGA 5,196/11 British India - *PERSONNEL SHIP (capacity 1,211)*: left Calcutta 5 May, Chittagong 8 May and Kyaukpyu 12 May in build-up convoy KRF4A: arrived Rangoon 14 May

EMPIRE CAPULET 7,044/43 *Glen Line - *MT SHIP*: left Calcutta 22 Apr and Kyaukpyu 4 May in follow-up convoy KRS1: arrived Rangoon

EMPIRE RANI 7,575/21 *British India ex German MARIENFELS - *MT/STORE SHIP*: loaded cased petrol at Calcutta and left there 22 Apr to load MT at Kyaukpyu: left there 29 Apr in assault convoy Charlie: arrived Rangoon River 2 May

ETHIOPIA 5,574/22 British India - *PERSONNEL SHIP (capacity 1,185)*: left Calcutta 8-9 May in build-up convoy KRF3: arrived Rangoon 14 May

GLENROY 9,809/38 Glen Line - *HM LANDING SHIP, INFANTRY (LARGE) (personnel capacity 980)*: left Kyaukpyu 30 Apr in assault convoy Baker: arrived Rangoon River 2 May: proceeded up river to Rangoon

6 May after second voyage from Kyaukpyu in follow-up convoy KRF1

HARPALYCE 7,269/42 Hain - *MT SHIP*: left Calcutta 7 May via Kyaukpyu in build-up convoy KRS3A: arrived Rangoon 14 May

IKAUNA 6,793/41 British India - *MT SHIP*: from Calcutta, left Kyaukpyu 8 May in build-up convoy KRS2: arrived Rangoon

ISLAMI 5,879/34 Mogul - *PERSONNEL SHIP (capacity 1,870)*: left Madras 4 May and Kyaukpyu 12 May in build-up convoy KRS4: arrived Rangoon 14 May

ITAURA 6,793/40 British India - *MT SHIP*: left Calcutta 7 May via Kyaukpyu in build-up convoy KRS3A: arrived Rangoon 14 May

ITOLA 6,793/40 British India - *MT/STORE SHIP*: loaded cased petrol at Calcutta and left there 28 Apr to load MT at Kyaukpyu: left there 4 May in follow-up convoy KRS1: arrived Rangoon

ITRIA 6,845/40 British India - *MT SHIP*: left Calcutta 26 Apr, Chittagong 29 Apr and Kyaukpyu 8 May in build-up convoy KRS2: arrived Rangoon

JALAVEERA 4,966/27 Scindia - *MT SHIP*: left Calcutta 2 May for Chittagong: left Kyaukpyu 12 May in build-up convoy KRS4 to arrive Rangoon 14 May

NANCHANG 2,489/22 China Navigation - *STORE SHIP*: from Chittagong, left Kyaukpyu 12 May in build-up convoy KRS4 to arrive Rangoon 14 May

NEVASA 9,213/13 British India - *PERSONNEL SHIP (capacity 1,822)*: left Calcutta 27 Apr, Akyab 29 Apr and Kyaukpyu 4 May in follow-up convoy KRF1 for Rangoon

ORNA 6,779/38 British India - *MT SHIP*: left Calcutta

7 May via Kyaukpyu in build-up convoy KRS3A: arrived Rangoon 14 May

PERSIMMON 8,244/44 Royal Mail PAMPAS - *HM LANDING SHIP, INFANTRY (LARGE) (personnel capacity 900)*: left Kyaukpyu 30 Apr in assault convoy Baker: arrived Rangoon River 2 May: listed for a second voyage from Kyaukpyu in follow-up convoy KRF1 for Rangoon

PRINS ALBERT 2,938/37 Belgian - *HM LANDING SHIP, INFANTRY (SMALL) (personnel capacity 350)*: left Kyaukpyu 30 Apr in assault convoy Baker: arrived Rangoon River 2 May: listed for a second voyage from Kyaukpyu in follow-up convoy KRF1 for Rangoon

RAJULA 8,478/26 British India - *PERSONNEL SHIP (capacity 1,621) AND HOSPITAL CARRIER*: left Madras 22 Apr and Kyaukpyu 30 Apr in assault convoy Baker: arrived Rangoon River 2 May: embarked released prisoners of war 4 May and left for Calcutta

RISALDAR 5,407/40 Asiatic - *MT/STORE SHIP*: loaded cased petrol at Calcutta and left there 22 Apr: loaded MT at Kyaukpyu and left there 29 Apr in assault convoy Charlie: arrived Rangoon River 2 May

SILVIO 7,177/43 ex EMPIRE HALBERD - *HM LANDING SHIP, INFANTRY (LARGE) (personnel capacity 1,000)*: left Kyaukpyu 30 Apr in assault convoy Baker: arrived Rangoon River 2 May: after second voyage from Kyaukpyu in follow-up convoy KRF1, badly damaged by mine explosion whilst returning downstream from Rangoon 8 May

SOFALA 1,031/37 British India - *CASED PETROL SHIP*: from Calcutta: listed for follow-up convoy KRS1 but did not sail

SONTAY 8,917/21 *Union-Castle ex French - *PERSONNEL SHIP (capacity 1,242)*: from Bombay,

VARSOVA. [Capt J F van Puyvelde]

Colombo and Trincomalee, left Madras 7 May via Kyaukpyu in build-up convoy KRF2: arrived Rangoon 11 May

SUIYANG 2,590/17 China Navigation - *CASED PETROL SHIP*: left Calcutta 7 May via Kyaukpyu in build-up convoy KRS3A: arrived Rangoon 14 May

VARELA 4,651/14 British India - *PERSONNEL SHIP (capacity 1,101)*: left Calcutta 9 May via Kyaukpyu in build-up convoy KRF3: arrived Rangoon 14 May

VARSOVA 4,701/14 British India - *PERSONNEL SHIP (capacity 1,112)*: left Calcutta 9 May via Kyaukpyu in build-up convoy KRF3: arrived Rangoon 14 May

WING SANG 3,560/38 Indo-China - *STORE SHIP*: carrying Royal Engineers' stores, from Calcutta and Chittagong, left Kyaukpyu 29 Apr in assault convoy Charlie: arrived Rangoon River 2 May

Other merchant ships including Royal Fleet Auxiliaries

BADORA 279/14 *Macneill - *HOSPITAL CARRIER*: from Kyaukpyu, listed for assault convoy Dog to arrive Rangoon River 2 May but did not sail

BEACON 528/14 Rangoon Port Commissioners - *PILOT VESSEL*: listed to leave Kyaukpyu 4 May in follow-up convoy KRS1 for Rangoon

CHANGTE 4,324/25 Australian-Oriental - *VICTUALLING SUPPLY ISSUING SHIP*: left Kyaukpyu 8 May in build-up convoy KRS2: arrived Rangoon

EASEDALE 8,032/42 Admiralty - *OILER*: at sea to refuel the main force

EMPIRE DOMBEY 813/44 *Anglo-Saxon - *TANKER*: left Kyaukpyu 29 Apr in assault convoy Charlie: arrived Rangoon River 2 May

EMPIRE DRURY 797/44 *Anglo-Saxon - *TANKER*: left Akyab 2 May for Kyaukpyu: listed to leave there 4 May in follow-up convoy KRS1 for Rangoon

EMPIRE ELAINE 7,513/42 *Cayzer, Irvine - *LANDING SHIP, CARRIER*: carrying craft and tugs from Calcutta, left Kyaukpyu 4 May in follow-up convoy KRS1A for Rangoon

EMPIRE MULL 797/44 *Anglo-Saxon - *TANKER*: carrying petrol, left Kyaukpyu 29 Apr in assault convoy Charlie: arrived Rangoon River 2 May

GOLD RANGER 3,313/41 Admiralty - *OILER*: left Trincomalee 26 Apr and Kyaukpyu 4 May in follow-up convoy KRS1: arrived Rangoon

HEYSER 1,164/43 *Anglo-Saxon - *TANKER*: left Kyaukpyu 4 May in follow-up convoy KRS1: arrived Rangoon

KARAPARA 7,117/15 British India - *HOSPITAL SHIP*: left Calcutta 28 Apr via Kyaukpyu: arrived Rangoon River: embarked released prisoners of war 4 May and left for Calcutta

KAROA 7,009/15 British India - *HOSPITAL SHIP*: left Calcutta 29 Apr and Kyaukpyu 3 May: arrived Rangoon River 5 May: moved seven miles up river 7 May and arrived Rangoon 16 May: with 231 patients aboard, left for Madras 19 May

NINGHAI 2,484/25 China Navigation - *STORE SHIP*: carrying coal, left Calcutta 29 Apr and Kyaukpyu 4 May in follow-up convoy KRS1 for Rangoon

OLWEN 6,470/17 Admiralty - *OILER*: at sea to refuel the main force

PHILOMEL 2,122/36 General Steam - *ARMAMENT SUPPLY ISSUING SHIP*: left Kyaukpyu 4 May in follow-up convoy KRS1 for Rangoon

SPINDLETOP 1,155/43 *Anglo-Saxon - *TANKER*: left Trincomalee 23 Apr and Kyaukpyu 29 Apr in assault convoy Charlie: arrived Rangoon River 2 May: continued to Rangoon

VITA 4,691/14 British India - *HOSPITAL SHIP*: left Madras 2 May: arrived Rangoon 9 May

Unnamed naval vessels carrying personnel and equipment

LANDING SHIPS, TANK
No LSTs were allocated to the assault convoys but two were listed for follow-up convoy KRS1; two for build-up convoy KRS3 and four were listed for build-up convoy KRS4. These are likely to have been drawn from the following: **LST 11**, **163**, **199**, **368**, **403**, **406**, **410**, **413**, **421**, **427**, **538**

LANDING CRAFT, INFANTRY (LARGE)
Participating craft included -
LCI(L) 121, **125**, **166**, **177**, **180**, **249**, **266**, **295**, **305**, **310** - all left Kyaukpyu 29 Apr in assault convoy Charlie: arrived Rangoon River 2 May

LANDING CRAFT, TANK
LCT 1054, **1143**, **1157**, **1238**, **1240**, **1242**, **2038**, **2120**, **2275**, **2287**, **2296**, **2297**, **2310**, **2339**, **2425**, **2440**, **2487** - all left Kyaukpyu 27-28 April in assault convoys Dog and Easy: arrived Rangoon River 2 May. LCT 1238 - suffered casualties when mined and sunk in the Rangoon River on 3 May

The battleship QUEEN ELIZABETH. [MPL 413]

Naval vessels in support

BATTLESHIPS
QUEEN ELIZABETH - left Trincomalee 27 Apr for the North Andaman Sea to provide bombardment support (Operation "Bishop")

RICHELIEU - Free French: left Trincomalee 27 Apr for the North Andaman Sea to provide bombardment support (Operation "Bishop")

ESCORT CARRIERS
EMPEROR - left Kyaukpyu 30 Apr: provided air cover for the assault convoys 1 May: arrived off the Rangoon River 2 May and provided air cover for the landings

EMPRESS - left Trincomalee 27 Apr for the North Andaman Sea

HUNTER, KHEDIVE - both left Kyaukpyu 30 Apr: provided air cover for the assault convoys 1 May: arrived off the Rangoon River 2 May and provided air cover for the landings

SHAH - left Trincomalee 27 Apr for the North Andaman Sea

STALKER - left Kyaukpyu 30 Apr: provided air cover for the assault convoys 1 May: arrived off the Rangoon River 2 May and provided air cover for the landings

CRUISERS
CEYLON, CUMBERLAND - both left Trincomalee 27 Apr for the North Andaman Sea (Operation "Bishop")

PHOEBE - left Kyaukpyu 30 Apr with convoy Baker: arrived Rangoon River 2 May: served as fighter direction ship: proceeded up river to Rangoon 6 May

ROYALIST - left Kyaukpyu 30 Apr as carrier force flagship: arrived off the Rangoon River 2 May

SUFFOLK - left Trincomalee 27 Apr for the North Andaman Sea (Operation "Bishop")

TROMP - Dutch: left Trincomalee 27 Apr for the North Andaman Sea (Operation "Bishop")

LANDING SHIP, HEADQUARTERS (LARGE)
LARGS - ex French CHARLES PLUMIER: left Kyaukpyu 30 Apr in assault convoy Baker: arrived Rangoon River 2 May: proceeded up river to Rangoon 6 May

LANDING SHIPS, HEADQUARTERS (SMALL)
NITH - frigate: left Kyaukpyu 29 Apr in assault convoy Charlie: arrived Rangoon River 2 May

WAVENEY - frigate: left Kyaukpyu 30 Apr in assault convoy Baker: arrived Rangoon River 2 May

FIGHTER DIRECTION SHIP
ULSTER QUEEN - carrying the Commander-in-Chief East Indies Fleet, left Trincomalee 8 May: arrived Rangoon 11 May

DESTROYERS
BLACKMORE - carried out weather reporting duties to the east of the Andaman Islands prior to the assault

NUBIAN - left Trincomalee 28 Apr to join the bombardment fleet (Operation "Bishop")

PALADIN - escorted the oilers EASEDALE and OLWEN, then joined the main fleet

PENN - left Trincomalee 27 Apr with the bombardment fleet (Operation "Bishop"), then escorted the oilers EASEDALE and OLWEN

RACEHORSE - left Trincomalee 27 Apr to patrol south of the Rangoon River (Operation "Gable")

REDOUBT, ROEBUCK - both left Trincomalee 27 Apr to patrol south of the Rangoon River: in action against

Japanese forces 30 Apr, between them sinking nine small vessels (Operation "Gable")

ROTHERHAM - left Trincomalee 27 Apr with the bombardment fleet (Operation "Bishop")

SAUMAREZ - left Kyaukpyu 30 Apr with the carrier force

TARTAR - left Trincomalee 27 Apr with the bombardment fleet (Operation "Bishop")

VENUS - left Kyaukpyu 30 Apr with the carrier force

VERULAM - left Trincomalee 28 Apr to join the bombardment fleet (Operation "Bishop")

VIGILANT, **VIRAGO** - both left Kyaukpyu 30 Apr with the carrier force

SUBMARINE
STRONGBOW - carried out weather reporting duties to the west of the Nicobar Islands prior to the assault

SLOOPS
CAUVERY - Indian: left Kyaukpyu 29 Apr with convoy Charlie: took the headquarters craft LCH 317 in tow 1 May: arrived Rangoon River 2 May

SUTLEJ - Indian: left Kyaukpyu 29 Apr with convoy Charlie: arrived Rangoon River 2 May

CUTTERS
BANFF - arrived Rangoon 8 May

LULWORTH - left Kyaukpyu 28 Apr with assault convoy Easy: arrived Rangoon River 2 May

SENNEN - arrived Rangoon 8 May

FRIGATES
BANN - left Kyaukpyu 27 Apr with assault convoy Dog: arrived Rangoon River 2 May

DEVERON - left Kyaukpyu 28 Apr with assault convoy Easy: arrived Rangoon River 2 May

HALLADALE - left Kyaukpyu 30 Apr with assault convoy Baker: arrived Rangoon River 2 May

LOSSIE - listed for follow-up convoy KRS1 to arrive Rangoon River 7 May

SHIEL - left Kyaukpyu 30 Apr with assault convoy Baker: arrived Rangoon River 2 May

TAFF, **TRENT** - both left Kyaukpyu 27 Apr with assault convoy Dog: arrived Rangoon River 2 May

CORVETTES
ASSAM - Indian: left Kyaukpyu 30 Apr with assault convoy Baker: arrived Rangoon River 2 May

LINARIA - left Kyaukpyu 28 Apr with assault convoy Easy: arrived Rangoon River 2 May

MINESWEEPERS
*BENGAL, ***BIHAR**, ***BOMBAY**, **CHAMELEON**, ***KHYBER**, ***KUMAON**, ***ORISSA**, **PICKLE**, **PINCHER**, **PLUCKY**, ***PUNJAB**, ***RAJPUTANA**, **RECRUIT**, **RIFLEMAN**, ***ROHILKHAND**, **VESTAL** [*Indian] - all left Akyab 29 Apr in assault convoy Able: arrived Rangoon River 1 May. KUMAON, ROHILKHAND proceeded up river to Rangoon 6 May

TRAWLERS
SANDRAY, **SCARAVAY** - both as danlayers, towing radar barges, left Kyaukpyu 27 Apr with assault convoy Dog: arrived Rangoon River 1 May

COASTAL FORCES DEPOT SHIP
BARRACUDA - Indian: listed to leave Kyaukpyu 29 Apr in assault convoy Charlie to arrive Rangoon River 2 May: arrived Rangoon 11 May

YACHT
VIRGINIA - for survey, left Kyaukpyu 27 Apr in assault convoy Dog towing one MFV: arrived Rangoon River 2 May: proceeded up river 6 May

MOTOR LAUNCHES
HDML 1272, **1299**, **1304**, **1456**, **1462**, **1463**, **1465**, **1467**, **1477**, **1478** - all left Kyaukpyu 27-28 Apr in assault convoys Dog and Easy: arrived Rangoon River 2 May. HDML 1463 - suffered casualties when hit by machine-gun fire 4 May

ML 205, **246**, **247**, **264**, **591**, **905** - all left Kyaukpyu 29 Apr in assault convoy Charlie: arrived Rangoon River 2 May. ML 591, 905 - both grounded and capsized 9 May

MOTOR MINESWEEPERS
BYMS 2007, **2008**, **2060**, **2148**, **2162**, **2181**, **2204**, **2232**, **2236** - all left Akyab 30 Apr in convoy Fox: arrived Rangoon River 2 May

MMS 198 - left Akyab 30 Apr in convoy Fox: arrived Rangoon River 2 May

LANDING CRAFT, HEADQUARTERS
LCH 101, **267** - both left Kyaukpyu 29 Apr in assault convoy Charlie: arrived Rangoon River 2 May

LCH 317 - left Kyaukpyu 29 Apr in assault convoy Charlie: broke down 1 May and taken in tow by the sloop CAUVERY to arrive Rangoon River 2 May

LANDING CRAFT, GUN (LARGE)
LCG(L) 5, **6**, **7**, **13**, **449** - all left Kyaukpyu 28 Apr in assault convoy Easy: arrived Rangoon River 2 May

LANDING CRAFT, ADMINISTRATION
LCQ 391 - left Kyaukpyu 28 Apr in assault convoy Easy: arrived Rangoon River 2 May

CITY OF CANTERBURY. [Capt J F van Puyvelde]

This section includes the ships and craft listed on 12 August 1945 to take part in Operation "Zipper" but diverted as a result of the Japanese surrender two days later.

Named ships carrying personnel, equipment and supplies

NAME OF SHIP Gross tonnage/Year of build Owner or *Managers, if British, or Nationality (and owner or *managers) - WARTIME FUNCTION [HM = His Majesty's commissioned ship: MT Ship = Cargo ship assigned primarily for carrying military vehicles]

ALMANZORA 15,551/14 Royal Mail - *PERSONNEL SHIP (capacity 230 British; 2,384 Indian)*: carrying follow-up troops, left Madras 3 Sep in assault convoy JME1F: arrived Morib beachhead 9 Sep: continued to Singapore

ANTENOR 11,174/25 *Alfred Holt - *PERSONNEL SHIP (capacity 179 British; 1,400 Indian)*: listed to arrive at the beachhead 17 Sep but diverted: left Madras 12 Sep for Singapore

ARAWA 14,462/22 Shaw Savill - *PERSONNEL SHIP (capacity 78 British; 1,289 Indian)*: left Bombay 2 Sep in assault convoy JMA2C: arrived Port Dickson beachhead 12 Sep: continued to Singapore

ARONDA 9,031/41 British India - *PERSONNEL SHIP (capacity 117 British: 1,611 Indian)*: at Bombay 30 Aug: listed to arrive at the beachhead 17 Sep from Chittagong

BAHARISTAN 5,479/28 Strick - *MT/STORE SHIP*: listed to arrive at the beachhead 12 Sep but diverted: left Rangoon 24 Aug for Singapore

BARPETA 3,194/14 British India - *LANDING SHIP, INFANTRY (LARGE) AND DEPOT SHIP (personnel capacity 400)*: listed to leave Cochin in assault convoy JMB2S to arrive Port Swettenham 12 Sep

BELNOR 2,871/26 Norwegian (*Christen Smith) - *STORE SHIP*: from Bombay, left Colombo 4 Sep in assault convoy JMG2 for the beachhead

BELPAREIL 7,203/26 Norwegian (*Christen Smith) - *MT SHIP*: from Calcutta, listed to leave Colombo 1 Sep in convoy JMG1 but did not sail

BOISSEVAIN 14,134/37 Dutch (KPM) - *PERSONNEL SHIP (capacity 1,068 British; 759 Indian)*: left Bombay 2 Sep in assault convoy JMA2C: arrived Port Dickson beachhead 12 Sep

BROCKLEYMOOR 7,368/44 *Runciman - *CASED PETROL SHIP*: listed to arrive at the beachhead 12 Sep but diverted: left Madras 26 Aug via Trincomalee for Hong Kong

CARLTON 7,210/42 Carlton - *MT/STORE SHIP*: from Madras, listed to arrive at the beachhead 18 Sep

CERION 2,588/38 Anglo-Saxon - *CASED PETROL SHIP*: left Bombay 27 Aug in assault convoy JMA1S to arrive at the beachhead 9 Sep

CHESHIRE 10,552/27 Bibby - *PERSONNEL SHIP (capacity 748 British; 1,189 Indian)*: listed to arrive at the beachhead 12 Sep but diverted: left Rangoon 30 Aug for Singapore

CHITRAL 15,346/25 P & O - *PERSONNEL SHIP (capacity 3,070)*: left Bombay 9 Sep: arrived Port Swettenham 20 Sep: continued to Hong Kong

CILICIA 11,136/38 Anchor - *PERSONNEL SHIP (capacity 198 British; 1,600 Indian)*: left Cochin 10 Sep for Port Swettenham: continued to Singapore

CIRCASSIA 11,136/37 Anchor - *PERSONNEL SHIP (capacity 139 British; 2,250 Indian)*: carrying follow-up troops, left Vizagapatam 2 Sep in assault convoys JMF1F then JME1F: arrived Morib beachhead 9 Sep: continued to Singapore

CITY OF AUCKLAND 8,336/14 *Hall - *MT/STORE SHIP*: listed to arrive at the beachhead 12 Sep but diverted: left Rangoon 2 Sep for Penang

CITY OF CANTERBURY 8,331/22 City - *PERSONNEL SHIP (capacity 1,312)*: carrying follow-up troops, left Madras 3 Sep in assault convoy JME1F: experienced difficulty in maintaining convoy speed but arrived Port Swettenham on due date, 9 Sep: continued to Singapore

CITY OF RANGOON 6,635/14 *Hall - *STORE SHIP*: loaded coal at Calcutta to arrive at the beachhead 9 Sep but diverted to Singapore

DERBYSHIRE 11,660/35 Bibby - *PERSONNEL SHIP (capacity 150 British; 2,389 Indian)*: listed to arrive at the beachhead 9 Sep but diverted: left Rangoon 30 Aug for Singapore

DEVONSHIRE 11,275/39 Bibby - *PERSONNEL SHIP (capacity 107 British; 1,907 Indian)*: listed to arrive at the beachhead 9 Sep but diverted: left Rangoon 30 Aug for Singapore

DILWARA 11,080/36 British India - *PERSONNEL SHIP (capacity 136 British; 1,825 Indian)*: listed to arrive at the beachhead 9 Sep but diverted: left Rangoon 30 Aug for Singapore

DUNERA 11,162/37 British India - *PERSONNEL SHIP (capacity 651 British; 1,498 Indian)*: listed to arrive at the beachhead 17 Sep but diverted: left Calcutta 8 Sep for Singapore

E SANG 3,370/34 Indo-China - *STORE SHIP*: left Bombay 24 Aug via Colombo in assault convoy JMG1 to arrive at the beachhead 9 Sep

EGRA 5,108/11 British India - *PERSONNEL SHIP (capacity 187 British; 707 Indian)*: listed to arrive at the beachhead 9 Sep but diverted: left Rangoon 2-3 Sep for Penang

EKMA 5,108/11 British India - *PERSONNEL SHIP (capacity 182 British; 1,025 Indian)*: listed to arrive at the beachhead 12 Sep but diverted: left Rangoon 30 Aug for Singapore

EMPIRE BEAUTY 7,297/43 *Stephens, Sutton - *MT/STORE SHIP*: left Bombay 29 Aug in assault convoy JMA2BS to arrive Port Dickson beachhead 12 Sep

EMPIRE BYNG 7,832/45 *P & O - *MT SHIP*: from Calcutta, left Trincomalee 30 Aug and Colombo 4 Sep in assault convoy JMA1S to arrive at the beachhead 9 Sep

EMPIRE CANNING 6,997/44 *Hogarth - *MT/STORE SHIP*: left Bombay 29 Aug in assault convoy JMA2BS: arrived Port Swettenham 12 Sep

EMPIRE CAPULET 7,044/43 *Glen Line - *MT/STORE SHIP*: listed to arrive at the beachhead 12 Sep but diverted: left Rangoon for Singapore

EMPIRE GENERAL 7,359/44 *Hain - *MT/STORE SHIP*: left Bombay 29 Aug in assault convoy JMA2BS to arrive Port Dickson 12 Sep

EMPIRE GUINEVERE 7,072/42 *Gould - *MT/STORE SHIP*: left Bombay 29 Aug in assault convoy JMA2BS: arrived Port Swettenham 12 Sep

EMPIRE IRVING 7,071/44 *Hall - *CASED PETROL SHIP*: listed to leave Bombay 6 Sep in follow-up convoy JMA3 but did not sail

EMPIRE METEOR 7,457/40 *Haldin & Philipps - *STORE SHIP*: left Bombay 29 Aug in assault convoy JMA2BS to arrive at the beachhead 12 Sep

EMPIRE MIRANDA 7,054/43 *Denholm - *MT/STORE SHIP*: left Bombay 29 Aug in assault convoy JMA2BS to arrive Port Dickson 12 Sep

EMPIRE NIGER 7,487/20 *British India ex German FRAUENFELS - *MT/STORE SHIP*: left Bombay 29 Aug in assault convoy JMA2BS to arrive at the beachhead 12 Sep

EMPIRE PRIDE 9,248/41 *Bibby - *LANDING SHIP, PERSONNEL (capacity 490 British; 1,646 Indian)*: left Bombay 31 Aug in assault convoy JMA1F to arrive Morib beachhead 9 Sep

EMPIRE PROME 7,100/45 *Runciman - *STORE SHIP*: left Bombay 29 Aug in assault convoy JMA2BS to arrive at the beachhead 12 Sep

EMPIRE RABAUL 7,307/45 *Moller - *MT/STORE SHIP*: from Calcutta, arrived at the beachhead 19 Sep

EMPIRE RANI 7,575/21 *British India ex German MARIENFELS - *MT/STORE SHIP*: left Bombay 6 Sep in

ESPERANCE BAY. [MPL 8119]

follow-up convoy JMA3: arrived at the beachhead 19 Sep

EMPIRE TAKORADI 7,318/45 *Reardon Smith - *STORE SHIP*: left Bombay 6 Sep in follow-up convoy JMA3: arrived at the beachhead 19 Sep: continued to Singapore

EMPIRE VICEROY 7,803/43 *Hall - *MT SHIP*: from Calcutta, listed to arrive at the beachhead 17 Sep carrying harbour craft

EMPIRE VOICE 6,828/40 *Booth - *STORE SHIP*: left Bombay 6 Sep in follow-up convoy JMA3: arrived at the beachhead 19 Sep

ESKBANK 5,137/37 *Weir - *STORE SHIP*: left Bombay 29 Aug in assault convoy JMA2BS to arrive at the beachhead 12 Sep

ESPERANCE BAY 14,204/22 Aberdeen & Commonwealth - *PERSONNEL SHIP (capacity 138 British; 1,376 Indian)*: left Bombay 2 Sep in assault convoy JMA2C: arrived Port Dickson 12 Sep: continued to Singapore

FELIX ROUSSEL 17,083/30 *Bibby ex French - *PERSONNEL SHIP (capacity 194 British; 2,093 Indian)*: carrying follow-up troops, left Cochin 1 Sep in assault convoys JMB1F then JME1F: arrived Morib beachhead 9 Sep: continued to Singapore

FLORISTAN 7,368/44 Strick - *MT/STORE SHIP*: left Bombay 6 Sep in follow-up convoy JMA3: arrived at the beachhead 19 Sep: continued to Singapore

FORT AKLAVIK 7,132/43 *Dodd, Thomson - *MT/STORE SHIP*: left Bombay 29 Aug in assault convoy JMA2BS to arrive at the beachhead 12 Sep

FORT CADOTTE 7,128/43 *Ropner - *STORE SHIP*: left Bombay 29 Aug in assault convoy JMA2BS to arrive at the beachhead 12 Sep

FORT CHESTERFIELD 7,127/43 *Hain - *MT/STORE SHIP*: left Bombay 29 Aug in assault convoy JMA2BS: unable to maintain convoy speed, so put into Colombo: arrived at the beachhead 19 Sep

FORT ENTERPRISE 7,126/43 *Hall Bros - *MT/STORE SHIP*: left Vizagapatam 30 Aug in assault convoys JMF1S then JMA1S to arrive Morib beachhead 9 Sep: continued to Singapore

FORT FINLAY 7,134/43 *Ropner - *MT/STORE SHIP*: left Madras in assault convoy JME2S to arrive Port Swettenham 12 Sep

FORT FRONTENAC 7,148/43 *J & C Harrison - *MT/STORE SHIP*: listed to arrive Port Swettenham 12 Sep but diverted: left Rangoon 30 Aug for Singapore

FORT GASPEREAU 7,134/43 *Watts, Watts - *MT/STORE SHIP*: left Vizagapatam 30 Aug in assault convoys JMF1S then JMA1S to arrive at the beachhead 9 Sep

FORT GLENORA 7,126/43 *Trader Navigation - *MT/STORE SHIP*: left Bombay 6 Sep in follow-up convoy JMA3: arrived at the beachhead 19 Sep

FORT HALL 7,157/43 *E R Management - *MT/STORE SHIP*: from Chittagong, arrived at the beachhead 19 Sep

FORT LAJOIE 7,134/42 *Lyle - *MT/STORE SHIP*: from Calcutta and Chittagong, listed to arrive at the beachhead 18 Sep but diverted to Singapore

FORT LOUISBOURG 7,130/41 *Thomson - *MT SHIP*: arrived at the beachhead 19 Sep

FORT MEDUCTIC 7,134/43 *Morrison - *MT/STORE SHIP*: left Bombay 6 Sep in follow-up convoy JMA3: arrived at the beachhead 19 Sep

FORT TURTLE 7,133/43 *Haldin & Philipps - *MT/STORE SHIP*: listed to arrive at the beachhead 9 Sep but diverted: left Rangoon 30 Aug for Singapore

FREDERICK BANTING 7,219/43 *City - *MT/STORE SHIP*: left Bombay 29 Aug in assault convoy JMA2BS to arrive Port Dickson 12 Sep

GEOLOGIST 6,202/44 *T & J Harrison - *MT/STORE SHIP*: left Bombay 29 Aug in assault convoy JMA2BS to arrive Port Dickson 12 Sep

GLENAFFARIC 7,782/20 Glen Line - *MT/STORE SHIP*: left Bombay 29 Aug in assault convoy JMA2BS to arrive at the beachhead 12 Sep

GLENGYLE 9,919/39 Glen Line - *HM LANDING SHIP, INFANTRY (LARGE) (personnel capacity 1,050)*: listed to leave Bombay to arrive Port Dickson 12 Sep but diverted: left Trincomalee 31 Aug for Hong Kong

GLENROY 9,809/38 Glen Line - *HM LANDING SHIP, INFANTRY (LARGE) (personnel capacity 980)*: left Madras 3 Sep in assault convoy JME1F: arrived Morib beachhead 9 Sep

GORJISTAN 5,888/29 Strick - *MT/STORE SHIP*: left Vizagapatam in assault convoy JMF2S to arrive at the beachhead 12 Sep

HARPALYCE 7,269/42 Hain - *MT/STORE SHIP*: listed to arrive at the beachhead 9 Sep but diverted: left Rangoon 30 Aug for Penang

HAVILDAR 5,407/40 Asiatic - *MT/STORE SHIP*: left Bombay 29 Aug in assault convoy JMA2BS: arrived Port Swettenham 12 Sep

HIGHLAND BRIGADE 14,134/29 Royal Mail - *PERSONNEL SHIP (capacity 130 British; 1,450 Indian)*: listed to arrive at the beachhead 17 Sep but diverted: left Rangoon 30 Aug for Singapore

HIGHLAND CHIEFTAIN 14,135/29 Royal Mail - *PERSONNEL SHIP (capacity 771 British; 874 Indian)*: left Madras 6 Sep in assault convoy JME2F to arrive at the beachhead 12 Sep

HIGHLAND MONARCH 14,139/28 Royal Mail - *PERSONNEL SHIP (capacity 213 British; 1,383 Indian)*: listed to arrive at the beachhead 17 Sep but diverted: left Rangoon 19 Sep for Singapore

IKAUNA 6,793/41 British India - *MT/STORE SHIP*: from Madras, arrived at the beachhead 19 Sep: continued to Singapore

INDRAPOERA 10,825/25 Dutch (Rotterdam Lloyd) - *PERSONNEL SHIP (capacity 31 British; 1,679 Indian)*: left Cochin 4 Sep in assault convoy JMB2F to arrive at the beachhead 12 Sep

ITAURA 6,793/40 British India - *MT/STORE SHIP*: listed to arrive at the beachhead 9 Sep but diverted: left Rangoon 2 Sep for Singapore

GLENAFFARIC. [Capt J F van Puyvelde]

ITOLA.
[Capt J F
van Puyvelde]

ITOLA 6,793/40 British India - *MT/STORE SHIP*: listed to arrive at the beachhead 9 Sep but diverted: left Rangoon 2 Sep for Singapore

ITRIA 6,845/40 British India - *MT/STORE SHIP*: from Madras, listed to arrive at the beachhead 18 Sep: arrived Singapore 1 Oct

LA PAMPA 4,149/38 Buries Markes - *MT SHIP*: from Bombay, Colombo and Trincomalee, arrived at the beachhead 19 Sep: continued to Singapore

LARGS BAY 14,182/21 Aberdeen & Commonwealth - *PERSONNEL SHIP (capacity 104 British; 1,162 Indian)*: left Bombay 2 Sep in assault convoy JMA2C: arrived Port Dickson 12 Sep: continued to Singapore

LLANSTEPHAN CASTLE 11,348/14 Union-Castle - *HM Indian LANDING SHIP, INFANTRY (LARGE) (personnel capacity 1,250)*: listed to leave Bombay to arrive Port Dickson 12 Sep but diverted: left Trincomalee 31 Aug for Hong Kong

LOSSIEBANK 5,627/30 *Weir - *MT/STORE SHIP*: left Bombay 6 Sep in follow-up convoy JMA3: arrived at the beachhead 19 Sep

MAHADEVI 5,459/43 Asiatic - *MT/STORE SHIP*: left Bombay 27 Aug in assault convoy JMA1S: arrived Morib beachhead 9 Sep

MALIKA 5,469/43 Asiatic - *MT/STORE SHIP*: left Bombay 27 Aug in assault convoy JMA1S to arrive Morib beachhead 9 Sep: turned back for repairs 28 Aug, after becoming holed on 27 Aug by the firing of a Bofors gun stowed in the hold

MONOWAI 10,852/25 Union SS of New Zealand - *PERSONNEL SHIP (capacity 100 British; 1,250 Indian)*: listed to arrive at the beachhead 17 Sep but diverted: left Madras 1 Sep for Singapore

MORETON BAY 14,193/21 Aberdeen & Commonwealth - *PERSONNEL SHIP (capacity 79 British; 1,744 Indian)*: listed to arrive at the beachhead 17 Sep but diverted: left Rangoon 2-3 Sep for Singapore

MYRTLEBANK 5,150/25 *Weir - *STORE SHIP*: from Bombay, listed to arrive at the beachhead 18 Sep but did not sail

NEA HELLAS 16,991/22 *Anchor ex Greek -

NEA
HELLAS
pre-war as
TUSCANIA.

PERSONNEL SHIP (capacity 1,406 British; 1,914 Indian): left Bombay 2 Sep in assault convoy JMA2C to arrive at the beachhead 12 Sep

NIEUW HOLLAND 11,066/27 Dutch (KPM) - *PERSONNEL SHIP (capacity 186 British; 1,684 Indian)*: left Bombay 2 Sep in assault convoy JMA2C: arrived Port Dickson 12 Sep: continued to Singapore

NOVELIST 6,133/40 *T & J Harrison - *STORE SHIP*: left Bombay 6 Sep in follow-up convoy JMA3: arrived at the beachhead 19 Sep

OCEAN ANGEL 7,178/42 *Barr, Crombie - *MT/STORE SHIP*: left Bombay 29 Aug in assault convoy JMA2BS: arrived Port Swettenham 12 Sep

OCEAN GYPSY 7,178/42 *J & C Harrison - *MT/STORE SHIP*: left Madras in assault convoy JME2S to arrive Port Swettenham 12 Sep: continued to Singapore

OCEAN PILGRIM 7,178/42 *Dene - *MT/STORE SHIP*: left Madras in assault convoy JME2S to arrive at the beachhead 12 Sep

OCEAN TRADER 7,178/42 *Glen Line - *STORE SHIP*: left Bombay 6 Sep in follow-up convoy JMA3: arrived at the beachhead 19 Sep

OCEAN VALOUR 7,174/42 *Souter - *CASED PETROL SHIP*: left Bombay 6 Sep in follow-up convoy JMA3: arrived at the beachhead 19 Sep: continued to Singapore

OCEAN VESTAL 7,174/42 *Kaye - *MT/STORE SHIP*: left Bombay 29 Aug in assault convoy JMA2BS to arrive at the beachhead 12 Sep

OCEAN VISCOUNT 7,174/42 *Bibby - *MT/STORE SHIP*: left Bombay 6 Sep in follow-up convoy JMA3: arrived at the beachhead 19 Sep

ORDUNA 15,507/14 Pacific Steam - *PERSONNEL SHIP (capacity 1,253 British; 1,597 Indian)*: left Bombay 31 Aug in assault convoy JMA1F to arrive at the beachhead 9 Sep

ORMONDE 14,982/17 Orient - *PERSONNEL SHIP (capacity 309 British; 2,150 Indian)*: left Madras 12 Sep: arrived Port Swettenham

PERSIMMON 8,244/44 Royal Mail PAMPAS - *HM LANDING SHIP, INFANTRY (LARGE) (personnel capacity 970)*: left Madras 3 Sep in assault convoy JME1F: lost a landing craft in rough seas 5 Sep: arrived Sepang beachhead 9 Sep, Morib beachhead 10 Sep and Port Dickson 12 Sep

PERSIMMON (right) as the cargo vessel PAMPAS and (below) as a Landing Ship, Infantry. [World Ship Photo Library/IWM HU69046]

PRINCESS BEATRIX 4,135/39 Dutch (Zeeland) PRINSES BEATRIX - *HM LANDING SHIP, INFANTRY (MEDIUM) (personnel capacity 420)*: listed to leave Vizagapatam to arrive Morib beachhead 9 Sep but diverted: left Trincomalee 17 Aug for Penang

PRINS ALBERT 2,938/37 Belgian - *HM LANDING SHIP, INFANTRY (SMALL) (personnel capacity 185)*: left Bombay 4 Sep and Colombo 6 Sep for the beachhead

PULASKI 6,345/12 Polish (Gdynia-America) - *PERSONNEL SHIP (capacity 1,323)*: carrying follow-up troops, left Madras 31 Aug in assault convoy JME1F: arrived Morib beachhead 9 Sep: continued to Singapore

QUEEN EMMA 4,135/39 Dutch (Zeeland) KONINGIN EMMA - *HM LANDING SHIP, INFANTRY (MEDIUM) (personnel capacity 420)*: listed to leave Madras to arrive Morib beachhead 9 Sep but diverted: left Trincomalee 17 Aug for Penang

RAJULA 8,478/26 British India - *PERSONNEL SHIP (capacity 303 British; 1,212 Indian)*: listed to arrive at the beachhead 9 Sep but diverted: left Rangoon 30 Aug for Singapore

RANCHI 16,738/25 P & O - *PERSONNEL SHIP (capacity 770 British; 2,093 Indian)*: carrying follow-up troops, left Cochin 1 Sep in assault convoys JMB1F then JME1F: arrived Morib beachhead 9 Sep: continued to Singapore

RISALDAR 5,407/40 Asiatic - *MT/STORE SHIP*: listed to arrive at the beachhead 12 Sep but diverted: left Rangoon 30 Aug for Singapore

RIVERCREST 6,998/44 Crest - *MT/STORE SHIP*: left Bombay 29 Aug in assault convoy JMA2BS: arrived Port Swettenham 12 Sep

ROCKSAND 7,177/44 ex EMPIRE ANVIL - *HM LANDING SHIP, INFANTRY (LARGE) (personnel*

capacity 1,355): left Madras 3 Sep in assault convoy JME1F: arrived Morib beachhead 9 Sep

SAINFOIN 7,144/44 ex EMPIRE CROSSBOW - *HM LANDING SHIP, INFANTRY (LARGE) (personnel capacity 1,355)*: left Bombay 2 Sep in assault convoy JMA2C: arrived Port Dickson 12 Sep

SALWEEN 7,063/37 *Henderson - *PERSONNEL SHIP (capacity 75 British; 1,400 Indian)*: listed to arrive at the beachhead 17 Sep but diverted: left Rangoon 30 Aug for Penang

SAMBURGH 7,219/43 *Weir - *CASED PETROL SHIP*: left Bombay 29 Aug in assault convoy JMA2BS: port order reversed: arrived Singapore 15 Sep then left for Port Swettenham 20 Sep

SAMDEE 7,253/43 *Brocklebank - *CASED PETROL SHIP*: left Vizagapatam 2 Sep in assault convoys JMF2S then JMA2BS to arrive at the beachhead 12 Sep

SAMFAITHFUL 7,210/44 *Royal Mail - *MT/STORE SHIP*: from Calcutta, arrived at the beachhead 19 Sep

SAMFIELD 7,219/43 *Cayzer, Irvine - *MT/STORE SHIP*: from Calcutta, arrived at the beachhead 19 Sep: continued to Singapore

SAMFLORA 7,219/43 *Union-Castle - *MT/STORE SHIP*: left Bombay 29 Aug in assault convoy JMA2BS to arrive at the beachhead 12 Sep

SAMGARA 7,219/43 *Alfred Holt, **SAMGAUDIE** 7,210/44 *Brocklebank, **SAMHAIN** 7,219/43 *Ellerman & Bucknall - *MT/STORE SHIPS*: all left Bombay 27 Aug in assault convoy JMA1S to arrive Morib beachhead 9 Sep

SAMHOLT 7,219/43 *Cunard White Star - *MT/STORE SHIP*: left Bombay 29 Aug in assault convoy JMA2BS to arrive Port Dickson 12 Sep

SAMLEA 7,210/44 *Ellerman & Bucknall - *MT/STORE*

RANCHI.

TEGELBERG.

SHIP: left Bombay 27 Aug in assault convoy JMA1S to arrive Morib beachhead 9 Sep

SAMLORIAN   7,255/44   *E R Management - *MT/STORE SHIP*: left Bombay 6 Sep in follow-up convoy JMA3: arrived at the beachhead 19 Sep

SAMOTHRACE 7,219/43 *Pacific Steam - *MT/STORE SHIP*: left Bombay 27 Aug in assault convoy JMA1S to arrive Morib beachhead 9 Sep

SAMPFORD 7,219/43 *Weir - *MT/STORE SHIP*: left Bombay 6 Sep in follow-up convoy JMA3: arrived at the beachhead 19 Sep

SAMRICH 7,219/43 *Shaw Savill - *MT/STORE SHIP*: left Vizagapatam 30 Aug in assault convoys JMF1S then JMA1S to arrive at the beachhead 9 Sep

SAMSKERN 7,210/44 *Radcliffe - *MT/STORE SHIP*: left Bombay 27 Aug in assault convoy JMA1S to arrive Morib beachhead 9 Sep

SAMSTURDY 7,210/44 *Common Bros - *MT/STORE SHIP*: left Bombay 29 Aug in assault convoy JMA2BS to arrive at the beachhead 12 Sep

SAMTHAR 7,219/43 *Royal Mail - *MT/STORE SHIP*: listed to leave Rangoon to arrive at the beachhead 18 Sep but diverted to Hong Kong

SAMTRENT 7,219/43 *Union-Castle - *MT/STORE SHIP*: left Bombay 29 Aug in assault convoy JMA2BS to arrive at the beachhead 12 Sep

SAMTROY 7,219/43 *Weir - *MT/STORE SHIP*: left Bombay 27 Aug in assault convoy JMA1S to arrive Morib beachhead 9 Sep

SAMTRUTH 7,210/44 *Haldin & Philipps - *MT/STORE SHIP*: left Bombay 29 Aug in assault convoy JMA2BS to arrive Port Dickson 12 Sep

SANSOVINO 7,177/43 ex EMPIRE CUTLASS - *HM LANDING SHIP, INFANTRY (LARGE) (personnel capacity 1,355)*: left Vizagapatam in assault convoys

JMF1F then JME1F: dropped astern of convoy 7 Sep but rejoined same day: arrived Morib beachhead 9 Sep: continued to Singapore

SEFTON 7,177/44 ex EMPIRE GAUNTLET - *HM LANDING SHIP, INFANTRY (LARGE) (personnel capacity 1,355)*: left Madras 3 Sep in assault convoy JME1F: arrived Sepang beachhead 9 Sep, Morib beachhead 10 Sep and Port Dickson 12 Sep

SOBIESKI 11,030/39 Polish (Gdynia-America) - *PERSONNEL SHIP (capacity 734 British; 1,200 Indian)*: left Bombay 9 Sep to arrive at the beachhead 17 Sep

STAFFORDSHIRE 10,701/29 Bibby - *PERSONNEL SHIP (capacity 70 British; 1,949 Indian)*: left Bombay 9 Sep to arrive at the beachhead 17 Sep

STANCLEEVE 5,970/42 Stanhope - *MT/STORE SHIP*: left Madras in assault convoy JME2S to arrive Port Swettenham 12 Sep

TAKLIWA 7,936/24 British India - *PERSONNEL SHIP (capacity 355 British; 1,000 Indian)*: listed to arrive at the beachhead 17 Sep but diverted: left Bombay 7 Sep for Chittagong and Hong Kong

TALMA 10,000/23 British India - *PERSONNEL SHIP (capacity 102 British; 1,446 Indian)*: listed to arrive at the beachhead 9 Sep but diverted: left Rangoon 2 Sep for Singapore

TAMAROA 12,405/22 Shaw Savill - *PERSONNEL SHIP (capacity 223 British; 1,221 Indian)*: left Madras 12 Sep for Port Swettenham: continued to Singapore

TAMELE 7,172/44 Elder Dempster - *MT/STORE SHIP*: left Bombay 29 Aug in assault convoy JMA2BS to arrive Port Swettenham 12 Sep

TEGELBERG 14,150/37 Dutch (KPM) - *PERSONNEL SHIP (capacity 679 British; 2,323 Indian)*: carrying follow-up troops, left Madras 3 Sep in assault convoy JME1F: arrived Morib beachhead 9 Sep: continued to Singapore

BUSHWOOD.
[A Duncan]

TREVAYLOR 5,257/40 Hain - *MT/STORE SHIP*: left Bombay 29 Aug in assault convoy JMA2BS to arrive at the beachhead 12 Sep

TWEEDBANK 5,627/30 *Weir - *MT/STORE SHIP*: from Bombay, arrived Port Swettenham 19 Sep

WARINA 3,120/18 British India - *STORE SHIP*: left Colombo 4 Sep in assault convoy JMG2 to arrive at the beachhead 12 Sep

WELSH PRINCE 7,354/44 *Furness, Withy - *MT/STORE SHIP*: from Madras, arrived at the beachhead 19 Sep

WING SANG 3,560/38 Indo-China - *STORE SHIP*: from Bombay, left Colombo 1 Sep in assault convoy JMG1 to arrive at the beachhead 9 Sep: continued to Singapore

WO SANG 3,373/34 Indo-China - *STORE SHIP*: left Bombay 23 Aug and Colombo 1 Sep in assault convoy JMG1 to arrive at the beachhead 9 Sep

WORCESTERSHIRE 11,402/31 Bibby - *PERSONNEL SHIP (capacity 1,253 British; 1,597 Indian)*: left Bombay 31 Aug in assault convoy JMA1F to arrive at the beachhead 9 Sep

Other merchant ships including Royal Fleet Auxiliaries

AMARAPOORA 9,342/20 *Henderson - *HOSPITAL SHIP*: listed to arrive Morib beachhead 9 Sep but diverted: left Madras 20 Aug and Trincomalee 28 Aug for Singapore

BELA 3,738/45 Anglo-Saxon - *TANKER*: carrying aviation fuel, listed for the operation but diverted to Penang

BRITISH GOVERNOR 6,840/26 British Tanker - *TANKER*: carrying fuel oil, from Bombay, left Colombo 4 Sep in assault convoy JMG2 for the beachhead: refuelled the destroyer BRECON at sea 9 Sep

BRITISH POWER 8,451/36 British Tanker - *TANKER*: arrived at the beachhead 19 Sep

BUSHWOOD 2,842/42 France, Fenwick - *ELECTRICAL SUPPLY SHIP*: listed to arrive Port Swettenham 18 Sep

CARPIO 1,847/21 MacAndrews - *ARMAMENT SUPPLY ISSUING SHIP*: left Trincomalee 1 Sep in assault convoy JMC1AS to arrive at the beachhead 9 Sep

CLAVELLA 8,097/39 Dutch ("La Corona") - *TANKER*: carrying fuel oil, left Bombay 6 Sep in follow-up convoy JMA3: arrived at the beachhead 19 Sep

CROMWELL 1,124/43 *Anglo-Saxon - *TANKER*: carrying aviation fuel, listed for the operation but diverted: left Trincomalee 15 Aug for Penang

DAGEID 6,361/31 Norwegian (A/S Ocean) - *TANKER*: carrying mixed fuel, from Trincomalee, listed for assault convoy JMA1S to arrive at the beachhead 9 Sep

DEVON CITY 4,928/33 Reardon Smith - *BOOM CARRIER*: left Trincomalee 3 Sep in assault convoy JMC2 to arrive Port Swettenham 12 Sep

DEWDALE 8,265/41 Admiralty - *LANDING SHIP, GANTRY*: listed to arrive Morib beachhead 9 Sep but diverted: left Trincomalee 28 Aug for Singapore

DORSETSHIRE 9,717/20 Bibby - *HOSPITAL SHIP*: listed to arrive Port Dickson 12 Sep but diverted: left Bombay 8 Sep for Rangoon

EASEDALE 8,032/42 Admiralty - *OILER*: listed for the operation but diverted to Penang

EMPIRE BELGRAVE 895/45 *Anglo-Saxon - *TANKER*: carrying aviation fuel, listed to arrive at the beachhead 17 Sep

EMPIRE BUTE 813/44 *Coastal Tankers - *WATER CARRIER*: from Colombo, listed to arrive at the beachhead 17 Sep

EMPIRE ELAINE 7,513/42 *Cayzer, Irvine - *LANDING SHIP, CARRIER*: left Trincomalee 1 Sep in assault convoy JMC1AS to arrive at the beachhead 9 Sep

EMPIRE ENSIGN 3,758/45 *British Tanker - *TANKER*: carrying mixed fuel, from Trincomalee, arrived at the beachhead 19 Sep

EMPIRE FAY 814/43 *Hemsley Bell - *TANKER*: carrying diesel, from Bombay, listed for assault convoy JMA2A to arrive at the beachhead 12 Sep

EMPIRE GYPSY 813/42 *Anglo-Saxon - *TANKER*: carrying aviation fuel, listed to arrive at the beachhead 17 Sep

EMPIRE LASS 813/41 *Rowbotham - *TANKER*: carrying fuel oil, from Bombay, listed for assault convoy JMA2A to arrive at the beachhead 12 Sep

EMPIRE TAVISTOCK 798/45 *Anglo-Saxon - *TANKER*: carrying mixed fuel, listed to arrive at the beachhead 17 Sep

EMPIRE TROTWOOD 797/44 *Anglo-Saxon - *WATER CARRIER*: arrived at the beachhead 19 Sep

ENNERDALE 8,219/41 Admiralty - *LANDING SHIP, GANTRY*: carrying 14 landing craft, left Madras 1 Sep in assault convoy JME1S: arrived Morib beachhead 9 Sep

FORT KILMAR 7,200/44 *Ellerman & Bucknall - *VICTUALLING SUPPLY ISSUING SHIP*: arrived at the beachhead 19 Sep

GRYFEVALE 4,434/29 Gryfevale - *DISTILLING SHIP*: arrived at the beachhead 19 Sep

HERMES 3,768/14 Dutch ("La Corona") - *TANKER*: carrying diesel, arrived at the beachhead 19 Sep

HEYSER 1,164/43 *Anglo-Saxon - *WATER CARRIER*: from Calcutta, arrived at the beachhead 19 Sep

HONG SIANG 3,703/12 Ho Hong - *NAVAL STORE ISSUING SHIP*: left Colombo 4 Sep in assault convoy JMG2 to arrive at the beachhead 12 Sep

KEDAH 2,499/27 Singapore Straits - *BASE AND ACCOMMODATION SHIP*: listed to arrive Morib beachhead 9 Sep as port party headquarters ship but diverted: left Trincomalee 28 Aug for Singapore

LULING 1,164/43 *Anglo-Saxon - *WATER CARRIER*: left Bombay 27 Aug in assault convoy JMA1S to arrive at the beachhead 9 Sep

MANELA 8,303/21 British India - *ACCOMMODATION SHIP*: for service as RAF depot ship, joined assault convoy JMD1B 31 Aug to arrive Morib beachhead 9 Sep: continued to Singapore

MANNINGTON 1,127/43 *Anglo-Saxon - *TANKER*: carrying fuel oil, from Bombay, listed for assault convoy JMA2A to arrive at the beachhead 12 Sep

MATIANA 9,045/22 British India - *TRANSPORT*: from Cochin, listed to carry port party and stores to arrive Port Swettenham 12 Sep but diverted to Singapore

NASSARIUS 8,246/44 Anglo-Saxon - *WATER CARRIER*: listed to leave Rangoon 7 Sep for the beachhead

OPHIR 4,115/28 Dutch (KPM) - *HOSPITAL SHIP*: left Trincomalee 3 Sep for the beachhead

PALESTINIAN PRINCE 1,960/36 Prince - *ARMAMENT SUPPLY ISSUING SHIP*: left Trincomalee 1 Sep in assault convoy JMC1AS to arrive at the beachhead 9 Sep

PHILOMEL 2,122/36 General Steam - *ARMAMENT SUPPLY ISSUING SHIP*: left Trincomalee 1 Sep in assault convoy JMC1AS to arrive at the beachhead 9 Sep

SALT CREEK 1,127/43 *Anglo-Saxon - *TANKER*: carrying fuel oil, from Bombay, listed for assault convoy JMA2A to arrive at the beachhead 12 Sep

SAN VITO 8,163/43 Eagle Oil - *TANKER*: carrying mixed fuel, from Trincomalee, listed for the operation but diverted to Penang

TAIREA 7,933/24 British India - *HOSPITAL SHIP*: from Bombay, arrived at the beachhead 19 Sep

TARENTUM 1,124/43 *Anglo-Saxon - *WATER CARRIER*: left Bombay 27 Aug in assault convoy JMA1S for the beachhead: unable to maintain convoy speed, dropped out night of 5-6 Sep

TORBORG 6,042/21 Norwegian (Mosvold) - *TANKER*: carrying fuel oil, left Trincomalee 3 Sep in assault convoy JMC2 to arrive at the beachhead 12 Sep

WALNUT BEND 1,124/43 *Anglo-Saxon - *TANKER*: from Bombay, left Trincomalee 3 Sep in assault convoy JMC2 to arrive at the beachhead 12 Sep

Unnamed naval vessels carrying personnel and equipment

LANDING SHIPS, TANK

LST 5, 11, 157, 163, 199, 280, 311, 315, 331, 337, 346, 368, 371, 373, 380, 382, 385, 403, 408, 410, 413, 421, 427, 538, 1021 - all left Madras in assault convoy JME1S to arrive Morib beachhead 9 Sep

LST 160 (S), **303** (S), **321** (P), **324** (S), **383** (P), **419** (S) - listed for the operation but diverted to Penang (P) and Singapore (S)

LST 8, 3006, 3007, 3008, 3009, 3010, 3017, 3019, 3020, 3024, 3035, 3036, 3037, 3501, 3502, 3503, 3507 - all left Bombay 29 Aug in assault convoy JMA2A: arrived Port Dickson beachhead 12 Sep

LST 3021 - left Cochin in assault convoy JMB2S to arrive at the beachhead 12 Sep

Also listed for the operation - **LST 164**

LANDING CRAFT, INFANTRY (LARGE)
LCI(L) 115, 121, 127, 136, 183, 217, 256, 266, 277, 305, 311 - all left Mandapam 31 Aug in assault convoy JMD1C: arrived Morib beachhead 9 Sep

LCI(L) 4, 33, 117, 122, 125, 180, 215, 216, 249, 252, 262, 270, 271, 293, 295, 299, 301, 310 - listed for the operation but diverted to Singapore in company with other LCIs not listed for "Zipper"

Also listed for the operation -
LCI(L) 114, 116, 177, 287, 290, 304, 312

LANDING CRAFT, TANK
LCT 451, 478, 489, 493, 736, 738, 742, 869, 913, 1055, 1056, 1057, 1058, 1059, 1060, 1102, 1104, 1105, 1111, 1139, 1143, 1144, 1146, 1147, 1148, 1151, 1152, 1153, 1154, 1156, 1158, 1159, 1160, 1161, 1174, 1195, 1237, 1240, 1241, 1309, 1318, 1320, 1329, 1331, 1333, 1334, 1335, 7016 - all from Madras, left Mandapam 29-30 Aug in assault convoys JMD1A and B: arrived Morib beachhead 9 Sep

LCT 1149, 1150 - both listed for the operation but diverted to Singapore

Also listed for the operation -
LCT 1176, 1213, 1239, 1321

Naval vessels in support

BATTLESHIPS
NELSON - left Penang 7 Sep: suffered power failure, which put both gyro compasses out of action 1405 8 Sep, followed by the failure of her electrical steering motors 1745 same day: manoeuvrability seriously impaired, so ship did not take up bombarding position at Morib beachhead 9 Sep but was held in readiness in case of emergency, then left for Singapore

RICHELIEU - Free French: left Trincomalee 5 Sep: joined the battleship NELSON 8 Sep: held in readiness for bombarding at Morib beachhead 9 Sep, then left for Singapore

ESCORT CARRIERS
AMEER - left Trincomalee 4 Sep: joined assault convoy JME1F 6 Sep: provided convoy air cover in the Malacca Strait 8-9 Sep: arrived at the beachhead 9 Sep

ATTACKER - listed for the operation but diverted to Penang, Sabang then Singapore

BEGUM - spare vessel with reserve aircraft embarked: damaged by grounding on departure from Trincomalee 4 Sep: put back into harbour and withdrawn from the operation

EMPEROR - left Trincomalee 4 Sep: joined assault convoy JME1F 6 Sep: provided convoy air cover in the Malacca Strait 8-9 Sep: sustained catapult damage 9 Sep which repaired same day, then left for Singapore

EMPRESS - left Trincomalee 4 Sep: joined assault convoy JME1F 6 Sep: provided convoy air cover in the Malacca Strait 8 Sep: sustained severe catapult damage 8 Sep and turned back to Trincomalee

The escort carrier BEGUM. [IWM A21737]

The cruiser CEYLON.

HUNTER - left Penang 7 Sep: provided convoy air cover in the Malacca Strait 8-9 Sep, then left for Singapore

KHEDIVE - left Trincomalee 4 Sep: joined assault convoy JME1F 6 Sep: provided convoy air cover in the Malacca Strait 8-9 Sep, then left for Singapore

PURSUER - left Trincomalee 5 Sep, joined assault convoy JME1F 6 Sep, then JMA1S: arrived at the beachhead 9 Sep and Port Swettenham 10 Sep

SEARCHER, SHAH - both listed for the operation but withdrawn

SMITER - listed for the operation to ferry RAF Spitfires but diverted: left Trincomalee 2 Sep for Hong Kong

STALKER - left Trincomalee 4 Sep: joined assault convoy JME1F 6 Sep: provided convoy air cover in the Malacca Strait 8-9 Sep, then left for Singapore

TRUMPETER - left Trincomalee 4 Sep: joined assault convoy JME1F 6 Sep: carried RAF aircraft which flown off 9-10 Sep

CRUISERS
CEYLON - left Penang 8 Sep: took up bombarding position off Morib beachhead 9 Sep, then left for Singapore

CLEOPATRA - listed for the operation but diverted: carrying the Commander-in-Chief East Indies Fleet, left Colombo 27 Aug for Sabang, Penang and Singapore

LONDON - listed for the operation but diverted to Sabang

NIGERIA - left Penang 8 Sep: took up bombarding position off Morib beachhead 9 Sep then left for Singapore

PHOEBE - listed for the operation but diverted: left Trincomalee 4 Sep for Sabang

ROYALIST - left Trincomalee 4 Sep as carrier force flagship: joined assault convoy JME1F 6 Sep for the Malacca Strait, then left for Singapore

SUSSEX - listed for the operation but diverted: left Trincomalee 31 Aug for Penang

LANDING SHIPS, HEADQUARTERS (LARGE)
BULOLO - left Madras 3 Sep in assault convoy JME1F: arrived Morib beachhead 9 Sep: continued to Singapore

LARGS - ex French CHARLES PLUMIER: left Madras 3 Sep in assault convoy JME1F: arrived Morib beachhead 9 Sep and Port Dickson 12 Sep

LANDING SHIPS, HEADQUARTERS (SMALL)
NITH - frigate: left Madras 3 Sep in assault convoy JME1F: arrived Morib beachhead 9 Sep and Port Dickson 12 Sep

WAVENEY - frigate: left Madras 3 Sep in assault convoy JME1F: arrived Morib beachhead 9 Sep

FIGHTER DIRECTION SHIPS
BOXER - listed for the operation but held in reserve

PALOMARES - listed for the operation but withdrawn after engine room fire damage

ULSTER QUEEN - left Madras 1 Sep in assault convoy JME1S: arrived Morib beachhead 9 Sep: controlled the air support at both Port Swettenham and Port Dickson beachheads

LANDING SHIP, DOCK
HIGHWAY - carrying 6 motor launches, left Madras 3

Sep in assault convoys JME1F then JME1S: arrived Morib beachhead 9 Sep

DESTROYERS

BICESTER - left Bombay 29 Aug with assault convoy JMA2BS

BLACKMORE - left Trincomalee 4 Sep with the carrier force: joined assault convoy JME1F 6 Sep for the Malacca Strait, then left for Singapore

BLEASDALE - left Trincomalee 4 Sep with the carrier force: joined assault convoy JME1F 6 Sep: arrived at the assault anchorage 9 Sep

BRECON - left Colombo 4 Sep with assault convoys JMG2 then JMA2B for the beachhead: refuelled at sea from BRITISH GOVERNOR 9 Sep: continued to Singapore

CALPE - left Trincomalee 4 Sep with the carrier force: joined assault convoy JME1F 6 Sep: arrived at the assault anchorage 9 Sep

CHIDDINGFOLD - left Trincomalee 4 Sep with the carrier force: joined assault convoy JME1F 6 Sep: arrived at the assault anchorage 9 Sep

FARNDALE - listed for the operation but diverted: left Trincomalee 5 Sep for Sabang: continued to Singapore

MYNGS - left Trincomalee 4 Sep with the carrier force: joined assault convoy JME1F 6 Sep: arrived at the assault anchorage 9 Sep, then left for Singapore

NUBIAN - left Penang 8 Sep, took up bombarding position off Morib beachhead 9 Sep

PALADIN - left Penang 8 Sep, took up bombarding position off Morib beachhead 9 Sep, then left for Singapore

PENN - left Trincomalee 2 Sep for Penang: joined the carrier force 8 Sep

PETARD - left Trincomalee 17 Aug: took up bombarding position off Morib beachhead 9 Sep

RACEHORSE - listed for the operation but diverted: left Trincomalee 30 Aug for Penang

RAIDER - listed for the operation but diverted to Penang

RAPID - left Trincomalee 4 Sep with the carrier force: joined assault convoy JME1F 6 Sep: arrived at the beachhead 9 Sep

REDOUBT - listed for the operation but diverted: left Trincomalee 30 Aug for Penang

RELENTLESS - left Penang 8 Sep with the battleship NELSON

ROCKET - listed for the operation but diverted to Sabang

ROTHERHAM - listed for the operation but diverted to Penang

SAUMAREZ - left Trincomalee 4 Sep with the carrier force: joined assault convoy JME1F 6 Sep for the Malacca Strait, then left for Singapore

TARTAR - left Penang 8 Sep, took up bombarding position off Morib beachhead 9 Sep, then left for Singapore

VERULAM - left Trincomalee 4 Sep with the carrier force: joined assault convoy JME1F 6 Sep: continued to Singapore

VIGILANT - listed for the operation but diverted: left Trincomalee 31 Aug for Penang

VOLAGE - listed for the operation but diverted to Penang

ZENITH - listed for the operation but withdrawn

SLOOPS
CAUVERY - Indian: left Colombo 4 Sep with assault convoy JMA1S: took up bombarding position off Morib beachhead 9 Sep

FALMOUTH - listed for the operation but diverted to Singapore

GODAVARI - Indian: listed for the operation but diverted: left Trincomalee 15 Aug for Penang

KISTNA - Indian: listed for the operation but diverted to Penang

NARBADA - Indian: left Mandapam 30 Aug with assault convoy JMD1A: took up bombarding position off Morib beachhead 9 Sep

SHOREHAM - left Vizagapatam 30 Aug with assault convoy JMF1S: arrived at the beachhead 9 Sep

CUTTERS
FISHGUARD - listed for the operation but diverted: left Colombo 3 Sep for Penang

GORLESTON - left Madras 3 Sep with assault convoy JME1F: continued to Singapore

LULWORTH - left Madras 3 Sep with assault convoy JME1F: detached 4 Sep to escort the personnel ship CITY OF CANTERBURY which arrived Port Swettenham 9 Sep

SENNEN - left Madras 1 Sep with assault convoy JME1S to arrive at the beachhead 9 Sep

FRIGATES
AWE - left Madras 1 Sep with assault convoys JME1S then JMA1F: served as radar picket: continued to Singapore

DART - listed for the operation but diverted: left Trincomalee 28 Aug for Singapore

DEVERON - left Colombo 28 Aug with assault convoys JME2S, JMF2S then JMA2BS

EVENLODE - left Mandapam 29 Aug with assault convoy JMD1B: continued to Singapore

INVER - left Trincomalee 1 Sep with assault convoy JMC1A

JED - left Colombo 2 Sep: assigned as RAF navigational aid ship

KALE - left Madras 1 Sep with assault convoy JME1S: assigned as radar picket: continued to Singapore

LOCH GLENDHU - left Colombo 6 Sep: listed for assault convoy JMA1S

LOCH GORM - listed for the operation: left Bombay 31 Aug

LOCH KATRINE, **LOCH LOMOND** - listed for the operation but diverted to Singapore

LOCH MORE - listed for the operation but diverted: left Trincomalee 28 Aug for Singapore

LOCH QUOICH - left Bombay 27 Aug with assault convoy JMA1S

LOCH RUTHVEN - from Bombay, listed for assault convoy JMA2BS: continued to Singapore

The sloop NARBADA.
[IWM A30693]

LOCH SCAVAIG - from Colombo, joined assault convoy JMD1B 31 Aug: continued to Singapore

LOCHY - from Colombo, listed for the operation

LOSSIE - left Mandapam 31 Aug with assault convoy JMD1C: assigned as RAF navigational aid ship

NADDER - left Colombo 27 Aug: continued to Singapore

ROTHER - listed for the operation but diverted to Singapore

TAFF - left Bombay 29 Aug with assault convoy JMA2BS

TEVIOT - left Colombo 2 Sep: assigned as RAF navigational aid ship

CORVETTES
MEADOWSWEET - listed for the operation from Colombo as air-sea rescue ship

MONKSHOOD - listed for the operation from Rangoon as air-sea rescue ship

SMILAX - left Colombo 8 Sep: listed for the operation as air-sea rescue ship

SNOWFLAKE - listed for the operation from Rangoon as air-sea rescue ship

MINESWEEPERS
BALUCHISTAN - Indian: left Colombo 15 Aug for the Malacca Strait

BENGAL - Indian: as danlayer, listed for the operation but diverted: left Trincomalee 17 Aug for Singapore

BIHAR - Indian: left Colombo 27 Aug for the Malacca Strait

BOMBAY - Indian: listed for the operation from Colombo

CARNATIC - Indian: left Colombo 26 Aug for the Malacca Strait but returned with defects

CHAMELEON - left Colombo 27 Aug for the Malacca Strait

DECCAN - Indian: as danlayer, left Colombo 27 Aug for the Malacca Strait

FRIENDSHIP - listed for the operation but diverted: left Colombo 15 Aug for Singapore

GOZO - listed for the operation but diverted: left Colombo 17 Aug: put into Trincomalee with defects 23 Aug: left 26 Aug for Singapore

KATHIAWAR, KHYBER - Indian: both left Colombo 15 Aug for the Malacca Strait

KONKAN - Indian: left Trincomalee for the Malacca Strait

KUMAON - Indian: left Colombo 15 Aug for the Malacca Strait

LENNOX, LIGHTFOOT - both listed for the operation but diverted: left Colombo 15 Aug for Singapore

MELITA - listed for the operation but diverted: left Colombo 26 Aug for Singapore

ORISSA, OUDH - both Indian: left Colombo 15 Aug for the Malacca Straits. OUDH as danlayer

PELORUS - listed for the operation but diverted: left Colombo 17 Aug for Singapore

PERSIAN - listed for the operation but diverted: left Colombo 15 Aug for Singapore

PICKLE - left Colombo 4 Sep

PINCHER, PLUCKY - both left Colombo 27 Aug for the Malacca Strait

POSTILLION - listed for the operation but diverted: left Colombo for Singapore

PUNJAB - Indian: as danlayer, listed for the operation but diverted: left Colombo 27 Aug

RAJPUTANA - Indian: left Colombo 15 Aug for the Malacca Strait

RECRUIT, RIFLEMAN - both left Colombo 27 Aug for the Malacca Strait

ROHILKHAND - Indian: left Colombo 26 Aug for the Malacca Strait

TRAWLERS
IMMERSAY, LINGAY - as danlayers, both listed for the operation but diverted: left Colombo 15 Aug for Singapore

BOOM DEFENCE VESSELS
BARCLOSE, BARFOIL, BARMOND - all from Trincomalee, listed to join assault convoy JMD1B

SURVEY SHIP
CHALLENGER - listed for the operation but diverted: left Trincomalee 1 Sep for Singapore

YACHTS
MAID MARION - for special forces' use, left Trincomalee 1 Sep in assault convoy JMC1AS: arrived Morib beachhead 9 Sep

WHITE BEAR - for survey duty, left Colombo 1 Sep in assault convoy JMG1: continued to Singapore

SALVAGE VESSEL
SALVIGIL - listed to leave Colombo in assault convoy JMG1 but did not sail

ESCORT MAINTENANCE SHIPS
BEACHY HEAD - left Colombo 9 Sep: continued to Singapore

GOMBROON - listed for the operation but diverted: left Rangoon for Singapore

MINESWEEPING FORCE REPAIR SHIP
CORBRAE - left Trincomalee 3 Sep in assault convoy JMC2 to arrive Morib beachhead 12 Sep

COASTAL FORCES REPAIR SHIPS
BARRACUDA - Indian: listed for the operation but diverted: left Trincomalee 15 Aug for Penang

MULL OF GALLOWAY - left Trincomalee 15 Aug for Penang then joined assault convoy JMC1AS to arrive Morib beachhead 9 Sep

RESCUE TUGS
ASSIDUOUS - left Trincomalee 30 Aug: joined assault convoy JMD1B for the beachhead

EMINENT - listed for the operation but diverted: left Trincomalee 10 Sep for Singapore

MOTOR LAUNCHES
HDML 1326, **1333**, **1336**, **1384**, **1386** - all from Trincomalee, arrived Morib beachhead 9 Sep

HDML 1080, **1082**, **1086**, **1098**, **1105**, **1106**, **1107**, **1108**, **1150** - all listed for the operation but diverted to Penang

HDML 1248, **1285**, **1288** - all assigned to the operation for survey duty

Also listed for the operation -
HDML 1334, **1335**, **1337**, **1376**, **1385**, **1398**

ML 187, **189**, **193**, **194**, **201**, **214**, **230**, **245**, **390**, **413**, **416**, **417**, **419**, **843**, **844**, **850**, **851**, **872**, **897**, **898**, **899**, **900**, **907**, **923**, **4001**, **4002** - all listed for the operation but diverted to Penang, during which ML 230 was sunk by gunfire after colliding with the tanker CROMWELL 17 Aug

Also listed for the operation -
ML 412, **438**, **440**, **474**, **476**, **477**

MOTOR MINESWEEPERS
BYMS 2006, **2007**, **2008**, **2162**, **2168**, **2203**, **2223** - all listed for the operation but diverted to Penang

Also listed for the operation -
BYMS 2005, **2060**, **2148**, **2181**, **2204**, **2217**, **2232**, **2236**

MMS 199, **200** - listed for the operation but diverted to Penang

Also listed for the operation -
MMS 107, **108**, **196**

MOTOR FISHING VESSELS
9 vessels assigned: numbers unknown

FIGHTER DIRECTION TENDER
FDT 13 - listed for the operation but held in reserve

LANDING CRAFT, HEADQUARTERS
LCH 101, **168**, **248** - all left Mandapam 31 Aug in assault convoy JMD1C to arrive at the beachhead 9 Sep

LANDING CRAFT, GUN (MEDIUM & LARGE)
LCG 5, **6**, **7**, **13**, **18**, **107**, **424**, **426**, **449** - all from Madras, left Mandapam 30 Aug in assault convoy JMD1A: arrived Morib beachhead 9 Sep

LANDING CRAFT, TANK (ROCKET)
LCT(R) 398, **419**, **434**, **435**, **436**, **438**, **440**, **458**, **459**, **460**, **484** - all from Madras, left Mandapam 30 Aug in assault convoy JMD1A: arrived Morib beachhead 9 Sep, except LCT(R) 460 which turned back 30 Aug with engine trouble

LANDING SHIPS, EMERGENCY REPAIR
LSE(LS) 1 - for LST repairs, left Vizagapatam 30 Aug in assault convoys JMF1S then JMA1S to arrive Morib beachhead 9 Sep

LSE(LC) 51 - for landing craft repairs, listed to leave Bombay 27 Aug in assault convoy JMA1S to arrive Morib beachhead 9 Sep

LANDING CRAFT, ADMINISTRATION
LCQ 381 - from Madras, left Mandapam 29 Aug in assault convoy JMD1B: arrived Morib beachhead 9 Sep

LCQ 389 - left Bombay 29 Aug in assault convoy JMA2A: arrived Port Dickson beachhead 9 Sep

LCQ 391 - from Madras, left Mandapam: arrived Morib beachhead 9 Sep

LCQ 491 - left Mandapam: arrived Morib beachhead 9 Sep

LANDING CRAFT, TANK (EMERGENCY REPAIR)
LCT(E) 303, **320**, **372**, **384** - all from Madras, listed for the operation: three left Mandapam 29 Aug in assault convoy JMD1B: arrived Morib beachhead 9 Sep

PUBLIC RECORD OFFICE FILE SOURCES

ADM 53 – 115317, 115368, 115409, 115437, 115476, 115508, 115724, 115725, 115766, 115785, 115819, 115836, 115892, 115901, 115932, 115933, 116099, 116356, 116408, 116454, 116491, 116529, 116535, 116580, 116598, 116632, 116742, 116743, 116991, 117339, 117377, 117519, 117521, 117660, 117671, 117760, 118254, 118256, 118341, 118481, 118483, 118676, 118717, 119050, 119699, 119725, 119743, 119746, 120221, 121446, 121520, 121889, 121986, 122054, 122209, 122226

ADM 186 – 796

ADM 187 – 19, 21, 22, 27, 28, 32, 39, 48, 52

ADM 199 – 426, 620, 652, 740, 774, 802, 852, 858-865, 868, 870, 873, 888, 902, 904, 909-912, 937, 943-947, 949, 1214, 1216, 1293, 1423, 1430, 1457, 2143, 2145, 2147, 2238, 2239, 2249-2251, 2268-2270, 2322, 2323, 2507, 2509, 2511-2513, 2515-2517

ADM 202 – 382-387, 395, 396, 409, 410

ADM 210 – 1, 4, 5, 6, 9, 15-17

ADM 234 – 331, 356, 358, 359, 376, 377

ADM 237 - 461

ADM 239 – 213, 234, 331

DEFE 2 – 92, 94, 179, 281, 283-286, 291, 292, 294, 312, 314, 315, 318, 319, 397, 555-557, 581-587, 589-592, 596, 599, 600-602, 605, 607, 628, 629, 631, 632, 638, 639, 646, 648A, 1778

MT 40 – 93, 103, 142-149

MT 59 – 585, 586, 628, 632

WO 106 – 3612, 4793

WO 203 – 1, 205, 208, 1594, 1595, 1650, 1653, 1659, 1663, 2783, 2784, 2834, 2975, 2981-2983, 3846-48, 3853, 4339, 4675, 4916, 4917, 4946, 5118, 5126

WO 204 – 1652, 1891, 4895, 8268

ACKNOWLEDGEMENTS

I would like to express my very sincere appreciation to all those who have very kindly assisted me and in particular to Arnold Hague; to Chris Page, his predecessor, David Brown, and Michael McAloon at the Naval Historical Branch; to Jenny Wraight, Admiralty Librarian; to Bob Todd of the National Maritime Museum; to Declan Barriskill and colleagues at the Guildhall Library; to Michael Crowdy; to the staff of the Public Record Office; to Anna Morling and, for the loan of some of his excellent photographs, to Captain J F van Puyvelde. As the official records are in some instances incomplete, I am most grateful to Geoffrey Hudson, in connection with Coastal Forces craft, and to Paul Motte-Harrison and Tony Chapman of the LST and Landing Craft Association, as well as to the following Association members, who supplied valuable supplementary information – A E S Carey, D Cawthorn, G F Green, R Jones, T V Jones, K Herbert, W L Kirley, C E Lear, J Morley, G Read, R Speight and G R Unwin.

INDEX OF OPERATIONAL CODE NAMES

relative to Section A

INDEX OF SHIPS

Page numbers of illustrations are shown in italics